But Don't Call Me White

BREAKTHROUGHS
IN THE SOCIOLOGY OF EDUCATION

Series Editors:

George W. Noblit, *University of North Carolina at Chapel Hill*

Joseph R. Neikirk, *Distinguished Professor of Sociology of Education*
University of North Carolina at Chapel Hill

In this series, we are establishing a new tradition in the sociology of education. Like many fields, the sociology of education has largely assumed that the field develops through the steady accumulation of studies. Thomas Kuhn referred to this as 'normal science.' Yet normal science builds on a paradigm shift, elaborating and expanding the paradigm. What has received less attention are the works that contribute to paradigm shifts themselves. To remedy this, we will focus on books that move the field in dramatic and recognizable ways—what can be called breakthroughs.

Kuhn was analyzing natural science and was been less sure his ideas fit the social sciences. Yet it is likely that the social sciences are more subject to paradigm shifts than the natural sciences because the social sciences are fed back into the social world. Thus sociology and social life react to each other, and are less able separate the knower from the known. With reactivity of culture and knowledge, the social sciences follow a more complex process than that of natural science. This is clearly the case with the sociology of education. The multiplicity of theories and methods mix with issues of normativity— in terms of what constitutes good research, policy and/or practice. Moreover, the sociology of education is increasingly global in its reach—meaning that the national interests are now less defining of the field and more interrogative of what is important to know. This makes the sociology of education even more complex and multiple in its paradigm configurations. The result is both that there is less shared agreement on the social facts of education but more vibrancy as a field. What we know and understand is shifting on multiple fronts constantly. Breakthroughs is to the series for works that push the boundaries—a place where all the books do more than contribute to the field, they remake the field in fundamental ways. Books are selected precisely because they change how we understand both education and the sociology of education.

But Don't Call Me White

Mixed Race Women Exposing Nuances of Privilege and Oppression Politics

Silvia Cristina Bettez
The University of North Carolina at Greensboro, USA

SENSE PUBLISHERS
ROTTERDAM/BOSTON/TAIPEI

A C.I.P. record for this book is available from the Library of Congress.

ISBN: 978-94-6091-691-5 (paperback)
ISBN: 978-94-6091-692-2 (hardback)
ISBN: 978-94-6091-693-9 (e-book)

Published by: Sense Publishers,
P.O. Box 21858,
3001 AW Rotterdam,
The Netherlands
www.sensepublishers.com

Printed on acid-free paper

Cover: Margo Rivera-Weiss
The artwork originally appeared in Other Tongues:
Mixed Race Women Speak Out, ed. Adebe deRango-Adem and
Andrea Thompson (Inanna Publications 2010).

DEDICATION

To sharing, learning, and loving across cultures.

TABLE OF CONTENTS

ACKNOWLEDGMENTS

Recently I have been writing and thinking about the importance of community building for those of us who engage in work to promote social justice. We all need support, not only to make it through difficult times, but also to reach our goals. A community of people has assisted me in myriad ways throughout the process of writing this book, from when I first began formulating my research up until the final manuscript draft – a seven-year total process.

If it weren't for my family and *familia*, both immediate and extended, this book would not be. It is because I have been incredibly loved and supported by both sides of my family that I feel so strongly about naming and claiming my own mixed race positionality and discovering more about others' mixed race experiences. My grandparents on both sides have been incredible role models of strength, love, and acceptance. Encouraged to work hard to reach my goals, I have experienced unconditional love and validation from more family members than I can name. So, I want to say thank you to my incredible extended family – grandparents, *abuelos*, aunts, *tías*, uncles, *tíos*, and cousins, *primos y primas*. My mom, Sonia Bettez, has always been an inspiration in more ways than I can name. She and her partner, Janice Kando, not only fed and housed me during my research and have supported me throughout my life, they serve as a shining example of deep, unwavering love across cultures. My dad, Donald Bettez, is the greatest. He and my mom both taught me a love of learning. He is always there for me; he revels in each of my accomplishments and reminds me to go easy on myself when things don't go as hoped. My sister, Vanesa, calls me her "angel of light." What she doesn't realize is that her incredible spirit is a continual source of strength for me. She is my tireless advocate and cheerleader. I love and appreciate all my family (including those who have passed); they are the original inspiration for this work.

In addition to my "biological" family, there is Mojgan Besharat, my chosen family and best friend, who has been there for me from the beginning to the end of this long process. Mojgan did an amazing job of transcribing over 10 interviews for me when "professional" transcriptionists refused to listen to participants' narratives. (I can't even get started on that story.) Mojgan always believed in me, encouraged me, and reminded me to have balance in my life between work and play. She is a most incredible, kind-hearted, intelligent, thoughtful, giving individual, and I am a better person for having her in my life. Another long-time friend that I must acknowledge is Victoria Alcoset; Vicki is not only a mixed sister who has been a great friend for decades, she and her partner housed me for two weeks during my research in the Bay Area. My wise *hermana*, Andrea Quijada, another mixed-race *compañera*, has been a true friend and my sounding board, both professionally and personally; I am thankful for her wisdom, humor, and love. Margarita Machado-Casas and I connected on the first day of our Ph.D. program, many years ago. She is a brilliant woman with boundless drive and energy, and although we no longer live in the same city, I trust that we will always support each other.

I have had the incredible fortune of having two wonderful mentors who are also friends. George Noblit believed in the power of this book long before I did. He not only is the epitome of what a good mentor should be – encouraging, challenging, supportive and kind – he's a great person with lots of integrity who practices what he preaches. Although Kathy Hytten is now more of a friend than a mentor, she is typically the first person I approach for work-related advice. Kathy is smart, generous and gently critical in ways that challenge me to be a continually better scholar.

As I have changed, grown and relocated, my support systems have shifted. Some of the following people are still in my life, others not, but all of them contributed to this process by providing me emotional support, financial support (sometimes simply feeding me), technical support (such as transcribing interviews when I was in a pinch or reviewing drafts), or a combination of all the above. I want to acknowledge and thank Kat Turner, Lisa Nickle, Becky Thompson, Michele Berger, Jim Trier, Annabelle Allison, Robin Criffield, Jane Lubischer, Jaynie Lara, Ana Bettez, Deb Eaker-Rich, Dee Gator, Amy Senta, Amy Swain, and Beth Hatt.

I want to thank my colleagues and students at The University of North Carolina at Greensboro. Smart, thoughtful people who are committed to promoting social justice surround me. My colleagues and department chair have encouraged me to follow my scholarly passions; their commitment to high quality teaching and scholarship motivates me to produce writing that matters in the struggle for equity while maintaining my obligations to students. The graduate students with whom I work consistently fuel my critical hope that we can indeed make the world a more equitable place for all people. I learn from my students every day and have no doubt that this book has been influenced by my interactions with them. I was incredibly fortunate to have Kathleen Edwards work with me as a graduate assistant over the past year. Kathleen is intelligent, organized, attends to detail and is an excellent critical thinker. She not only meticulously went through each sentence of the book helping me to refine the writing, she brainstormed with me regarding the analysis whenever I felt stuck, contributing brilliant ideas. This book truly would not be what it is without her keen insights and technical support.

I am thankful to all who made the final, finished product possible. The editors at Sense Publishers not only agreed to publish my book, but have been patient, kind and accommodating. Thanks also to editor Kara Stephenson Gehman who agreed to proofread the final book on very short notice in record time. The writing is tighter and smoother as a result of her contribution. Margo Rivera-Weiss is a mixed race artist who graciously donated the artwork for the cover (the artwork originally appeared in *Other Tongues: Mixed Race Women Speak Out*, edited by Adebe deRango-Adem and Andrea Thompson). Please check out Margo's website http://www.margoriveraweiss.com; she has some fantastic, beautifully colorful art. Finally, I want to thank the participants who entrusted me with their life stories; I tried to hold and tell their individual and collective narratives with care and integrity. Collectively, the participants were an amazing group of women; individually, they shared selflessly, many of them going above and beyond by helping me connect with other participants, securing interview locations, and even opening their homes to me. They revealed intimate, often painful details of their lives, responded to challenging questions and challenged me back. Their words are gifts for which I am incredibly thankful.

This book is a collective project on many levels, and I am forever grateful to everyone who helped me in this process.

EXPOSING METHODS AND POSITIONALITY

America should wake up to the accelerating colorization of the US and realize that mixed race people are the future of this country. We are not "different." – Diana

I believe that the more intimately interconnected people feel – the more we take the time to learn about and connect with people across cultural differences – the less separation, segregation, and oppression there will be. Connecting with others in a way that has the potential to minimize oppression, however, requires striving to understand the complex operations of privilege related to race, class, gender, and sexuality. My beliefs about the importance of cross-cultural connections, my desire to do work that dismantles oppression, and my personal mixed race identity led me to seek out life stories by mixed race women, individuals who simultaneously embody racially/ethnically oppressed and privileged identities and, thus, could speak directly to the challenges of deconstructing hierarchies built on emphasizing *inequity* in differences (Adams, Bell, & Griffin, 1997). For this project, I conducted extensive interviews with 16 biracial women in three parts of the United States; each has one White parent and one parent who is a person of color. I approached this research with a sociological lens searching for meaning related to issues of social justice: What can these women's stories tell us about how to better communicate cross culturally? How do their multiple positionalities – of gender, race, class, and sexuality – affect the ways in which they claim agency and are limited by structure? What do their stories reveal about racial politics?

Wanting to learn more about how the women might describe their experiences of communicating cross-culturally, I was struck by the many stories of participants naming their identities in large part by *distancing* themselves from identifications with Whiteness. Diana's experience while visiting Manhattan is perhaps most telling:

I was getting out of the cab on the wrong side; I was getting out in the street. And I didn't see this guy on the bicycle, and I opened the door and he almost ran into me. And he said, "You dumb, White bitch!" And I said (angrily and emphatically), "I am not White!"

Diana shared this story twice, both in the group and in an individual interview. When told in the group, participants burst into laughter in response to her story and another participant, reflecting on Diana's story, reiterated, "You can call me stupid and a bitch, but don't call me White!" To be called "White" was the worst insult of all.

Yet, given that all of the women have White heritage, and most could "pass" for White, acknowledging Whiteness was unavoidable. Subsequently, as much as the women collectively rejected Whiteness, discussions of Whiteness permeated the interviews revealing complicated dynamics of racial performance, racism, and the workings of White supremacy.

This work is deeply personal for all of us – the participants and me. In addition to uncovering answers to the questions listed above, this book is also an effort to create a shift in thinking about mixed race identity and conceptions of hybridity. As will be explained in greater detail in Chapter 2, dominant discourses have exposed mixed race people in particular ways that position us as objects. We have been feared, despised, labeled as traitors, monitored, exoticized, and rendered invisible. My intention as the interviewer, writer, and participant-researcher is to bring the complexities of our stories to life by centering the words and experiences of mixed race women so that we can become subjects who do the exposing (to readers) rather than be victimized as exposed objects of oppressive narratives. People can be exposed unwillingly by others or choose to expose themselves with a purpose. Throughout the book, there are multi-layered stories of exposure, both forced and chosen. The details of the exposures in turn expose sociological nuances of privilege and oppression as both the participants and I theorize the narratives through a critical macro/micro, structure/agency lens.

To expose oneself requires one to risk, to be vulnerable. As the author, I feel simultaneously protective of the stories and proud of the courageous risk-taking displayed by the women who shared intensely personal stories – of privilege, oppression, and emotional life moments – with what ultimately will be a mixed audience. This particular group of women turned out to be a researcher's dream; they often analyzed their own stories as they told them, describing institutional privilege and oppression. As the writer and researcher, I conscientiously took a sociological, critical theory perspective to the work, striving to make explicit connections between the micro (the women's stories of particular life experiences) and the macro (the context and structures that influenced their stories); often, however, the women made such links themselves without my prompting. These women are "secret agent insiders" to Whiteness, letting you, the reader, in on their knowledge. Readers who are people of color may likely have heard or even said what is revealed about Whiteness, but perhaps never thought about it as situated in the contexts described here. White readers, depending on exposure to issues of race, may never have heard such descriptions of Whiteness, some of which may be shocking, angering, or guilt inducing, but ultimately, we hope, will contribute to an increased awareness of race-based oppression. Mixed race readers may find solace in the shared stories. Much of what the participants share is never revealed in mixed – White/of color – company. Through the participants' personal exposures and collective stories, we are exposed to larger systematic workings of privilege and oppression.

AUDIENCE

It is my intent that this book be accessible and useful for a wide range of people. First and foremost, I want it to be a resource for all who are interested in mixed race issues, cross cultural communication, and social justice work, and wish to minimize racial conflict and other forms of oppression. I envision this work being of interest to a wide range of activists and scholars, including sociologists, sociologists of education, feminists, anti-oppression/social justice scholars, critical multicultural educators, and qualitative researchers; however, I also hope it is read by people who are indifferent to the academic theories, and simply want to learn from the mixed race women's stories shared here. If you fall into the latter category, you may want to skim some of the remaining sections of this chapter and the next chapter.

As a qualitative researcher operating within the new paradigm of critical qualitative research (Lincoln & Denzin, 2003), I believe in the importance of making the research methods and paradigms clear for the reader. Thus, in the remainder of this chapter, I expose my methodology, techniques, and intent through detailed descriptions of my (a) participant selection processes, (b) research paradigms, (c) project goals, (d) original research questions, (e) data collection methods, (f) data analysis and interpretation techniques, and (g) research trustworthiness. I end the chapter with several short stories that illuminate my multiple positionalities and expose a variety of my own related experiences and viewpoints.

PARTICIPANT SELECTION AND OVERVIEW

Hoping to understand how mixed people navigate both dominant and subordinate cultures, I recruited participants who have one White parent and one parent who is a person of color – first generation mixed White/of color people, for lack of a better term. Curious about people's reflections on schooling and evolving identity formation, I focused on adults. For a variety of reasons, I limited participants to women in order to engage in feminist research that "emphasizes the sources of power that women find" (Richardson, Taylor, & Whittier, 2001, p. 2), to encourage freer storytelling within group interviews[1], and to unpack the particularly scrutinized position of partner choices, given that they bear children.

Expecting that people's experiences might be quite different depending on where they were raised and lived, I purposefully planned to conduct interviews in a variety of U.S. cities. Before beginning this research, I conducted a pilot project in the Southeast, interviewing six young women in central North Carolina. Striving for the corners of the United States, I decided to conduct interviews for this project in the Northeast (Boston, MA), the Northwest (San Francisco/Oakland, CA), and the Southwest (Albuquerque, NM).

I approached this project with very broad research questions. Foremost, I wanted to simply collect the life stories of women, describe their experiences with family, friends, school, and work, and see what themes and patterns emerged. I recruited participants through snowball sampling (Glesne, 2006, p. 35) via a recruitment flier[2] emailed to friends, family, and colleagues who helped distribute the information. I began receiving phone calls immediately after the flier was sent, and, given the small number of participants desired, I did not need to recruit using other methods. I responded to everyone who inquired about the project and interviewed all who met the criteria of the study and could meet during the time I would be visiting each city. In the end, I had a total of 16 participants: five from the Oakland/San Francisco area, four from Albuquerque, and seven from Boston.[3]

In Table 1-1, I provide an overview of participant data in terms of age, parents' races/ethnicities, childhood locale (where they grew up for most of their lives), current location, capacity to "pass" as White, sexuality, formal education level, childhood socioeconomic status, and current class status. It is important to remember that these are temporal and sometimes fluid identifications. Participants ranged in age from 24 to 58, with the average age being 32. Five of the participants had moms of color, 11 had dads of color. The races/ethnicities included: Black/African American, Mexican, Peruvian, Filipina/o, Somali, Japanese, and White (including Jewish, Norwegian, and Polish). I had hoped to include people of American Indian descent, but only two people with Native heritage responded, and neither of them could meet with me during the times I was scheduled to visit their city. Most of the participants grew up in cities, some in suburbs of cities, and only two in small towns. They were all living in the Bay Area, Boston, or Albuquerque at the time of the interviews. The table indicates the capacity to pass; participants described a continuum of passing from almost always being perceived as White to almost never, but only three participants could never pass for White. As will be described in detail in Chapter 6, participants generally never desired to pass, but to varying degrees were presumed to be White by others.

Eight of the women self-identified as queer, lesbian, and/or bisexual; the other eight identified as straight. The number of queer-identified participants may be particularly high, in part, because I spread the word through my personal network. I identify as queer, as do many of my friends, so it would follow that several of their contacts may be queer-identified as well. However, the Boston participants had no direct connections to any of my friends, having learned about the project through a mixed race organization, and there were three queer/bi participants out of seven.

This was a highly formally educated group of women. All but one participant had at least her bachelor's degree. The participant who did not have her bachelor's degree was one of the younger participants (age 26). She had attended cosmetology school upon graduating high school but dropped out due to sexual harassment. She expressed a desire to return to school and get her degree but was not sure in what field. Ten of the participants had taken at least some graduate courses. Three were in the process of getting their master's degrees and four others already had master's degrees. In addition, the majority of them shared stories about doing well in school throughout their lives.

It is harder to define class status than some of the other positionality variables. In follow-up emails after the interviews, I asked participants to identify both their historic and current socioeconomic levels (i.e., working class, lower middle class, middle class, etc.). All but three participants – Brittney, Ruth, and Katherine – responded to my request. Given the importance of multiple positionalities, I felt it was important to report their class status, which I determined based upon the information they shared about their lives in the interviews. Some people simply stated their class position in a few words such as, "I am middle class." Several, however, qualified their responses and puzzled over the class categories. For example, Susan said, "I don't know the official guidelines for what income positions you where, but I think we are middle class." Marta said:

> I was raised working class (my dad was a cabinet maker and we owned a small home). I am currently middle class in my income/job but I hope I retain my working class values and sensibilities. Also, I wanted to point out that working class is just part of the lower class income spectrum - there is also poverty class. As I'm sure you're aware many folks with working class jobs actually earn middle class incomes – plumbers, electricians, or some other trades, and even though there isn't job status and more possible health issues from the work, this is very far from a poverty class existence.

Alana explained her class background in equally complex terms:

> I was raised middle class. I was also raised around a great deal of wealth and did not actually understand my class standing until I found myself in circles with predominantly working class people of color. I always assumed that I was working class because I grew up in apartment buildings with my single mom as opposed to living in a large house. Though I am a financially struggling grad student, I still consider myself to be a member of the middle class because I don't think one ever moves down, so to speak, the class hierarchy. I still have access to certain privileges and power through my cultural capital. If you are qualifying my current class standing just based on income, I probably would be lumped into the working class, but I was raised middle class.

Their self-positioning stories serve as a reminder that class status is derived from a complex set of factors including but not limited to income, the type of job someone holds, cultural capital, and instilled class values (Bourdieu, 1986). Furthermore, how people view themselves in terms of class is impacted by the class positionality of the people around them. For example, Alana explained above that she assumed she was working class growing up because of the wealth that surrounded her, but later realized she was more middle class. Race and class operate both independently and interdependently. Glimpses of this are provided in the women's stories; it is evident that the intersections of race and class status positions create perspectives as either insiders or outsiders or a combination of both.

Bettie's (2003) discussion of class in the opening to her ethnography *Women without Class* is useful here. She argued, "As I came to understand these negotiations of class as cultural (not political) identities, it became useful to conceptualize class not only as a material location, but also as performance" (p. 50). Class, she explained, is expressed through speech, grammar, accents, mannerisms, and dress (p. 51). Bettie chose to use the terms "working-class performers" and "middle-class performers" in her work to remind readers that there are exceptions to the class-origin equals class-performance rule. I will return to this concept of performance in the next chapter, but in this instance, I can state that all the participants asserted or "performed" a middle class standing, lower to upper, at the time of the interviews, and most were raised middle class.

Thus, this project provides insights into the specific experiences of formally educated, mostly middle class, straight and queer, mixed race women with varying skin colors. Although I feel such contextualization is necessary to guide you in your reading (in fact I have included an extra participant table in Appendix A that can be removed and used to locate the women as you are reading their stories), I am troubled by the labelling as well. These labels are sometimes chosen, sometimes given, and sometimes temporal, yet using them runs the risk of promoting essentialization of identity. However, the participants' own complications of labels serve as reminders that identifications are ever-evolving and shifting. As I wrote, I envisioned the women – how they talked, what they looked like, their tones of voice, body language, and the collection of their stories. A drawback of choosing a thematic analysis is that it is quite difficult to accurately represent the uniqueness and deep dimensionality of each individual participant. Due to confidentiality agreements, I cannot include pictures. I considered providing detailed physical descriptions, but it seems that such framing would only further essentialize and exotify. Instead, I provide selective, purposeful, physical descriptors of individuals in relation to specific stories throughout. Physical attributes could be another category of analysis – the bodied experience – but such work would require, I believe, pictures as well as descriptions and explicit consent and understanding of such inclusion by the participants. Ultimately, I hope that readers will respect that these are portraits of people's lives – people who risked sharing intimate, sometimes painful, stories – while remembering that each snapshot is also a moment in time.

Appendix A: Participants Overview

Name	Age	Mom	Dad	Childhood Location	Current Location	Pass	Sexuality	Education	Childhood Class	Current Class
Maria	34	White	Mexican	Phoenix	Albuquerque	Yes	Queer	MA	Lower middle	Middle
Ana	32	British	Filipino	Los Angeles	Albuquerque	Yes	Queer	BA	Middle	Upper
Brittney	26	White	Black	Albuquerque	Albuquerque	No	Straight	HS Diploma	Middle	Working
Janet	25	White	Mexican	Kansas City	Albuquerque	Yes	Straight	BA	Middle	Lower middle
Linda	30	Japanese	White Polish	San Francisco	Oakland	Yes	Queer	BA	Working	Working/low middle
Marta	46	White Jewish	Peruvian	suburb of San Francisco	Oakland	Yes	Queer	BA	Working	Middle
Alana	32	White	Black	LA	Oakland	No	Queer	Getting MA	Middle	Middle
Bobbi	26	White	Somali	Phoenix	San Francisco	Yes	Straight	MA	Middle	Middle
Tina	24	White	Mexican	suburb of San Francisco	Oakland	Yes	Straight	Getting MA	Working/ middle	Middle
Diana	58	White	African American	Buffalo	Boston	Yes	Straight	MA	Working	Upper middle
Ruth	34	Russian Jewish	African American	Chicago	Boston	No	Queer	MA	Lower middle	Middle
Joanna	23	Black	White	suburb of Philadelphia	Boston	Yes	Queer	Getting MA	Lower middle	Middle
Katherine	27	Black	White	suburb of Philadelphia	Boston	Yes	Straight	Getting MA	Middle	Middle
Elizabeth	31	Filipina	White	upstate NY	Boston	Yes	Straight	MA	Middle	Middle
Mindy	33	Filipina	White	SE Massachusetts	Boston	Yes	Straight	BA, some grad	Working	Lower middle
Susan	36	Norwe-gian	Mexican	Minnesota	Boston	Yes	Bisexual	BA	Upper middle	Middle

7

INTERPRETIVIST, CONSTRUCTIVIST PARADIGM

This is an exploratory, ethnographic study, based primarily on interviews. I began with a few specific questions that I hoped to have answered, but the main goal was to hear people's life stories. Glesne (2006) argued:

> The particular research mode with which you will find greatest comfort and satisfaction will depend on your personality, background, values, and on what you believe is important to know about the world around you. (p. 8)

Goodall (2000) similarly stated, "Ethnographic fieldwork and the writing that comes of it is less a formal method of inquiry than it is a disciplined attitude and conversational style that I have learned to make a way of life" (p. 21). I don't feel like I choose qualitative research as much as it chooses me. Doing critical ethnographic work is a "natural" extension of how I view the world and what interests me.

Ethnography has a history situated in a positivist paradigm in which the ethnographer sets out to "discover" how cultures operate through "objective" observation and non-leading questions (Glesne, 2006; Goodall, 2000; Lincoln & Denzin, 2003; Van Maanen, 1988). Clifford (1983) wrote that historically ethnographers emphasized "objectively" gathering stories. He cited Malinowski, who in his ethnographic book *Argonauts*, published in 1922, "was greatly concerned with the rhetorical problem of convincing his readers that the facts he was putting before them were objectively acquired, not subjective creations" (Clifford, 1983, p. 123).

However, there has been a shift in the role of the ethnographic researcher among those who write about ethnography as a discipline and those who conduct ethnography; the role of the ethnographer is now realized as one that is as much about interpretation and construction as it is about documenting experience. Ethnographers have moved away from a realist paradigm to more interpretive and/or constructivist paradigms (Clifford, 1983; Glesne, 2006; Goodall, 2000; Lincoln & Denzin, 2003). Lincoln & Guba (2000) argued that "objectivity is a chimera: a mythological creature that never existed, save in the imaginations of those who believe that knowing can be separated from the knower" (p. 181). Clifford (1983) maintained that, "experiential, interpretive, dialogical, and polyphonic processes are at work, discordantly, in any ethnography" (p. 142). Ethnography is about the "interpretation of cultures" and "representations of dialogue" (Clifford, 1983, p. 131 & 134). Others have similarly argued that ethnography is not about pursuing or establishing a single "truth" but is about creating and uncovering various constructions of social reality (Glesne, 2006; Goodall, 2000; Lincoln & Denzin, 2003; Lincoln & Guba, 2000).

It is from the interpretivist, constructivist paradigm that I approach my work as a researcher. I assume that meaning is constructed through negotiation among individuals, both between the participants and also between participants and myself as the participant-researcher. I believe that "ethnography is an embodied practice" (Conquergood, 2003, p. 353). I approached my work as a participant-researcher, which at times required participant-observation. Clifford (1983) argued:

> Participant-observation serves as shorthand for a continuous tacking between the "inside" and "outside" of events; on the one hand grasping the sense of specific occurrences and gestures empathetically, on the other stepping back to situate these meanings in the wider contexts. (p. 127)

I walked this line of being both an insider and an outsider, of being both a participant and a researcher.

As a participant-researcher, I have a prominent presence in this work. During both group and individual interviews, my role continuously shifted from asking questions to answering them, from facilitator to participant, and from listener to interpreter. Along with my participants, I also shared my own stories. I always kept sight of my role as a researcher, and in some interviews my role primarily entailed asking questions and listening. However, some individual interviews were much more dialogical in nature by virtue of connections in age, experience, and a multitude of other factors, including prompting by the participants. In the group interviews, I positioned myself explicitly as both facilitator *and* participant and encouraged participants to ask questions of each other and of me.

As a participant-researcher, I took a reflexive approach to my work. Reinharz (1997) argued that we "*create* the self in the field" (p. 3). I created myself – as a combination researcher-participant – in multiple ways through interactions with my participants. My positionality as a middle class, mixed race woman created an initial point of connection and often, a level of comfort with my participants. In addition, other factors of social positionality often united us; for example, Latina participants were able to bring in words and phrases in Spanish, and I could respond knowingly, which enhanced our connection. My queer positionality also created a point of connection with queer participants. I came out to all of the queer participants in hopes of creating a sense of comfort for them to share stories that related to their sexual identities.

Other times factors of social positionality divided us. For example, as I met with Diana, she spoke of being able to slip in and out of Ebonics yet she never did so with me; I wondered how different our interview interaction, and her speech, might have been if she had read me as someone able to understand and speak Ebonics. In acknowledgement of my presence as a participant-researcher, I include my voice as both a participant and a researcher in the writing of this study. Lincoln and Guba (2000) stated that reflexivity "demands that we interrogate each of our selves regarding the ways in which research efforts are shaped and staged around binaries, contradictions, and paradoxes that form our lives" (p. 183). Because this work is directly connected to the "contradictions" and "paradoxes" of my life as a middle class, formally educated, queer, mixed race woman, I have consciously asked myself and others who have assisted me in this research process, "What is it that I might be missing here?" I am continually conscious of issues historically related to validity, though more contemporarily thought of in terms of trustworthiness.

PROJECT GOALS: CRITICAL, SELF-REFLEXIVE ETHNOGRAPHY

Validity is problematized in constructivist paradigms. Whereas in the past ethnographers such as Malinowski struggled to claim that researcher objectivity could help to ensure valid results, as a "new ethnographer" (Goodall, 2000) I struggle instead to position my subjectivity. Acknowledging subjectivity, qualitative researchers offer strategies to ensure data as trustworthy while they argue that there is no one true or "valid" interpretation on the data. To describe trustworthiness in the context of my study, I first need to describe the goals of my project and my research approach. Geertz (2003) defined the aim of anthropology as "the enlargement of the human discourse" (p. 153). First and foremost I think of my project, and qualitative work in general, as adding to human discourse. My goal was to "search for pattern and meaning rather than for prediction and control" (Reinharz, as cited in Lather, 2003, p. 192). I believe, like Clifford (1983) that with ethnographic writing, "it is more than ever crucial for different peoples to form complex concrete images of one another, as well as of the relationships of knowledge and power that connect them" (p. 119). I take a *critical* constructivist approach to this research. "Critical theory is committed to unveiling the political stakes that anchor cultural practices" (Conquergood, 2003, p. 351). In writing about the women in my study, I strove to maintain at least some of the complexities of their lives and interactions and to also locate their experiences in wider contexts of institutional and social power. Thus my approach is interpretive, constructivist, self-reflexive, and critical, particularly in the sense that it attends to issues of social power.

ORIGINAL RESEARCH QUESTIONS

I approached this work with three main, and broad, research questions. The first was: How do these women navigate their "hybridity," and why does it matter? By hybridity, I refer to the women's embodied mixed race existence and the meaning of their life choices in relation to wider discourses. I wanted to explore "hybrid" experiences in various areas of life, including education, family, social life, dating/partnering, and careers. Lincoln and Guba (2000) asserted:

> Critical theorists, constructivists, and participatory/cooperative inquirers take their primary field of interest to be precisely that subjective and

intersubjective social knowledge and the active construction and cocreation of such knowledge by human agents that is produced by human consciousness. (pp. 176–177)

I was interested in understanding how the participants actively constructed their experiences as mixed race women and what their intersubjective social knowledge might tell us about issues related to race, gender, and power. I utilized the term "hybridity" strategically. In many contemporary postcolonial writings about hybridity (Bhabha, 1994; Grossberg, 1996; McLaren, 1997), it is discussed in abstract ways, disconnected from the actual lives of "hybrid" (mixed race) people and their experiences. I wanted to center these women's voices in relationship to the theoretical conceptions of hybridity to serve as a reminder that hybridity, for some, is a lived experience.

The second research question I had as I approached this project was: What do the participants' stories demonstrate about the ways people might better communicate and comprehend one another across lines of racial difference? In autobiographical writings, mixed race people often allude to having enhanced skills for moving in and out of various ethnic/racial communities (Camper, 1994; O'Hearn, 1998; Walker, 2001). In my pilot project, several of the participants talked at length about the ways in which they navigated cultural codes and expectations within various racial/ethnic communities. I wanted to examine the women's stories for what they might tell us about cross cultural communication and comprehension.

My third research question was: Are there shared experiences identified with by mixed race women in the U.S. that cross racial/ethnic lines? I am interested in both the diversity and commonalities of the experiences of mixed race people. Mengel (2001), who conducted general research on the multiracial experience and conducted interviews with multiracial Asian individuals, argued:

There appears to be a commonality, a level of comfort, a place where one does not have to code-switch, a level of unspoken understanding that is experienced by mixed race in the company of others like them that is not found in their experiences with monoracial people. (p. 122)

Mengel argued that multiracial individuals create "panethnic" identities that are based on "mixedness" (p. 112). My study focuses on the experience of individuals living in the United States. Although there may be a shared, mixed, panethnic identity, individual racial formation is affected and bound by the accompanying history of racial politics in which people live. How individuals situate themselves racially is impacted by the discourses of race that abound in the particular areas where they grew up and currently reside; in other words, location and context matter. My goal is to situate the women's stories while analyzing them for interconnecting themes.

Even as I uncover the potential unities among mixed race women, I also remain committed to naming the disjunctures of "the" multiracial experience. Ifekwunigwe (2001), in her mixed race research, asked:

How do we create political alliances forged from shared marginal status while also acknowledging the varied and inherently hierarchical power dynamics within, between, and among such disparate and differently racialised groups? (p. 45)

Mixed race status is an identification that exists amid a multitude of other identity categories and characteristics; these identifications carry the potential for disparate positions in institutional hierarchies. In other words, multiracial identifications and their subsequent implications are affected by socioeconomic status, gender, location, skin color, family make-up, sexuality, and countless other factors. Given this complexity, I wanted to learn about the contextualized experiences of mixed race women and analyze the narratives for the ways they implicate, and are implicated by, the social and institutional structures in which we live.

Although not an original research question, one of the main findings and issues explored is: What do these women's stories reveal about racial politics, particularly in relation to social constructions of Whiteness? I am someone who cares deeply about issues of social justice, and I believe that we are required to explore and name issues of oppression such as racism and White supremacy. Therefore, when participants raised these topics, I asked several probing follow-up questions to elicit more information regarding their experiences and opinions related to issues of social justice. These women provided unique perspectives on issues of racial oppression as individuals who sometimes straddle racial and ethnic cultural borderlands of privilege and oppression.

DATA COLLECTION METHODS

With my leanings toward ethnography, I would have liked to have immersed myself in a location with a group of people over time to conduct research. However, at the time of my research, there was no one place where I could access a variety of mixed race people consistently over time. Thus my research was predominately interview based. I conducted two semi-structured individual interviews[4] with each participant (except Bobbi, with whom I conducted a follow-up via email). Most interviews were approximately 1.5 hours long, but the total individual interview time with each participant ranged from 2 hours 20 minutes to 6 hours.

I began each interview with a statement to the effect of, "I have some broad questions for you, but I really would like for you to tell whatever stories you wish to tell. I will ask you follow-up questions based on what you say. If there is a story you wish to share that doesn't fit within any of my questions, please do so." In her book on qualitative research, Glesne (2006) asserted that an interviewer should employ probes to learn as much as possible in response to each main question. Interviewing, she says, is a "'what-else' and 'tell me more' endeavor" (p. 96). This is how I approached my work; I probed for clarification, specific examples, self-analysis, and explanation. I conducted interviews in locations convenient for the participants. Although a few interviews were conducted in local libraries, most were conducted in homes or workplaces, thus providing a fuller picture of participants' lives.

In addition to individual interviews, I conducted a group interview in each city. Fortunately, all but one participant (Janet) were able to participate in a group interview. Each group interview was approximately 2 hours in length. I had only five pre-set group interview questions.[5] In the group interview, participants were encouraged to ask each other questions. We also established ground rules, which included an acknowledgment that each person had the right not to answer a question posed to her.

Beyond the individual and group interviews, I incorporated, to a smaller extent, a few other data collection methods, including short follow-up questions via email, participant-observation, artifact analysis, and document review. The women in this research did not lend themselves easily to participant-observation, especially since most of the participants did not belong to cohesive mixed race groups. I was, however, able to attend a social for the mixed race group in Boston that included two of the participants and approximately 15 other mixed race people. At the event, a meeting at a Boston bar for happy hour, I introduced myself as a visiting researcher and a mixed race woman. I did not take notes during the event but wrote up field notes afterwards. Attending this event was the only formal opportunity I had for participant-observation outside of the interviews.

Some participants did, however, share artifacts and documents with me. I encouraged the participants to bring to the interviews any writings, artifacts or pictures that might help them tell their stories. Several of the participants shared pictures of themselves and/or friends and family. This helped me to obtain a fuller view of them in relation to significant people in their lives. Some of the women shared pictures of themselves as children; often defining features of "race" shifted over time. Maria, for example, had skin color several shades darker as a child and teen than she did at the time of our interviews. One participant, Marta, shared with me an album of pictures of art she had created. A few participants gave me personal writings related to being mixed race. Two participants shared their "MySpace" online accounts, which allowed me to see some of their friends and provided insights into how they presented and described themselves in another context. I interviewed nine of the participants in their homes, allowing further insight into their lives. At five of those homes, I had the opportunity to peruse participants' bookcases, which provided information on possible common ground with me and others based on what they might have read.

After the interviews were completed, I asked a few follow-up questions via email; some participants also sent me follow-up emails without specific prompting.[6] I conducted all of the interviews personally and audio recorded them, with participant permission. During the interviews, I took extensive written field notes that included the participants' words, as well as the setting and interactions before and after the interviews. Thus, my collective data ultimately consisted of a combination of individual interviews (two per person), group interviews, email correspondence, observation field notes, documents (written stories, pictures, shared journal entries, emails), and a personal field journal.

DATA ANALYSIS AND INTERPRETATION

Using inductive thematic analysis (Johnson & Christensen, 2004), I began to examine my field notes for codes and themes during the data collection. Johnson and Christensen (2004) defined inductive analysis as "immersion in the details and specifics of the data to discover important patterns, themes, and interrelationships; [it] begins by exploring, then confirming, [and is] guided by analytical principles" (p. 362). I transcribed the group interviews first, coded them for themes, and looked for patterns. This served as my initial analysis and enabled me to create an initial coding schema. I then began to transcribe the individual interviews.[7] While I waited for the final transcriptions, I coded my written field notes and typed up an overview of each interview from the notes. Glesne (2006) stated:

> Coding is a progressive process of sorting and defining and defining and sorting those scraps of collected data… that are applicable to your research purpose. By putting like-minded pieces together into data clumps, you create an organizational framework…. Eventually, you can place the various data clumps in a meaningful sequence that contributes to the chapters or sections of your manuscript. (p. 152)

Interviews were transcribed verbatim. I sorted and organized each data scrap under a code such that nothing was omitted. After coding the group interviews and the first few individual interviews, I searched for common codes in order to more succinctly organize the data. Those original codes expanded and metamorphosed until all the data was accounted for from each interview.

Throughout the process I was committed to reflexivity, meaning that I attempted to be "as concerned with the research process as [I was] with the data" (Glesne, 2006, p. 125). In addition, I asked myself questions such as: Do stories exist that dispute this analysis? Whose voices are most prominent in this section? Who is being left out and why? What follow up questions should I ask? What are the words that are hardest to hear? What are the stories that feel most personally affirming? Am I including both affirming and disaffirming stories in my final product?

Through the use of the described coding process, I identified six major themes that have become the data chapters of this book. The themes include: (a) (shifting) racial and ethnic positionalities, (b) negotiating structural constraints, (c) claiming agency through fluid identities, (d) forced "passing," (e) discussions of Whiteness, and (f) bridge building and educating others.

RESEARCH TRUSTWORTHINESS

Glesne (2011) explains that some researchers "create [a] claim that their work is plausible or credible" while others "reject attempts at such claims and focus on whether the inquiry, 'advances a social agenda or offers cultural criticism' (Schwandt 2007, 311)'" (p. 49). In this section I explain why I think my work is "credible;" however, throughout the book I also demonstrate how the inquiry offers a social justice agenda. I attended to trustworthiness in several ways, including member checks (Glesne, 2006; Lather, 2003; Lincoln & Guba, 1985), triangulation (Glesne, 2006; Lather, 2003), peer review and debriefing (Glesne, 2006), and thick description (Clifford, 1983; Glesne, 2006). I attempted to conduct member checks with all participants. During the original coding and analysis, I did an extensive member check with one of the participants, Maria, asking for her input on my interpretations. I also provided a draft of the book to all the participants I could locate[8] (10 total), and requested their reactions and input[9]. Four of the 10 acknowledged receiving the book draft but provided no feedback, two had only minor edits, three had substantive suggestions (only one major suggested change per person) related to content and/or analysis, and one had no changes but provided significant feedback that contributed to the ending of the book. I decided to incorporate the responses of those who had substantive content-related suggestions primarily in footnotes.

Triangulation includes the use of "multiple data sources, methods, and theoretical schemes" (Lather, 2003, p. 191) and is recommended by many as a way to strive for trustworthiness (Creswell, 1998; Glesne, 2006; Lather, 2003). I utilized multiple data methods and sources including individual interviews, group interviews, document and artifact review, participant-observation, multiple geographic locations, and reflections on my own personal experience as a mixed race woman. I also examined and articulated the stories in relation to several theoretical frameworks, as I will explain in the next chapter.

I engaged in peer review and debriefing with others at length – mentors, peers, and friends – about my codes, analysis, and interpretation. Each time I asked, "Is there anything you see that I am missing?" These debriefings and peer reviews challenged me to consider alternate data organizational structures and assisted me in recognizing multiple viewpoints relating to the data.

In the process of my writing and analysis I strived for "rich, thick description...[to] allow the reader to enter the research context" (Glesne, 2006, p. 38). In addition, I made a "conscious search for negative cases and unconfirming evidence" for my working analyses (Glesne, 2006, p. 37). I consciously worked to include any contradictions to my overall conclusions, allowing the reader to obtain the fullest picture possible in relation to each issue addressed. Lather (2003) argued that critical researchers should demonstrate "catalytic validity," which she defined as the degree to which research helps participants to rethink their lives and energizes them to engage in efforts toward social justice (p. 191). During second interviews, participants' self-disclosures of actions they took, or wished to take, as the result of the first interviews demonstrate "catalytic validity." As a critical researcher, this type of validity is especially important.

Thus, I conscientiously worked to attend to issues of trustworthiness throughout the research process. My main goal was to maintain critical reflexivity and act ethically throughout the research and writing process in order to represent the participants and information in ways that are plausible given the data.

POSITIONALITY AND SUBJECTIVITY

Post-structuralists and post-modernists have criticized the notion that a qualitative researcher has a bounded and impenetrable sense of self that can be used as an objective tool in the field. Instead, a researcher is a co-participant as she/he positions her-/himself in relation to participants, and participants position themselves in relation to how a researcher is perceived or behaves (Ellis, 2004; Gergen, 2000). (Chavez, 2008, p. 474)

There are five main positionalities from which I approach this work. I am (a) a mixed race woman, (b) an ethnographer, (c) a sociologist, (d) a feminist, and (e) a critical theorist – I attend to issues of structure and power and strive to promote social justice. These positionalities help locate my relationship to the participants and readers. As a mixed race woman, I am both a participant and a researcher in this project. As a critical ethnographer and sociologist, I approach the data from an interpretivist, constructivist paradigm paying attention to systematic issues of power and oppression. As a feminist I strive to "illuminate the social and structural roots of our gendered experiences" (Richardson, Taylor, & Whittier, 2001, p. 2).

These positionalities are influenced by my *"subjective positions* [which] refer to 'life history and personal experiences' that also affect our research" (Chiseri-Strater & Sunstein, as cited in Goodall, 2000, p. 133). Goodall (2000) argued that, "Subjective positionings are usually derived from *deeply felt lived experiences* because they recall a life's self-defining moments, decisions, or turning points" (p. 133). Varying opinions exist as to how much a researcher should reveal her/himself. I return here to the concept of exposure; I purposely risk taking a personal stance in my research and writing. The women's stories are exposed here, and I choose to reveal, through the following vignettes, some of my influencing life moments in order to situate myself as both a participant and researcher.

Hispanic Festival, Lawrence, Massachusetts, 1975

White woman: Hi Sonia, who is this you have with you?

Mom: (proudly) This is my daughter, Silvia

White woman: She's so pretty. When did you adopt her?

I am the daughter of a dark skinned Latina and a White father. In the scene above I was 5 years old attending a "Hispanic Festival" with my mom. We had recently moved from Lawrence, a working class town with a predominately Latina/o and Black population to Andover, a virtually all-White, upper middle class town. My parents moved before I started kindergarten; they wanted me to attend "good schools." I remember that day at the "Hispanic Festival" vividly; I was happy to be back in Lawrence because it felt familiar. The air was filled with *música Latina – salsa, cumbia,* and *merengue.* Aromas from various food vendors reminded me of my mom's cooking. The Spanish that was spoken was familiar even though I could not discern the words. My mom and I were having fun that day. She bought me *empanadas* and *limonada.* We danced on the concrete next to the DJ table. I didn't notice back then how my light skinned hand contrasted against my mom's brown complexion. Later in life, as I further acquired several of my mom's mannerisms, facial expressions and attitude, I would be told on several occasions – usually by my father, "You certainly are your mother's daughter!" But not that day. That day was one of several times when someone would attempt to deny that I am my mother's daughter.

Being mixed is a core part of my identity. My mother is Colombian, born and raised in Bogotá; my father is French-Canadian, born and raised in Massachusetts. I was born in Bogotá and raised most of my life in Massachusetts, in a suburb of Boston. My dad met my mom in Colombia while doing work in her *barrio* through a church program. They fell in love, got married, and, soon after, had me. When I was less than a year old, we moved to the United States. My mom, knowing that the more you speak a language the faster you learn it, refused to speak anything but English at home; we learned English together. My dad, although fluent in Spanish and a bilingual elementary school teacher, never spoke to me in Spanish. Both my parents thought we would return to and live in Colombia indefinitely and assumed I could learn then. As a result, English is my first language. My mom, who is extremely bright and very driven, spoke English within a year. I did not learn Spanish until I was seven years old when we finally returned to Bogotá. However, instead of settling there, we stayed for only one year. I attended a bilingual elementary school in Bogotá for second grade and gained fluency in Spanish at my grade level.

My experiences as a light skinned, biracial, bicultural, and bilingual woman have instilled in me a passion to learn more about the mixed race experiences of other women. There have been formative moments in my life where being mixed became particularly salient.

Middle School Locker Room, North Andover, Massachusetts, 1983

(Setting: A group of girls are huddled in the locker room talking. I am standing 10 feet away getting my things together after gym class. My small, worn purse lies on the table in front of me.)

Tracy: Hey guys, did you notice my new pocket book?

Tara: Oh my god, I totally love it. Is it a Dooney & Bourke?

Tracy: Yeah, my dad got it for me when we took our trip to Florida. I told him that I needed one to go with my new outfit.

Tracy: (looking over at me, in a fake voice) Your pocket book is cute too.

(The girls in the huddle giggle and continue to talk. A few minutes later they begin to leave. Before they reach the door I speak)

Me: (face turning red, blurt out) Tracy, you're a fucking snob!

Tracy: Why don't you go ride your llama!

Me: What is that supposed to mean?

Tracy: Well you're from Colombia aren't you? Why don't you go back to where you came from!

Throughout K – 12, except for the year I lived in Colombia, I struggled to find my place among my wealthy, predominately White peers. I did well in school academically, but among my peers I felt like an outsider in many ways. Even though at times I blended in, there were always moments when my classmates reminded me that being Colombian made me different. Rarely did I claim my voice and stand up to them, and when I did, they quickly reminded me that I did not belong. I stood out not only in terms of race, but also in terms of class. Many of my peers' parents held jobs as top executives, doctors, and some were even professional sports players. My mom was a social worker, and my dad was an elementary school teacher; although we had plenty of money, I often felt like my classmates looked upon me as if I was poor. Additionally, I had a feminist analysis that positioned me, yet again, as an outsider in relation to my peers. My feminist mom consciously taught me about gender bias, and as a teenager I was able to detect sexism that was invisible to most of the people around me. I longed for the company of peers who had a similar gender role analysis, and I wanted to learn more about feminism. When the time came to explore options upon high school graduation, with my parents' encouragement and support, I decided to pursue a degree in Women's Studies. Having felt trapped, and at times alienated, in a predominately White high school, I was determined to attend a university where diversity was valued.

My desire to be on a diverse campus that had Women's Studies as a major led me on a path to the University of California at Santa Cruz (UCSC). I visited UCSC during spring break. There were virtually no students around, but the fliers on campus advertised a variety of cultural groups and events, making it seem as if people of color would have a large and central presence on campus.

My first semester at Santa Cruz I took a "Women Writers" class through the Women's Studies department. Being a naïve 18 year old, and having been misled by the multitude of fliers around campus relating to campus diversity groups, I was surprised to find that all the other women in the class were White. The instructor was also a White woman; however, the course included readings by an ethnically and racially diverse group of women authors. In class discussions, I discovered that my perspective in response to the readings was most often contradictory to the other students, and I knew that my "different" perspective was due, at least in part, to the fact that I am mixed. They, however, assumed that I was White (like them), and when I shared my perspective, I was dismissed because what I said did not match their beliefs.

Women Writers Class, UCSC, 1988

Scene One

> Classmate: The author sounds really angry, so angry that her work is not accessible. I don't think she has to be that angry to get her point across. I didn't really like this reading.

> Me: Of course she's angry; she's talking about her life, about being discriminated against as a Black woman.

> Classmates: (Stares of annoyance)

> Classmate: Still…

> Me: (Silence)

Scene Two

> Classmate: I think that women are more oppressed than people of color.

Me: (to myself "What????") (angrily) Women are people of color.

Classmate: I know, I just ... You don't have to get angry.

Me: (Silence)

My anger and inability to relate to my classmates' perceptions left me tongue-tied. At times I tried to speak up, but I was typically dismissed until they learned that I am Latina, a "woman of color." At UCSC at that time, being a person of color carried clout; it was cool to be a person of color – in a problematic, tokenized way. Thus, only when I identified as such, did others want to hear what I had to say, but then my words were subsequently superficially glorified and my perspectives essentialized.

The most life-changing experience from that class resulted from being introduced by my tutor to the book *Borderlands/La Frontera,* by Gloria Anzaldúa (1987). Having failed the required UCSC writing entrance exam, I was assigned to work with a tutor who, it turned out, was another mixed race student of color. I talked with her about my experiences in the Women Writer's class, explaining my struggles of feeling like an "other" while simultaneously feeling bad about calling myself a "woman of color" as a white skinned woman. However, because of my life experiences, I did not identify as White. I felt caught between the identifications of "White woman" and "woman of color," forced to choose an identification as a woman of color but feeling like that did not acknowledge the entirety of who I am. No other option for self-identification had occurred to me until I was introduced to *Borderlands*. In this richly contextualized book Anzaldúa writes about a variety of borderlands including physical, psychological, sexual, and spiritual borderlands. She defines a new space, a new identity – the *mestiza* consciousness – a place where there is a tolerance for ambiguity and room for growth. In *Borderlands* I found a home where I could claim all parts of me, the mestiza identity.

It had never occurred to me to call myself "mixed" before reading Anzaldúa's book; I could not imagine claiming a mixed race identity because of the prevalence of binaries in society. The mestiza literally embodies the message that connection across difference and tolerance for ambiguity is imperative. Without the acceptance of plurality and ambiguity, mestiza people don't exist. For the mestiza this creates what Anzaldúa (1987) calls "psychic restlessness." She said, "Cradled in one culture, sandwiched between two cultures, straddling all three cultures and their value systems, la mestiza undergoes a struggle of flesh, a struggle of borders, an inner war" (p. 78). I know this war on a personal level. I have lived it. It is crazy-making. But for me waging the inner war is worth it because my existence and the existence of other mestizas, mixtures of people of all kinds, helps to keep people from placing individuals into categories of *us* and *them*. After reading the words of Anzaldúa (1987), I began to accept my identity by "developing a tolerance for contradictions, a tolerance for ambiguity" (p. 79). This does not negate the value of honoring distinct cultures, even for those of us who are mixed, but it allows for points of connection in the face of difference.

As I learned to embrace the ambiguity of my identity, I learned to cherish the ways it enhanced my ability to connect to others. Because of my bicultural identity I was forced to move between and within cultural groups that did not always feel like home. Maria Lugones (1990) argued in her text, "Playfulness, 'World'–Travelling, and Loving Perception," that "outsiders" to the mainstream White/Anglo culture acquire "flexibility in shifting from the mainstream construction of life to other constructions of life where she is more or less 'at home'" (p. 390). She calls this flexibility "'world' travelling" and recommends "to women of color in the U.S. to learn to love each other by travelling to each other's 'worlds'" (p. 390). I have been fortunate in my life to have been invited to travel into the "worlds" of other women of color. Those experiences helped me to heal from the effects of being the victim to what is called "arrogant perception" (Frye, as cited in Lugones, 1990, p. 390). Arrogant perception, Lugones says, is "systematically organized to break the spirit" of people (p. 391).

Many of my middle school, high school, and college classmates viewed me through this lens of arrogant perception and positioned me as the subordinate, stereotyped "other." Sometimes, even those who expressed interest in my opinions, as the women eventually did in my Women Writers class, often seemed to do so from a self-serving position rather than through a desire to make a connection. Lugones calls us to action, to perceive others through "loving eyes" (p. 391), by traveling to each other's worlds in a way that is playful and non-judgmental, a way that promotes identification rather than separateness. She said, "The reason why I think that travelling to someone's 'world' is a way of identifying with them is because by travelling to their 'world' we can understand *what it is to be them and what it is to be ourselves in their eyes.* Only when we have travelled to each other's 'worlds' are we fully subjects to each other" (p. 401). Although throughout my life I have experienced the benefit of "world" traveling, I have often felt unsure of where to call home.

I am fortunate to have two incredibly loving extended families. On both sides my grandparents, aunts, and uncles love(d) me for who I am. This support carries me through all the arrogant perception challenges I face. However, even though they love me, they don't always understand my mixed race life. After being introduced to the concept of mixed race identity, I wanted to make connection with other mixed race people in hopes of finding shared experiences.

When in college as an undergraduate, I concentrated much of my studies on learning about the experiences of mixed race people. My work culminated in an undergraduate thesis based on interviews with eight mixed race women titled, *Women of Mixed Heritage Living on the Borders of Whiteness and Color: Reconstructing Whole Selves.* The interviews, and the accompanying readings, helped me to find connection with others and validate my identity as a mixed race woman. Since then I have also learned to embrace identities as a Latina and as a woman of color. I embrace all three positionalities simultaneously. Although I have a wide range of interests and have held a variety of roles since that time, I longed to return to conducting qualitative research with mixed race people, thus leading me to this project.

Although my undergraduate research focused on women's mixed race experiences, the motivation for that project was to learn about others in hopes, primarily, of better understanding myself and learning how to create a solid mixed race identity. What I gained from that work, and my life experience as a woman who straddles two ethnicities and cultures, was not only a stronger sense of security with my multiple, ambiguous, sometimes conflicting positionalities, but a desire to engage in work – personal, academic, and paid – that centers on forging connections across cultural difference. Through my work over the years as an activist, community educator, college instructor, and scholar, I have always strived to eradicate oppression through education. In each role, my goal has been to find ways to promote equity. This – eradicating oppression and promoting equity – is the primary goal that motivates my work with this project.

It is from these positionalities that my theoretical frameworks and supporting literature emerge. I recognize that:

> Ethnography is from beginning to end enmeshed in writing. This writing includes, minimally, a translation of experience into textual form. The process is complicated by the action of multiple subjectivities and political constraints beyond the control of the writer. In response to these forces ethnographic writing enacts a specific strategy of authority. (Clifford, 1983, p. 120)

I am conscientious of my multiple subjectivities, my positionalities, and the political implications of my work. I maintain a critically self-reflexive approach to writing this ethnographic account and strive to maintain integrity and respect in relationship to the participants, readers, and myself – tasks that sometimes are in direct contradiction to each other. I acknowledge and draw upon the work of other ethnographers, mixed race people, sociologists, feminists, and critical theorists to position these stories and my work in relationship to the voices and work of others.

Collectively, the participants' voices, my writing, and the situated theoretical frameworks add to the discourse on mixed race research and reveal sociological nuances related to the intersections of race, class, gender, and sexuality and their relationships to issues of power, structure, and agency.

RESISTING THEORETICAL DISEMBODIMENT: CLAIMING SPACE IN THE RESEARCH AND THEORIES CONVERSATIONS

Sociology, Hybridity, and Mixed Race Studies

Read books about how White people benefit from White power. – Susan

Little did I know when I began this research in 2005 that a few years later U.S. citizens would elect a mixed race president. Ironically, the prominence of Barack Obama has simultaneously highlighted mixed race experience and hidden it. Although it is well known that Obama is the son of a White mother and a Black African father, that fact is often overshadowed by descriptions of him as "the first *Black* president." There are power plays daily in news media regarding the connections between Obama's character and his race. An image flashes on television of Obama in an elderly home smiling with White residents followed by a picture of him as a child with his White grandparents. Even without words, the message is conveyed as to why this Black man can occupy such a White space with perceived ease – he is mixed. Yet comments about his "Blackness" predominate. In a 2010 episode of *The Daily Show with John Stewart*[10], Stewart explicitly illuminated how Obama is often caught between stereotypes. When cool and collected, he is positioned as uncaring and aloof, but any displays of emotion threaten to place him in the category of "the angry Black man." One thing is clear, despite assertions that we have reached a "post-racial era," race still matters, and racism and White supremacy abound in ways often difficult for many to detect.

There are multiple angles from which to approach mixed race issues. In this chapter, I discuss the academic theories and literature that I both employ and critique in my analysis and interpretation, including (a) sociology of education and sociological race theories, (b) the social construction of race and gender, (c) translocational positionalities and theories of performativity, (d) hybridity theory, and (e) mixed race studies theory and research. As mentioned in Chapter 1, if you are uninterested in the academic theories and desire to learn mostly from the mixed race women's stories, you may wish to skim this chapter. However, it is important to recognize that context matters, and these stories are situated within these theoretical contexts.

SITUATING THE RESEARCH WITHIN BOTH SOCIOLOGY AND
SOCIOLOGY OF EDUCATION

Sociologists in general, and sociologists of education in particular, have had a prominent role in unveiling and unpacking various mechanisms and manifestations of oppression. Through evolutions of functionalism, conflict theory, interactionism, and critical theory, ideas about the way society operates as a whole, and specifically how schools function, have shifted from a macro perspective to a micro perspective to a combined macro-micro analysis.

Although the field of sociology of education is vast, there is a general split between those who operate in the old versus "the New Sociology of Education" (Weis, McCarthy, & Dimitriadis, 2006). The old paradigm, situated in functionalism – a theory that views school as maintaining social order through a meritocratic system – "assumed the most important question was that of 'access' to educative institutions – what blocked it or what might encourage it" (Weis, McCarthy, & Dimitriadis, 2006, p. 2). Conflict theorists (see Bowles & Gintis, 1976; Weber, 1978), creating the emergence of a New Sociology of Education, revealed that U.S. schooling practices ultimately function in dominant groups' interests. The new sociology of education scholars "looked at the complex interrelationship between the stratification of knowledge and social stratification" (Weis, McCarthy, & Dimitriadis, 2006, p. 4). Reproduction theorists such as Pierre Bourdieu and Basil Bernstein argued that educational institutions reproduce social inequalities through complex, sometimes indirect, processes (McDonough & Nuñez, 2007).

Bourdieu is perhaps best known for his concepts of cultural capital and social capital. Cultural capital consists of knowledge, attitudes, forms of presentation, and behaviors that are favored in the dominant culture (Bourdieu, 1977; McDonough & Nuñez, 2007). This capital is most often possessed by socioeconomically and racially (White) privileged individuals and is passed along from one generation to the next. Within the formal education context, this means that privileged parents pass on their cultural capital to their children who then possess the capital that assists them in being successful in school, which in turn helps them maintain their privileged status and pass it along to the next generation. Social capital refers to the connections that can be made through social network resources that can be used to gain success and advancement in dominant society. Bourdieu focuses on how social capital can reproduce social hierarchies and inequity (Stanton-Salazar, 2004). Cultural and social resources can only become cultural and social capital if they are "used and valued in the context in which they are used and converted" (McDonough & Nuñez, 2007, p. 146). The women's stories are replete with examples of cultural capital gained through status. Stories of both access to and lack of social capital also surface.

Sadovnik (2001) explained that Bernstein "[e]xamined how speech patterns reflect students' social class backgrounds and how students from working-class backgrounds are at a disadvantage in the school setting because schools are middle-class organizations" (p. 22). Bernstein has been critiqued as a deficit theorist (Karabel & Halsey, 1977). However, he rejected that critique, stating that it was not the language itself that created the disadvantage but the unequal power relations between the distinct socioeconomic classes of students. The quotes in this book reveal that all of the women in the study possess the general speech patterns of the dominant culture. We also learn that ultimately each has achieved academic success in school, for some, very high degrees of success.

Postmodern, critical theory emerged based primarily on the work of Brazilian educator Paulo Freire (1995, 2000, 2001). Although not all critical theorists would identify as sociologists of education, critical theory has become a valuable lens used by sociologists to examine the purposes and processes of schooling (Bennett deMarrais & LeCompte, 1999; Sadovnik, 2001). Critical theory uses concepts from several other theories to combine both a macro and microanalysis of social phenomena, for example schooling. Critical theorists strive to uncover how schooling reproduces dominant class interests and how students are influenced and respond; critical theorists argue that schools mostly help dominant groups maintain power, but subordinate groups have the potential to resist domination (Bennett deMarrais & LeCompte, 1999).

Lauder, Brown, and Halsey (2009), in their overview of current trends in British sociology of education, acknowledged a similar "cultural turn" (p. 576), including a new understanding that the education system not only reproduces but also *constructs* inequity. This turn also includes a heavy focus on "identity and cultural politics," as evidenced by a study of the research paper themes published within the *British Journal of Sociology of Education*, finding that 80% of the 294 articles fell within these two themes (Power & Rees, as cited in Lauder, Brown, & Halsey, 2009, p. 576).

This research project is situated within this cultural turn toward the new sociology of education. Given the notable gaps in academic achievement based on race (Noguera & Wing, 2006), it is clear that race is an important factor to consider in how power operates in educational systems. Sociologists of education have long examined issues of race in education (see Hallinan, 1988; Jencks & Phillips, 1998; Noguera, 2004; Valenzuela, 1999); however, work within sociology of education that explores the stories of mixed race individuals is virtually non-existent. A search[11] in the *Sociology of Education* journal revealed only one entry related to the experiences of mixed race people (see Herman, 2009). A similar search conducted in the *British Journal of Sociology of Education* yielded only three entries focused on mixed race individuals, each of which was about specific cultures, not a cross-representation of mixed race people. Work on mixed race topics is also notably scarce in the larger sociology literature.

Telles and Sue (2009), in the *Annual Review of Sociology*, examined "a large, interdisciplinary, and somewhat scattered literature, all of which falls under the umbrella term race mixture" (p. 129). Taking a social constructivist approach to race, they argued that "race is of sociological importance because humans are categorized by race, hierarchized according to these categories, and treated accordingly" (p. 130). They asserted that race mixture was a strong topic of concern among sociologists in the earlier part of the 20th century, but various factors "led to a diminished interest in the topic of race mixture and multiracialism" until the last decade when interest re-emerged inspired by debates regarding the inclusion of a multiracial category on the 2000 U.S. census (Telles & Sue, 2009, p. 132).

One of the central arguments in recent scholarly discussions of race mixture is that interracial relationships and multiracial identification will eliminate racism (D'Souza, 1995; Patterson, 2000). D'Souza declares, "The country is entering a new era in which racial categories are rapidly becoming obsolete, mostly because of intermarriage" (as cited in Telles & Sue, 2009, p. 133). Mixed race people are often hailed as the answer to racial divides (Nakashima, 1992; Trueba, 2004). The argument's logic is that as interracial marriages and couplings rise, racial differences will become increasingly blurred, and racial conflict will consequently decrease (Hoetink, 1985; Trueba, 2004).

This argument, about the potential positive impact mixed race people and interracial unions can engender, stands in stark contrast to earlier debates by White racist colonialists who argued that human beings were of different species, with Whites being superior (Young, 1995). Mixed race people, and thus interracial unions, signaled the potential demise of the "great White race;" race mixing was viewed with fear, hatred, and contempt. Although some argue that mixed race people provide hope for a better future, hatred, fear, and resentment towards White/of color multiracial people continue today among racist White supremacists (Parker & Song, 2001) and others who do not consider themselves "racists" but rebuke interracial coupling nonetheless (Bonilla-Silva, 2006).

Research that focuses on multiraciality is needed to unpack these ongoing debates and augment understandings of how racial constructs intersect with gender, sexuality, and social class. The mixed race discourse is rapidly growing but still limited; sociological analysis and ethnographic data on the topic are particularly wanting. Although there are increasing numbers of academic books dedicated to race mixing (see DaCosta, 2007; Downing, Nichols, & Webster, 2005; Ifekwunigwe, 2004; Parker & Song, 2001; Root, 1992, 1996; Sexton, 2008) as well as novels and anthologies with personal narratives by mixed race people (see Anzaldúa & Keating, 2002; Camper, 1994; O'Hearn, 1998; Walker, 2001), there are few ethnographic studies examining the experiences of mixed race people. Much ethnography regarding mixed race individuals concentrates on multiracial identity development and takes a psychological perspective (see Collins, 2000; Funderburg, 1994; Gillem, Cohn, & Throne, 2001; Kich, 1992; Standen; 1996). Few ethnographic studies (Ifekwunigwe, 1999; Korgen, 1998) conducted with mixed race people move beyond identity development analysis to include a larger sociological perspective, and these works do not include examinations of schooling experiences.

Telles and Sue (2009), in their attempt to problematize "the assumed relationship between miscegenation/intermarriage/multiracial identification and a lack of racism" (p. 134) turned to studies on Latin America (see Wade, 2004) to argue that race mixing can actually serve to maintain racial boundaries rather than erode them. They questioned how trends of multiracial identification will impact racial hierarchies (p. 135). "Sociologists are not only concerned with race mixture in and of itself, but also with how mixed-race persons are categorized in a particular society and how this, in turn, affects race relations and the social structure more broadly" (Telles & Sue, 2009, p. 136). Telles and Sue (2009) specifically called for sociologically analyzed "qualitative and ethnographic data" on race mixing to increase understanding of racial dynamics (p. 140). My writing in this book is an answer to that call. What these women's stories reveal is a complex configuration of how mixed race people's existence, actions, and beliefs might impact race relations in the United States. As of now, the debate is dichotomized; some believe that the increasing existence of mixed race individuals will decrease racial conflict while others believe that race mixing will intensify racial inequity. Through personal narrative, these women reveal nuances of thought about race mixing that simultaneously increase and decrease racial boundaries and conflict.

This book exemplifies a breakthrough in both sociology and sociology of education because it incorporates research with mixed race people, a topic, which up until now, has been virtually absent from the literature; in the proceeding chapters, the women's narratives reveal more nuanced ideas regarding social stratification, stratification of knowledge, interracial conflict, and interracial understanding. In addition, this work resists theoretical disembodiment. Although theories often spring from lived experience, frequently the theory becomes disembodied and decontextualized. Bourdieu (1987-88) stated, "… all sorts of historical agents, starting with social scientists such as Marx, have succeeded in transforming what could have remained as an 'analytical construct' into a 'folk category,' that is, into one of those impeccably real social fictions produced and reproduced by the magic of social belief" (p. 9). In other words, social scientists examine phenomena and then create their own renditions that are acted upon and people respond accordingly; we remake the world in our own image. This has occurred with the concept of hybridity which has been extracted from people's lived "hybrid" experiences, theorized, and reworked in a manner that disregards embodied "hybrid" living; it decontextualizes and simplifies. This project recontextualizes hybrid theories and examines sociological theories, hybrid theories, and Whiteness theories through the multifaceted lens of mixed race lived experiences.

RACE AND GENDER AS SOCIAL CONSTRUCTS

The Social Construction of Race

Although the term race is used throughout this book, I want to emphasize that race is a social construct (Omi & Winant, 1994). The concept of race was originally based on the notion of biology, but it is now commonly accepted that race is socially constructed (Furedi, 2001; Olumide, 2002; Omi & Winant, 1994; Spickard, 1992). However, although race may not be defined biologically, the implications of racial categorizations continue. "Throughout American history, the U.S. government has used racial designations as a tool of dominance, serving to separate and penalize those not defined as white" (Williams, 2008, p. 22). Omi and Winant (1994) argued that race, as with gender, is one of the first observations noted in meeting a person. They assert that without a racial designation one is left without a complete identity because race identity is so integral to U.S. society. Thus, although race is not "real" in a biological sense, race marking, racism, and the consequences of such are real in the everyday lives of people. While it is problematic to utilize the term "mixed race" because it has the potential to reify racial categorization, it is also important to recognize that racial categorization continues to define people. Currently the federal government defines five racial categories: American Indian or Alaska Native; Asian; Black or African American; Native Hawaiian or Other Pacific Islander; and White.[12] In addition, the government recognizes one ethnicity: Hispanic or Latino. To use the term "mixed race" to describe my project would, according to government definitions, have excluded Latino/as who are not considered a race by government delineation. However, Latino/as often view themselves and are treated as peoples from a distinct racial category. As such, for the purpose of this study, I include people who are White and Latina under the term "mixed race."

Like various "minority" monoracial groups who have been the targets of racist attacks, verbal and physical, many mixed raced people have also experienced racism. Mixed race people sometimes experience racism when being identified with one racial group. For example, a biracial Black/White person may experience racism for being recognized as Black. However, there are also a variety of derogatory terms that have been used to refer specifically to mixed race people including "mulatto," "octoroon," "half-breed," and "half-caste" (Mengel, 2001). Multiracial people have been represented as confused, fragmented, and even as race traitors (see Root, 1992; Williams, 2008; Young, 1995). It is important to continually question the use of racial categories, including the category "mixed race," as a reminder that race is socially constructed. However, because race is real in its material consequences, and we have yet to escape racial designations, using race-based terms is necessary to unpack operations of power.

Many British authors place any terms that include the word "race" in quotation marks, such as the term "mixed race" or "multiracial" (see Ifekwunigwe, 2004; Parker & Song, 2001). The quotations symbolize acknowledgement of and emphasis on race as a social construct. One prominent British author focused on mixed race issues, Jayne Ifekwunigwe (1999), initially invoked the French term *métis*, in place of the label "mixed race," which she explained is "synonymous with the derogatory English 'half-caste' and 'half-breed'" to circumvent the issue of which existing term to use (p. 43). She argued that her goal in "redeploying" the term in the English context was to de-center race. However, upon reflection, she changed her mind and in later writings decided not to employ the term in the English context for fear that using a French-African term in that way could further marginalize mixed race subjectivities (p. 44). She has now returned to using the term "mixed race" in quotes. Downing, Nichols, and Webster (2005), in an effort to help readers best find resources on "interracial themes," provided an overview of language related to multiracial people and issues. They reminded us that "meanings of words change over time" and recommended that people seeking information use broad terms such as "interracial" for keyword searching (p. 9). Interracial, they argued, is used synonymously with the term multiracial. However, I would caution that interracial can also refer to an interaction between members of different races, and thus has little to do with mixed race individuals.

The wide range of possible terms and the multitude of potential arguments for the preference of any one term demonstrate that we have yet to find terminology that adequately describes and defines us. I have decided to predominately use the term mixed race in my work. For flow of text, at times I will use the terms multiracial and biracial interchangeably with mixed race.

The Social Construction of Gender

Like race, gender is also socially constructed (Butler, 1990, 1993; Lorber, 2001). Judith Butler examined the relationship between the materiality of the body and the performativity of identity, particularly gender identification. She stated "gender is an identity tenuously constituted in time, instituted in an exterior space through a *stylized repetition of acts*" (1990, p. 179). She argued that gender and sex are performative and culturally constructed. Just as race is often assigned through phenotype and particular marking characteristics, such as skin color, gender is often assigned on the basis of a sex category that is primarily determined by the genitalia that people have at birth. However, "a sex category becomes a gender status through naming, dress, and the use of other gender markers" (Lorber, 2001, p. 40). Long before puberty, children are named in a variety of ways as occupying the gender of either a boy or a girl. Gender thus becomes a social institution that serves as "one of the major ways that human beings organize their lives" (p. 41). This is evidenced through the social division of labor and heterosexual marriage.

29

Although gender may be socially constructed, "once gender is ascribed, the social order constructs and holds individuals to strongly gendered norms and expectations" (p. 48). Thus, although gender is socially constructed, because it is a major organizing institution, we must acknowledge that people are primarily categorized in groups as men or as women. People, who through their actions, dress, appearance, and self-definitions resist dominant gender norms – for example as transgendered, intersexed, and butch – reveal the constructedness of gender categories. Nonetheless, social forces of domination often disregard "alternative" gender constructions and require people to choose between either man or woman. This plays out in myriad ways, including through the use of language, as we will see in participant Marta's self-naming in relation to the gendered terms Latino and Latina. Because oppression is sustained by an interlocking matrix of domination created through race, gender, class, sexual orientation, and other social categories (Collins, 2000), distinct implications for race mixing among men and women exist historically. This will be further discussed in the sections on multiracial discourses and hybridity.

TRANSLOCATIONAL POSITIONALITY AND PERFORMATIVITY

Often, work related to race and gender is approached in terms of "identity politics" (Power & Rees, 2006). I myself began this work wanting to learn how these women navigated their "hybrid identities." Yet I have always been troubled by this term "identity" – a prominent concept in psychoanalysis. Much work on mixed race people is grounded in identity theories and attempts to explain how and why people identify in certain ways. Authors who analyze data through an identity theory lens sometimes advocate specific aspirational identifications in order to help individuals reach greater self-acceptance and/or enlightenment (Kich, 1992). This work has been useful in bringing hidden mixed race experiences and issues to the fore. Yet, as a sociologist, I have often found analysis through identity theory troubling because so much emphasis is placed on individual work and action, sometimes to the exclusion of outside influencing factors such as the communities and structures in which people live, the relationships they have with others, and the language and knowledge readily available to engage in such work.

As I delved into existing research involving mixed race individuals, I found the predominant focus on identity development limiting. Thus, in my analysis of this data, I foreground Anthias's (2002) concept of translocational positionality. She argued, "The notion of narratives of location and positionality appears to be a more useful analytical device for what is produced in the texts than the notion of identity" (p. 493). I concur with Anthias that the concept of identity "obscures" and reintroduces essentialism (p. 494). A narrative of location "tells a story about how we place ourselves in terms of social categories such as those of gender, ethnicity and class at a specific point in time and space" (p. 494). The stories these mixed race women share reveal "conventional norms or rules" (p. 499) and, thus, tell us something about the (perceived) context, social place, and hierarchies they are navigating in their lived experiences.

To accomplish my analysis, in addition to a sociological, critical perspective, I take a poststructuralist lens to this work, recognizing that discourse matters; meaning is created through discourse and people are constituted by and in stories (Anthias, 2002, p. 499). Reality is constructed and performed through narrative; it is both constitutive of and constituted by discourse. Narratives define positionality; how stories are situated and their constructed meanings provide information about the hierarchies of social positions. Therefore, it is important to remember that "narratives are never innocent of social structure and social place, simultaneously reflecting and making sense of our social position in the order of things while never being merely representational of this order" (p. 500).

Positionality, Anthias (2002) explains,

> relates to the space at the intersection of structure (as a social position/social effects) and agency (as social positioning/meaning and practice). The concept involves processes of identification but is not reducible to these, for what is signaled are the lived practices in which identification is practiced/performed as well as the intersubjective, organizational and representational conditions for their existence. (pp. 501–502)

This concept of translocational positionality recognizes the importance of context (with a focus on location) and allows for variability in negotiations of structure and agency. This more aptly allows for unveiling and understanding the multiple layers of complexity inherent in these mixed women's lives.

To assist in approaching these narratives through an analysis of translocational positionality, I emphasize the work of others on performativity. Hey (2006) examined how Butler's definition of performativity might be used in theorizing critical ethnographies in sociology of education. She argued, "Performativity conceptualizes the paradox of identity as apparently fixed but inherently unstable, revealing (gender) norms requiring continual maintenance" (Hey, 2006, p. 439). In other words, the concept of performativity – repetitions of actions related to particular social positions such as gender – reveals (and reproduces) norms. A Butlerian view replaces the concept of "identity" with "the subject as a fictive accomplishment of 'identification'... saturated by wish fulfillments" (Hey, 2006, p. 445). However, although I wish to disrupt fixed notions of identity by utilizing the term positionality, I am cognizant of the fact that many of the women refer to their particular "identities." Thus, in the text, although I will most often refer to the concept of shifting positionalities, at times I will use the word "identity," particularly in relation to social identity categories such as race, class, gender, and sexuality. In the text as a whole, the women themselves disrupt fixed notions of identity through discussions of fluid and shifting "identities," even though they may use that the term "identity" in their personal narratives in ways that on the surface may seem fixed.

I approach these stories with a theoretical analysis based on the belief that identifications matter because they tell stories not only about individuals but also about larger societal norms and structures. Interrogating performativities of positionalities – located within particular contexts – for patterns and disjunctures has the potential to increase our understandings of social processes, which can create new possibilities for more socially just processes.

One of my goals of this work is determining how these women's descriptions of their experiences and thoughts as mixed race individuals living in contemporary U.S. society might aid us in promoting social justice. In order to create new visions, we must first understand current operations of positionality power dynamics as they relate to intersections of race, gender, class, and sexuality.

> The narrational aspects of location/dislocation are important for sociological understanding and political contestation and can be seen as both outcomes and effective social processes. These narrations of individuals are the stories that they tell and retell about their collective placement, about their place in the social order of things. (Anthias, 2002, p. 512)

These stories can be situated in the context of a wide range of discourses and theories. I highlight a few here that are most directly related to mixed race issues.

HYBRIDITY DISCOURSES

Hybridity is currently a popular concept in a variety of contemporary academic discourses. Discussions of hybridity can be found in multiple fields, including sociology, women's studies, cultural studies, postcolonial studies, and education. These discourses directly and indirectly speak to multiracial experiences and the social construction of race. However, they are largely theoretically abstract, neglecting the embodied experiences of mixed race people.

History of the Term "Hybridity"

The term hybridity stems from biology and the selective interbreeding of plants. However, in the mid 1800s the term was used to refer to humans and became associated with the eugenics movement (Young, 1995). White colonialists wanted to promote the idea that human beings were of different species to justify slavery and exploitation of people of color. At this time, mixed race women were scrutinized in the effort to show that, as a different species, mixed race women were infertile. When this line of reasoning was destroyed by the evident capacity of mixed race women to procreate, racist scientists developed arguments about different "types" of people (Young, 1995). For example, in *The Races of Men,*

Knox (1850) argued, "the hybrid was a degradation of humanity and was rejected by nature" (as cited in Young, 1995, p. 15).

The term hybridity has always been entwined in racial debates and often carries a history of racist politics (Young, 1995). Hybrid persons signaled the potential demise of the "great White race." "Hybrid" identities simultaneously offered hope to people of color, because the hybrid existence, and specifically the fertility of the hybrid woman, proved that people of color were indeed people and not another species that could be exploited at will. At the same time, some mixed race children were daily reminders for women of color of sexual assault they had endured.

The New Conception of Hybridity

The new postcolonial concept of hybridity is in many ways removed from its biological origins and placed instead into a theoretical *space* of culture. Bhabha is the most prominent writer linked with the recent reconceptualization of the term hybridity. He stressed the interdependence of hybrid parts (e.g., the colonizer and the colonized) and challenged the assumption that cross cultural encounters will automatically be regulated by a dominator/dominated relationship. Instead, such encounters create what Bhabha (1994, 1996) described as "the Third Space." This hybrid space, Bhabha argued, breaks down binary categories and enables a form of subversion by the colonized of the colonizer. In this in-between, hybrid, "Third Space," a new space of negotiation emerges where "power is unequal but its articulation may be equivocal" (Bhabha, p. 58, 1996); in other words, the colonized may claim power in this space through discourse. Bhabha argued that this hybrid space is one of empowerment for the colonized agent. However, this "Third Space" theory is often articulated by voices that represent the dominant culture, namely male academics (see, for example, Grossberg, 1993; McLaren, 1997), and the voices of the subaltern – people who represent oppressed minority groups, including mixed race women – are marginalized.

Ashcroft, Griffiths, and Tiffin (2003) promoted Bhabha's notion that the hybridity of the postcolonial subject is a source of strength. They defined hybridity as "the creation of new transcultural forms within the contact zone produced by colonization" (p. 118). This is a zone in which hybridity combines the colonizer and colonized worlds. Ashcroft, Griffiths, and Tiffin did acknowledge, however, that the term "hybridity" has often been used in postcolonial discourse to mean simply "cross-cultural exchange." They pointed out the danger in doing so; it can lead to "negating and neglecting the imbalance and inequality of the power relations it references" (p. 119).

Young (1995), in contrast to Bhabha, argued that the theories advanced today about postcolonialism and ethnicity continue to promote the colonial discourse of the nineteenth century rather than dismantle it. He explained that the current celebration of hybridity is an extension of the nineteenth century fascination with people having sex and feeds into the pseudo-scientific cultural construction of race. Hybridity in its new form conveniently forgets the sordid colonialist history of interbreeding through rape. Although there are conflicting views on the new concept of hybridity and its potential to break down the colonizer/colonized binary, it is clear that the term "hybridity" has taken up new space and meaning in what is termed "postcolonial dialogue."

Despite the newfound attention to hybridity in postcolonial discourses, Stam (1998) reminded us, "hybridity has been a perennial feature of art and cultural discourse in Latin America – highlighted in such terms as *mestizaje, indigenismo, diversalite, creolite, raza cósmica*" (p. 2). He argued that hybridity, as both a term and concept, has recently been "recoded" by the postmodern, postcolonial, and post-nationalist movements. Hybridity, Stam stated, has existed and been discussed for centuries and has always been "deeply entangled with colonial violence" (p. 2). This reconceptualization is power-laden, asymmetrical, and co-optable. This newly redefined hybridity term

> fails to discriminate between the diverse modalities of hybridity, such as colonial imposition (for example, the Catholic Church constructed on top of a destroyed Inca temple), or other interactions such as obligatory assimilation, political cooptation, cultural mimicry, commercial exploitation, top-down appropriation, bottom-up subversion. (Stam, 1998, p. 3)

In other words, not only has the concept "hybrid" been co-opted from terms and concepts related to signifiers of "race-mixing," but it has been so broadly defined that it fails to define anything and simultaneously succeeds in making the power relations involved in colonizer/colonized positionality once again invisible.

The New Hybridity and Mixed Race Women

Contemporary cultural studies writers such as Grossberg (1993) and McLaren (1997) take up the postcolonial concept of the hybrid *space* and splice it with the writing of Women's/Chicana Studies scholar Gloria Anzaldúa. In her groundbreaking book, *Borderlands/La Frontera,* Anzaldúa (1987) wrote about how mixed people inhabit a *mestiza consciousness*. Although there are resemblances between Anzaldúa's ideology and the postcolonial concept of hybridity, there are differences. The fundamental difference is that at the heart of her writing she spoke literally about the *experience* of "una nueva raza" (a new race) of mestizo/as (p. 5). Unlike cultural studies authors, Anzaldúa's conception of the borderlands, both literal and theoretical, includes mixed race *people*. She argued that *mestizas* feel a "psychic restlessness" as they are "caught" in the "battleground" of racial debates.

Yet often, the postcolonial concept of hybridity overlooks the experience of actual hybrid persons, and instead focuses on the theoretical construct of crossing borders (Bhabha, 1996; Grossberg, 1993; McLaren 1997). McLaren (1997), for example, in his chapter "The Ethnographer as postmodern *flâneur*: Critical reflexivity and posthybridity as narrative engagement," discussed hybridity and mestizaje. At the beginning of the chapter, McLaren (1997) stated that the *flâneur* "or dandy whose aim is to be aimless ... must negotiate the everyday scene of postmodern hybridity" (p. 149). In the next sentence he indicated that hybridity is comprised of "intercultural social relations within frenetic narratives" (p. 149). Throughout the chapter, McLaren utilized the terms "hybridity" and "hybrid" to refer to various types of mixing, as in the example above in which he described hybridity as intercultural relational mixing; he also referred to "hybridized spheres" as those that mix together both public and private spheres (p. 150). McLaren also discussed the concept of "mestizaje." He aligned his concept of mestizaje with that of Anzaldúa, stating, "Mestizaje identity as articulated by McLaren, Anzaldúa, and others refers to a counter narrative that builds community within the margins of culture" (p. 156). Mestizaje, in his conception, is created through discourse; it is not the lived experience of mixed people. The experience of the "hybrid" or mestiza is removed and even he, as a (White, middle class male) postmodern *flâneur*, can assume "a narrative identity built upon cultural hybridity in a world undergoing a process of structural hybridity on a global basis" (p. 163). Hybrid existence is co-opted and romanticized as primarily a site of critical reflexivity.

Grossberg (1993) used hybridity to "describe three different images of border existences" (p. 91). The first is the image of a "Third Space," as defined by Bhabha and described earlier in this chapter. The second is the image of "liminality," which refers to how the subaltern lives on the border (p. 91). The third is "border-crossing" which marks an image of "between-ness" created by mobility. Grossberg (1993) argued, "These three versions of hybridity are conflated in various ways, as in Gloria Anzaldúa's (1987:37) description of the Atzlan [*sic*]" (p. 92). Thus, Grossberg undermine mestizas' literal lived experiences of liminality by claiming that concepts are being conflated, rather than acknowledging that it is the actual mestiza, the living and breathing woman, who inhabits mestiza consciousness or the "Third Space." The hybrid positionalities of Third Space, liminality, and border crossing are made open to everyone and, once again, the mestiza herself is rendered invisible while her theoretical consciousness is co-opted. These new conceptions of hybridity are also problematic because they overlook the historical violence related to race mixing as well as the embodied experience of mixed race people living today.

In the original conception of hybridity, hybrids were literal people who were posed as *both* the ultimate threat to dominant power *and* hope for the colonized to be treated as (equal) human beings. This debate about mixed race people continues today in the United States; the arguments have changed, but interracial people continue to stand for a possibility of hope for some and demise for others. Women, with the ability to get pregnant, often sit at the heart of this debate.

Today, people of mixed heritage are often hailed as the answer to racial divides. For example, Trueba (2004) argued that as interracial marriages increase and racial differences become increasingly blurred, racial conflict will decrease. Alternatively, some conservatives cite people of mixed heritage as proof that reparations for racial injustice, such as affirmative action programs, are no longer needed (see Williams, 2008). At the same time, both White people and people of color have made arguments that mixed race people will be the demise of cultural preservation (see Williams, 2008; White supremacist websites). White supremacists argue that race mixing should not occur, naming miscegenation as the ultimate sin. Some people of color, after being subjected to years of assimilation and cultural genocide, also view mixed race people as a threat to cultural preservation and argue against interracial coupling.

Discourses on hybridity and race mixing are used in a variety of ways: to end racism (as in Trueba's 2004 argument that mixed race people will decrease racial conflict), to promote social justice (as seen in the work described later by Maria P.P. Root, 1992, 1996), and to promote critical theory (as used, for example, by McLaren (2000) when he stated ,"I have tried in a modest way to advance a critical pedagogy of whiteness that will serve a form of postcolonial hybridity," (p. 150). Yet all of these approaches largely ignore the experiences of the women who embody this debate.

I purposefully situate these women's stories in the hybridity discourse as a reminder that this debate has a historical legacy that was initially located upon mixed race bodies, women's bodies in particular. The current theoretical conception of postcolonial hybridity often disregards embodied hybrid experiences. This is not to say that there is an authentic hybrid experience, for I do not want to essentialize hybrid existence, but these stories of hybridity continue to get mapped upon the bodies of mixed race people as political debates about racial coupling and conflict persist.

MIXED RACE THEORY AND RESEARCH

Although there is a growing body of work related to multiracial experiences and identifications, the amount of writing on this topic is still relatively minimal. When I first began exploring this topic in 1990, there were virtually no academic books written by or for mixed raced people, with the exception of *Borderlands* by Anzaldúa written in 1987 (which has now gained recognition as an academic text but, at that time was not considered as such). Although there were some personal narratives written by and about mixed race people (see Creef, 1990; Moraga, 1983), the first academic book dedicated specifically to that subject, *Racially Mixed People in America*, by Maria P. P. Root, did not appear until 1992. This text was a compilation of essays, some written by mixed race people, incorporating a variety of disciplines including psychology, sociology, and social work. Root (1992) explained that there were several factors that silenced multiracial voices, including isolation of interracial families, forced monoracial identification by the government, and the then "recent pride in being a person of color" that "demanded full-fledged commitment to the racial and ethnic minority group in order to pass 'legitimacy tests'" (p. 8). Root argued that the "biracial baby boom" which started around 1967 after anti-miscegenation laws were repealed, forced people to acknowledge the existence of multiracial experiences. Additionally, she asserted, "The topic of racially mixed people provides us with a vehicle for examining ideologies surrounding race, race relations, and the role of the social sciences in the deconstruction of race" (p. 10). The book offered a comprehensive look at multiracial experiences through both sociological and psychological analyses. The tenor of the book was a celebration of mixed race people; it included arguments for why people should claim mixed race identities and why mixed race voices and experiences matter in understanding the race relations discourse. For example, Nash (1992), one of the authors in the book, argued, "Multicultural people have a special role to play in combating stereotypes" (p. 330) and provided hope that racial divides will decrease. Although perhaps celebratory at the cost of minimizing the complexity of mixed race experiences, *Racially Mixed People in America* was a well-developed, comprehensive, and much needed edited text at the time it was published.

In 1996, Root edited a second book of essays entitled *The Multiracial Experience*. The included authors provided an in-depth look at the impact of mixed race people and multiracial discourses in relation to identity formation, other social categories such as gender, and multicultural education. This edited collection was more critical and politicized than the first volume; simultaneously, several of the writings continued to highlight the positives of multiracial people and identification.

Since the two edited collections of academic writings by Root, there have been two other edited collections published that mark "mixed race" issues as a legitimate field of ethnic studies and sociological inquiry: *Rethinking 'Mixed Race'* (Parker & Song, 2001) and *'Mixed Race' Studies: A Reader* (Ifekwunigwe, 2004). Both of these books were edited by British authors and include writings by academics from both Great Britain and the United States. Parker and Song edited *Rethinking 'Mixed Race'* in 2001. They acknowledged that mixed race people and the topic of mixed race can elicit hatred, fear, and resentment, as expressed, for example, on White supremacist websites. However, at the same time, "proponents of interracial love can express a naïve celebration of 'mixed race' relationships and children as 'living proof' of the transcendence of racism and the ultimate expression of multicultural harmony" (Parker & Song, 2001, p. 1). The editors' goal was to avoid such extreme positions and "think critically about 'mixed race' in a variety of settings, through a variety of methodologies and perspectives" (p. 1). Indeed, the writings cover a variety of topics including: the intersection of eugenics and mixed race people (Furedi, 2001); the distinctiveness of mixed race experiences based on race and place (Ifekwunigwe, 2001); the importance of questioning who is included and excluded in mixed race discourse to move beyond the Black/White binary (Mahtani & Moreno, 2001); and the interplay between racialization and physical characteristics (Mahtani, 2001); The writings incorporate sociological, theoretical, empirical, and personal methodologies and perspectives.

In 2004, Jayne O. Ifekwunigwe published a *Mixed Race' Studies* reader in which she argued, "'Mixed Race' Studies is one of the fastest growing, as well as one of the most important and controversial areas in the field of 'race' and ethnic relations" (p. 1). Ifekwunigwe's carefully crafted anthology provides an insightful overview of the history of 'mixed race' through three main themes: (a) the origins of views of miscegenation as pathological; (b) contemporary discourses that celebrate mixed race people and mixed race as a social category; and (c) the debates about "the politics, policies, practices and paradigms of 'multiraciality' and their critiques" (Ifekwunigwe, 2004, p. 18). Authors in this collection challenged readers to understand the U.S. history of anti-miscegenation sentiment, to rethink the justifications for racial categories and the implications of the social construction of race, and to critically think about mixed race issues in relation to current political debates.

In 2005, Downing, Nichols, and Webster published *Multiracial America*, "a resource guide on the history and literature of interracial issues" (p.1), which is an invaluable resource for those who are interested in scholarship on mixed race studies. The resources are plentiful, but based upon their thorough review of the literature, it is apparent that there are still relatively few academic articles and books written on the topic of mixed race.

These burgeoning academic texts mark multiracial experiences as an emerging field of legitimate and necessary scholarship related to issues of race. They also demonstrate the growing complexity of mixed race issues. Earlier writings on the mixed race experience (see Root, 1992, 1996) written, to some extent, by and for mixed raced people, concentrated on naming the rights of mixed race people and asserted that multiracial individuals can and do live healthy lives. Historically, mixed race people were labeled as degenerate and developmentally inferior (Knox, 1850; Nott & Gliddon, 1854; Young, 1995). Root's texts served to normalize and name the multiracial experience. Although there are critical pieces that examine mixed race in relationship to larger political issues, the prominent message might be encapsulated as "We can identify ourselves however we want and that is okay," as evidenced by the opening bill of rights in the second anthology (Root, 1996, p. 7). Although as a mixed race woman I appreciate this, as an educator working to promote social justice, I am invested in understanding the political implications of certain individual choices. The celebratory tone of Root's texts was perhaps necessary at the time to combat years of historical pathologizing of mixed race people. They mark an important part of the path that has led to the continued enunciations of the mixed race experience as can be seen in the subsequent anthologies.

In addition to increased writings on the mixed race experience, an active multiracial movement has been growing over the past ten years. In 1996, Brown and Douglas documented the six largest multiracial organizations: I-Pride in San Francisco, CA; The Biracial Family Network in Chicago, IL; The Interracial Family Circle in Washington, DC; Multiracial Americans of Southern California; PROJECT RACE, in Roswell, GA; and AMEA in Berkeley, CA. They found that that only two of the organizations (I-Pride and AMEA) were founded by multiracial people; those two organizations were organized to respond to the needs of mixed raced people. The other four groups were primarily founded by White women who were creating spaces to deal with racism they encountered as a result of being in interracial marriages. Mengel (2001) labeled the distinctness of these groups as *interracial* – "groups initiated by White people romantically involved in interracial relationships," and *multiracial* – "groups initiated by mixed race people" (p. 104). Mengel notes that often reporters and researchers in search of the voices of mixed race people seek out these organizations; however, because most of the organizations are led by White parents, the direct voices of mixed race people are absent. He argues, "The parents of the mixed race individual, unless multiracial themselves, simply cannot be the authorities through which this shared history can be passed" (p. 107).

Discussions and examinations of multiracial movements have continued in the recently published book *Mark One or More: Civil Rights in Multiracial America* in which Kim Williams (2008) traced the history of multiracial movements and examined their intersectionality with civil rights. She charted dozens of multiracial organizations across the United States. Williams was interested specifically in the connections between multiracial organizations and policy outcomes; she found that few organizations had any bearing on these outcomes. However, there were about 20 multiracial movement leaders who pushed for a multiracial category on the 2000 U.S. Census (p. 15). Like Brown and Douglas (1996), Williams (2008) found that "middle-class, suburban, interracially married white women tend to serve as the public face of local multiracial advocacy" (p. 82). Through her research among these leaders she also found "a thematic if ill-defined assertion that interracial love and the acknowledgement of multiracial people could, if recognized, help American society moved beyond an impasse ... of racial polarization" (p. 102). Thus, her findings coincide with the celebratory aspect of mixed race history as noted in the edited books by Root (1992, 1996) and Ifekwunigwe (2004).

Williams's (2008) work is especially powerful because it lays out the history of the multiracial movement and articulates it in relationship to civil rights ideals and legislation. In addition to exposing the uncritical celebration of mixed people as the saviors of racial divides, she explained that African Americans concerned with civil rights view the multiracial movement and multiracial people who insist on multiracial identities with suspicion and concern. Williams quoted Jesse Jackson, who described the multiracial movement as "a diversion, designed to undercut affirmative action" (p. 102). Williams's work recognizes Black elites' fears that the opportunity to mark a multiracial identity might lead to a "mass desertion from black identification" (p. 114). Simultaneously, she acknowledged the time in United States history when mixed race people were considered to be inferior human beings by White supremacists (p. 23). Williams pinpointed the multiple sides of the mixed race debates in which mixed race people are caught (and participate). In one corner, there are the acritical, naïve proponents of interracial love that argue that mixed people are the cure for racism and racial divisions. In another corner, there are civil rights activists who fear that people who identify as multiracial will lead to the demise of affirmative action and other hard won civil rights for African Americans. In yet another corner are White racists who argue that mixed race people (especially those who are part White) are leading to the demise of the country. Her work highlights the contentious political debates around mixed race people. In relation to the politics of including categories for multiracial people on the census, she succinctly stated, "Think of it this way: Democrats wanted multiracial recognition *without* adverse civil rights consequences; Republicans wanted multiracial recognition *with* adverse civil rights consequences" (Williams, 2008, p. 21).

Williams' work is located alongside other texts that examine the impact and implications of multiracial identities and multiracial movements in contemporary U.S. society. Based on a critical analysis of in-depth qualitative research, DaCosta (2007) examined the multiracial social movement and how the topic of "multiracials" went from being ignored, or treated as taboo, to becoming "a recognizable social category and mode of identification" (p. 2–3). Her work stands out as being both theoretically sophisticated and grounded in qualitative research that incorporates the voices of mixed race individuals. In examining how multiracial persons have been "made," DaCosta (2007) focused on "the cultural, institutional, and political factors that motivated mixed race people in the Unites States to organize collectively" (p. 11).

Williams' and DaCosta's books expanded upon the writings in Dalmage's (2004) edited book, *The Politics of Multiracialism*. The authors in Dalmage's book examined the "Multiracial Movement" to demonstrate its impact on multiracial identification and political policies. Contributors provided insights into some of the ways multiracialism and racial categorization are used to maintain White supremacy (DaCosta, 2004; Ferber, 2004). Chapters dedicated to the perspectives of White people reveal how multiracials blur the boundaries of Whiteness (Gallagher, 2004) and how White mothers of multiracial children embrace color-blind ideologies (Karis, 2004). Authors explored how mixed race people and identifications might disrupt, maintain, and complicate ongoing debates about racial boundaries, racial oppression, racial privilege, and related racial politics.

Similar discussions can be found in the sociological writings about the impact of multiracial identities in Brunsma's (2006) edited text, *Mixed Messages: Multiracial Identities in the "Color-Blind" Era*. Several of the authors thoughtfully expanded theories related to shifting color lines, dilemmas and manipulations of multiracial identifications, and multiracial socialization. Yet once again, research incorporating the voices of mixed race individuals is relatively minimal.

The discourse of mixed race issues is still limited but rapidly growing. As noted earlier, few ethnographic/qualitative studies exist and the majority of those take a psychological perspective examining multiracial identity development. In the following section, I provide an overview of the works that move beyond identity theory analysis to include broader macro levels of analysis.

Macro-Micro Analyzed Ethnographic Research

In her book *From Black to Biracial: Transforming Racial Identity among Americans*, Kathleen Odell Korgen (1998) described her interviews with 40 adults who had one White parent and one African American parent. Korgen argued that there has been an historical transformation in how biracial persons identify themselves. She found that two-thirds of her participants over 30 years of age self-identified as exclusively Black, while less than one-third under 30 years old identified racially as Black. She explained, "while it is increasingly accepted for black-white persons to claim both their black and white heritage, the possibility of being simply white is still not socially sanctioned" (p. 53). She found that most of her younger participants identified as biracial. She argued that "the dialectic between society and identity continues. As society becomes globalized and the economy shifts... identities adjust by becoming more fluid" (p. 95). This fluidity, as evidenced among the transformation of identity in biracial Americans "reveals the fluidity and subjectivity of race" (Korgen, 1998, p. 118).

Jayne Ifekwunigwe's (1999) *Scattered Belongings*, is also ethnographic, based on a two year Bristol, England-based project that involved 25 mixed race participants representing the White-English and English-African diaspora. The testimonies she gathered "illustrate the ways in which, acting *métis(se)* subjects can and do negotiate, challenge and subvert all of the subject positions – 'One' (White) the 'Other' (Black) or 'Neither' (*métis(se)*)" (p. 21). She highlighted the testimonies of six women and illuminated "painful psychosocial consequences for *métisse* women whose lived reality defy the false one drop rule" (Ifekwunigwe, 2004, p. 184). All the women had White English, German or Irish mothers and Black fathers. They also had "other Black continental, African, African Caribbean or African American safety nets" (p. 186) – surrogate sisters and other-mothers. Ifekwunigwe argued that "Additive Blackness" can be a survival strategy for *métis(se)* people who are "unwilling or unable to sever ties with their White British or White European origins" (1999, p. 183). Ifekwunigwe (2004) maintained that "embracing an exclusive Black identity – as a political strategy – is counterproductive ... [because] Black identity masks the many differences that exist across cultures, nations, ethnicities, religions, gender, regions, and generations"

(p. 190). Ultimately Ifekwunigwe (2004) argued for an understanding of multiple subjectivities that interrogates "taken-for-granted constructs of 'race,' nation, culture and family and their confluent relationships to gendered identities" (p. 193).

There are two other notable writings based on ethnographic work that do not apply a multiracial identity development perspective to the narratives. Mahtani (2001) interviewed 35 multiethnic women in Toronto, Canada, and described their varied senses of belonging. She reported that many of the women in her study "explained that their ability to cross over demarcations in racial divides made it easier to transcend other social cleavages" (p. 185). Mahtani found that her participants claimed to occupy both center and marginalized spaces and "some even likened their multiethnic status to an ability to understand marginality" (p. 187). She argued that multiethnic people can experience their mixedness in paradoxical yet positive ways.

In 2004, Kristen Renn added to the sparse qualitative work on mixed race identity by publishing her research with 56 multiracial college students in which she used an ecology model to examine how peer culture shapes identity in various spaces. Renn found a *monoracial identity pattern* among 27 students who identified some or all of the time with only one of their heritages (p. 95). There was also a *multiple monoracial identities pattern* exhibited by 27 of the students; these were students who identified as "both x and y" or "half x and half y" (p. 124). Fifty of the participants claimed a *multiracial identity* – this included a variety of self-labels that were nonmonoracial (p. 155). The least common identity pattern was the *extraracial identity* in which participants resisted identifying in U.S. racial categories. Thirty-four of the participants fell into what Renn described as the *situational identity pattern,* which was comprised of students who, consciously or unconsciously, publicly identified with more than one of the four patterns based on the context (p. 219). Renn (2004) argued, "Perhaps the most important finding of this study is that, for mixed race students, achieving a singular racial identity outcome is not necessarily reasonable or desirable" (p. 243).

Collectively, these ethnographic studies reveal that there are multiple ways – influenced by age, generation, experiences, peers, and racial politics – in which mixed race women might identify. The research in this book both adds to this scant ethnographic research and goes beyond current forms of analyses to delve further into what the stories of mixed race women can reveal about current race relations and politics.

CONCLUSION

The mixed race women's stories shared throughout this book unfold in multiple contexts and are situated in particular theoretical frameworks. I analyze the stories through sociological critical theory and poststructuralist lenses with a particular focus on how these women's stories contribute to debates and understandings about racial oppression/privilege and theories of social justice. This is an atypical sociology of education study given that the research is not conducted in a school, nor do I centralize formal education. Yet this work is highly relevant to the field. Schooling often mirrors larger society, and these women's stories highlight the myriad ways that social stratification is connected to stratification of knowledge. Their raced, classed, and gendered experiences situated them in multiple, sometimes conflicting, positions in relation to knowledge – in particular, knowledge of operations of Whiteness. Sociology of education as a field has been so focused on schooling that larger operations of social and institutional power often have been overlooked. Discussions of race within sociology of education have ignored the experiences of mixed race people. This work centers the words of mixed race individuals themselves, rather than White parents, in a way that is neither uncritically celebratory nor pathologizing, nor limited to identity development.

Race and gender are understood to be social constructs that are enacted through performativity in an interwoven web with class, sexuality, and other social positionalities. The fluid and ever-shifting translocational positionalities described in the narratives are examined for patterns and themes. The stories that they tell enrich theories of hybridity, add to mixed race studies, and further the debates about the complicated workings of racial oppression and White supremacy.

The themes and patterns that emerged through my analysis of the collective body of stories constitute the heart of the chapters that follow. Each chapter is focused on a particular theme. In line with feminist methodology, I foreground the data, letting the stories, for the most part, speak for themselves. Of course, my own positionality and theoretical lenses influence my organization. While this is, in and of itself, a form of analysis, I highlight participant voices and stories (at times with my voice as a participant-researcher) before incorporating my analysis at the end of each chapter. Finally, in the concluding chapter, I offer my collective analysis of the research as a whole, as it relates to the literature and theories highlighted in this chapter.

CHAPTER 3

RACIAL AND ETHNIC POSITIONALITIES

Floating Around in the Borderlands

I think educators need to understand, among many other things about racial identity, that no matter the age of the person or what they seem like, it's not necessarily something that everyone has come to accept to understand about themselves. It is always changing; it is not something that we should assume everyone has dealt with in a way that they feel is finite, in a way that is not going to change. – Katherine

Katherine was my first interview in Boston. We planned to meet the afternoon I arrived in the city. My dad, who lives 45 minutes outside Boston, excited about my research, offered to drive me. Due to unexpected traffic (almost an oxymoron when thinking about Boston), we were already running half an hour late. I called Katherine, and she graciously said she would wait for me to arrive; we would meet in front of the CVS drugstore in Harvard Square. Twenty minutes later I arrived, immediately exhilarated by the college crowds milling the streets. I jumped out of the car, quickly thanked and kissed my dad goodbye and stood at the front of the store where Katherine and I were to meet. I looked at everyone around me, wondering of every woman I saw, "Does she looked mixed?" Nothing. A few cell phone calls later Katherine and I realized that we were at two different CVS stores in Harvard Square, and she came to rescue me from a morning of perpetually leaning towards what was just out of reach.

Katherine was strikingly beautiful, exactly whom one might think of when the image of someone mixed race comes to mind, a combination of features that make you wonder, "What might her background be?" I feel trepidation as I write that description because I trouble the notion of essentializing and exotifying the mixed race "look." Nonetheless, that was my initial impression of her, and I wondered what her first impression was of me, did I also look mixed race? At a fast pace, Katherine led me to the nearby Harvard Education School Library where we had previously arranged to talk. As we walked, I tried to pay attention to landmarks and street signs while making small talk so that I could later find my way back to the T stop. She walked with the grace of a dancer, and as I was trying to make a mental note of the clothes she was wearing (as a good ethnographer does), I tripped while walking up the stairs to the interview room and immediately blushed. *Suave.*

45

The interview began with ease in the small yet surprisingly modern furnished library study room. We sat across the table from each other. I pulled out my recorders, and the words began to flow. Katherine shared stories of her life. Over the next couple of interviews with her and others, I began to recognize themes of how the participants form their racial and ethnic positionalities.

There are many ways one could describe racial and ethnic positionalities, and the main themes that emerged from the women's stories were: claiming women of color identities; rejecting White identities; and shifts and challenges to identity. Language, home culture, relationship to each parent, geographical location, physical appearance, school, and friends influenced this process of identification, which included both self-identification and external identifications by others. I use the term "identity" loosely here. As explained in Chapter 2, I do not view identity as fixed; rather, the stories reveal how racial and ethnic identifications explain the women's positionalities – both their self-positioning and positioning by others.

It is important to remember that this was a select group of mixed race women. These were women who responded specifically to a call for mixed race women, so it makes sense that most of these women would identify primarily as mixed race rather than with one ethnic group or racial identity. This was also an incredibly educated group; all of the women but one had at least a bachelor degree, three were in the process of obtaining graduate degrees, and four held advanced degrees. However, there was a fair amount of diversity in terms of where they grew up, their socioeconomic backgrounds, their current class positions, the jobs they held, physical appearance, their racial and ethnic backgrounds, and sexuality.

SELF-POSITIONING THROUGH PARENTS

When asked, "Tell me about who you are," almost all of the women positioned their racial/ethnic identities through their parents. For example, Joanna said, "My mom is Black and my dad is White;" Marta said, "My dad is an immigrant from Peru, and he's mestizo; my mother is Ashkenazi White Jewish;" and Ana said, "My mom is White, she's British and my dad is Filipino." There were a few exceptions to this. Mindy said, "I'm half Filipino and half White American." In the group interview Alana said "I'm mixed with Black and White," but in her individual interview she said, "I was born in '79 in Los Angeles to a Black man and White woman." However, beyond simple explanations of racial and ethnic identifications, there were a variety of ways that the women positioned themselves, and were positioned by others, and for several of the women, racial and ethnic self-identifications changed over time and within different contexts.

Katherine's opening quote is a reminder that identity formation is a constant process. Many of these women had shifting racial/ethnic identities, and I suspect they will continue to change. In addition, sometimes other social and personal identities took center stage. I began each individual interview with the invitation, "Tell me about yourself." Knowing that the interviews were about mixed race women, most participants began their responses with their ethnic identities, usually naming themselves through their parents as described above, but often those racial/ethnic descriptions were accompanied by other important identity markers. For example Linda said, "I am a 30-year-old, queer, hapa[13], gender queer, filmmaker, writer, friend, sister, daughter, San Francisco native." Maria, often sarcastically witty in her remarks, said, "I'm someone who's totally in a relationship crisis" (she broke up with her partner of 5 years a few months after the interview). She then quickly gave an analysis of the difficulties associated with answering my question as a mixed race person in relation to racial/ethnic identity. She stated,

> So this is always interesting being asked that because who I am always comes around to who my parents are separately, and then being both those is who I am. So like there are other people who can say, "Oh, I'm Black," even though both parents could have really distinct identities around that culture.

After explicitly naming the complexity of answering that question, she then described herself, similar to other participants, through her parents, then adding, in this case, her age. "My mother is German and Swiss. My grandmother is German. My dad is Mexican, and I'm 34."

WOMEN OF COLOR IDENTITIES AND HERITAGE OF COLOR IDENTITIES

Although many of the women were light skinned, and several could pass for White, all but 2 of the 16 women in the project identified as women of color, in addition to identifying as mixed. Some of the women claimed that identification strongly, without hesitation. They would make statements beginning with the phrase, "As a woman of color...," and at times some spoke specifically about claiming that label. For women with dark skin, their women of color positionality was often not a question, as exemplified by Alana's statement, "I totally identify [as a woman of color]. I don't have white skin privilege, I'll never be White." Linda, who was at times perceived as White, described why she claimed the label she did. "So what I identify as basically is a person of color, because politically that's what seals it for me. And that's what my conscientization[14] was around, around social inequity and social justice." She acknowledged that it is a "privilege being able to choose" her identity. For others, the label "woman of color" was something they were newly claiming as their own. Janet, for example, now 25, talked about how she used to think of herself more as White:

> Yeah, I definitely see myself when I was younger identifying as more White than I do now. I think maybe it was just because I had a lot of White friends, half of my family was all White, and they were the family I was around more than the family on my father's side, and I think there's definitely been times where...there's only moments like where I questioned it, but I think a lot of

time I didn't think about myself as a person of color. It was just like very invisible to me. And I definitely started seeing my identity differently when I moved out here [to Albuquerque], and I think that's part of just growing up and just thinking about it more, and being confronted with it more and then studying media and in that just talking about a lot of race issues that come up in media … and the fact that there's just a lot more Brown people out here. I have more Brown friends out here, and talking with them about things…yeah I think those are all reasons.

As a follow up I asked her, "So you now identify as a woman of color?" She answered affirmatively without hesitation and talked about her recent involvement with a local women of color organization. Janet moved from Kansas City, where there were few Brown people, to Albuquerque, which has a high population of Brown people. Also, upon arriving in Albuquerque, she began to work for a media justice organization. These experiences helped her begin to identify as a woman of color.

There were only two women who were hesitant to call themselves women of color, although they did not consider themselves White either. There was a sense, with both of them, of not knowing where the identity boundaries lay in race constructions. They were struggling to find comfort defining themselves in a racially dichotomized society in which they were often perceived as White. In the Oakland group interview Tina said:

> So I think that I'm just like a newborn in the way that I'm just learning how to articulate my identity and really appreciate it … When I go to women of color meetings or conferences, I feel really uncomfortable, because I pass as White. And I have privilege in that, you know? It's just really uncomfortable and hard. As of right now, I don't know how I identify, as mixed is probably the best way.

In the Boston group interview, Mindy hesitantly identified herself as the one person in the group who did not claim a "woman of color" identity. In that group interview, I asked the question, "Do all of you consider yourselves women of color?" Everyone said "yes" in unison, except for Mindy, who responded:

> I don't. Only because people take me for White so much. I don't identify, and I know I'm not necessarily that, society doesn't treat me as a woman of color because they don't see it in me so I don't have any experiences of that. So it's kind of interesting trying to nail down identity because I'm not a White person, but I'm not a woman of color because I just don't have those experiences.

Mindy was not quite sure how to position herself. Throughout her interviews she talked about the disconnect she felt from constantly being perceived as White while not feeling White. She said, "People identify me as White, but I mean, you know, that's fine, but that's not something I hold for myself because I think being identified that way and actually being that is really very different." Mindy explained that the difficulty was that "people will look at you in a certain way and expect you to know certain things." Because she was constantly being faced with expectations of acting White that she could not meet, she developed "intimacy issues" and was anxious about letting people get to know her. One strategy Mindy used to make connections with people without facing those expectations was to chat and blog online. She said, "[through computers] I find a different way to interact with people where those insecurities are not brought to the fore so readily."

In contrast, Joanna talked about how identifying as a person of color was more comfortable for her than claiming to be Black. In response to my question and Mindy's hesitation to claim the label woman of color, Joanna said:

It's interesting because I tend to reject the identity of calling myself Black. Once in a blue moon it is relevant in whatever context I'm talking about, but I do strongly identify as *not* White. I just call myself Brown, or a person of color. Whereas if somebody asked me if I were Black, I would probably give them a long complicated answer. Whereas if somebody asked me if I were White, I would say no. Whenever somebody asked me if I were Black I would go into a whole spiel about my race politics and my identity, and my experience growing up, you know?

Although in rare cases people assume she is White or Jewish, Joanna has what might best be described as tan skin. In an individual interview Joanna explained:

Once in awhile I'll call myself Black when it's relevant to the conversation, [for example] if I'm referring to being the only Black person in a certain setting. Sometimes it's just easier than saying a person of color or whatever. But, I think that, like the duality of it is very important to me because I grew up with both of my parents and they are still together and close to both of their families. I have trouble just calling myself Black and denying – it feels to me like denying my father and his family. And I'm not okay with that. And also, it feels like denying a part of who I am. Especially because I don't look like, you know, being a biracial is a big part of how the world views me, because I'm racially ambiguous and I get upset when other people try to force some identity on me.

Joanna is an anomaly in sometimes rejecting the label Black. Throughout their interviews and in describing the way they identified, all but one of the other women revealed that in some situations and at some times in their lives they identified themselves in relation to their heritage/race of color, for example as Black, Japanese, Mexican, or Filipina. Besides Joanna, Brittney who has brown skin, and who like Joanna is also mixed Black and White, was the only other person who hesitated to claim only her heritage of color and said, "I've never said that I was one race. I've never identified myself as one race…Just because I have darker skin doesn't mean that I should just claim one." No other participants seemed to hesitate to use their heritage of color as a primary identity. Some like Maria, who was most likely to call herself Latina or Mexican, preferred to identify with their heritage of color, or as a woman of color, rather than mixed.

DEFINITELY NOT WHITE

In contrast to claiming their heritage of color without needing to name their Whiteness, none of the women accepted the label White if it was not qualified as being in combination with their heritage of color; in other words, if it wasn't made clear that they were mixed. Even Mindy, in explaining that she doesn't claim the label woman of color added immediately, "I'm not a White person." The story shared in the opening chapter by Diana in which she responded to the person who called her a "dumb, White, bitch" by yelling back, "I am not White" exemplifies the verve with which many of the women rejected the label White. The sentiment "But don't call me White!" was echoed throughout the interviews. There were times when the women would refer to being part White or would claim to be White *and* Black, Filipina, etc. but no one ever consciously claimed to be exclusively White.

SHIFTS AND CHALLENGES TO IDENTITY

For many of the women, how they identified in terms of race and/or ethnicity changed both over time and in different situations. Some women shifted from claiming a primarily mixed race identity to a monoracial identity of color, and others shifted from a monoracial identity to a mixed race identity. Even those who maintained the same racial/ethnic label often shifted in the core ways they viewed themselves racially and ethnically in relation to those around them. Perhaps most notable in the stories is the message that identity is not fixed. Our identities shift in response to institutional pressures, life changes, and perceptions and challenges by those around us. For example, Diana experienced a shift from identifying exclusively as Black to also claiming a biracial identity. Diana was the oldest participant in the group, age 58, and grew up in an era in which there was no option to claim biraciality. She said:

> I went to historically Black schools, and I was raised as a Black person, because in my generation you could be one thing *or* the other. And so I was always a Black person until about 10 years ago when I started thinking about being biracial.

Although Diana was sometimes assumed to be White by others, she was raised as a Black child, in a Black neighborhood, and attended predominately Black schools during a time in which anyone with any Black ancestry was considered to be

Black. However, due to the changing climate of racial politics and the emergence of a multiracial movement in the mid 1990s, Diana began to recognize the option of claiming a mixed race identity in addition to her identity as a Black person. At the time of the study, she had been exploring what her biracial identity means and was writing a book about her life experiences and "the evolution of thought on biracialism."

Alana, who is also mixed Black and White but is about 25 years younger than Diana, experienced the opposite identity shift upon entering college. She explained:

> I definitely grew up identifying as a biracial person. And that identity was definitely being half White and half Black. And it changed, I guess, as I realized I was never perceived as White even though I have cultural Whiteness. But then when I got into college and gained a more radical liberal consciousness I dropped the biracial identity, and just identified with being a Black person and being a Black woman, and later being a Black queer woman. And I think that more recently, as I'm sort of thinking about like privilege and power in my position as I'm doing community work and social justice work or education, I'm thinking more about my mixed race identity more so in terms of like cultural Whiteness as a form of cultural capital[15] and how I have a lot of that privilege and sort of rethinking about my mixed race identity. Also in terms of queer spaces, it shows up because I never identify as sort of a rigid border construct of a queer identity, like gay, lesbian, bisexual. I like everything; I like a lot of things. So I feel I could just kind of float around in the borderlands in a lot of different ways.

For Alana, college became a space where she was able to name her identity in new ways; she shifted from a primarily biracial identity to claiming an identity as a Black woman. However, post-college, conscientiously acknowledging her White privilege, she began reclaiming a mixed race identity. Her description – as it moves from Black *person*, to Black *woman*, to Black *queer woman* – also highlights the intersectionality of identities and translocational positionalities. In this instance she emphasizes the connections between race, gender, and sexuality explicitly, and socioeconomic status implicitly through her use of cultural Whiteness as cultural capital.

Like Alana, Tina also marked college as a turning point in her shifting racial identity. She explained that those around her shaped her identity from a very young age, and college provided her the space to begin to reclaim her own identity. She said:

> When I was in fourth grade I found familiarity with other Mexican kids. And I wanted to hang out with them. I was like, "I'm Mexican!" And I identified as Mexican even though I lived with my White mother. And so it was really hard for me because I wasn't accepted by kids...And so slowly I began to

transition into, I guess I identified more as White.... So for the past six years now I've been trying to juggle this identity of being mixed race, and trying to negotiate spaces in which I feel comfortable to identify as a woman of color... I think that if I never went to college I wouldn't be thinking about being mixed race at all, because I wouldn't have been exposed. Actually it was probably in high school. But I wouldn't have been exposed to, I guess, just the ability or the tools to analyze or to be looking at myself.

Tina's racial/ethnic self-identification was complicated by the fact that her Mexican father, who is light skinned with light hair, is White-identified and politically conservative. Tina explained that her dad is "completely different" from the rest of his family, "He's Republican, and everyone else in my family is Democrat. He's anti-immigration. I mean it's just weird." However, Tina spent lots of time with her extended family, who are Mexican-identified, who consequently instilled in her a primary ethnic identification as Mexican.

It's weird because when I was younger, I felt like I looked a lot like my family members. So that made me feel like I identify more as Mexican. I was always around Spanish speakers, but I don't know any Spanish. When I was growing up, I felt like that was my culture. That's how I grew to know myself and identify.

Yet outside of her home culture – because of her light skin, her inability to speak Spanish, and her Valley Girl accent – people of color constantly challenged her when she claimed to be Mexican. Although she felt "different than other [White] people" she felt that Latinas, "didn't really validate" her since she didn't speak Spanish. When she tried to insert herself in women of color spaces she got "these really weird looks... like a sort of, 'Oh look at this White girl trying to be an ally.'" All of this led her to "be defensive of my mixed cultural background and really start to kinda like educate myself."

Like Tina, Marta also had a White-identified father, although he could not pass for White. She explained,

My father is mestizo and he's definitely brown skin[ned]. But my birth certificate says he's White, because Latinos unless they're obviously of *Indio* [Indian] or African descent are considered White. So he identifies as being White, even though he's not treated that way. He has a pretty heavy accent, and he's always looked at as being foreign or whatever. But you know that was his identity, so it took me a while to have an identity that wasn't that.

Similar to Tina's experience, Marta's dad's White self-identification led her to identify as White at first, but that identification changed over time and continually changes within different contexts. She says, "How I identify does change depending on what group I'm in. I feel like if I'm with a group of Jews then they take me as being Jewish, and if I'm in a Latin group then they take me as being

Latin[16]." As the oldest woman in the Oakland group, age 46, she demonstrated a notable comfort with her identity. In an educative role, toward the end of the group interview, Marta explained that her self-acceptance was the result of a difficult, long, and continuing process. She said:

> I didn't get here right away. Because initially, I mean my identity went from I don't know, not really having a racial identity – just being – and then getting politicized about it, back when it was "Third World," yeah, way back in the 70s. Back then I felt real pressure to just say I am Latina, I'm Latina, you know, and not talk about the White part with other people of color. They [people of color] were like, "Don't talk about that." I was like "Oh, okay, whatever." But then I was like, "Fuck it, if they don't accept me for who I am then too bad," you know? This is who I am. It took a long time for me to be okay with everything, with who I am. It's always a work in progress.

Our identities are a work in progress because there are constant challenges and revelations associated with race relations and race politics. These race politics are connected to politics of gender, sexuality, and social class. Note that in her storytelling she is challenged by people of color to claim the label "Latina" – a term, given the way the Spanish language works[17], that not only racializes her but also labels her gender. In the earlier quote where she uses the term "Latin," without the "a" at the end, Marta rejects that gender positioning. As a queer person who considers (her/him)self to be "as much male as female" s/he consciously claims what s/he perceives to be a "nongendered" term. I use the terms "(her/him)self" and "s/he" purposefully in this instance to emphasize the trap of gendered language; I want to respect Marta's fluid gender identity, yet I find it difficult to do so in the English language, which genders pronouns. Given that Marta never explicitly challenged the English terms in our discussions, and for reading fluidity, I will use the terms "she" and "her" in the rest of text when referring to Marta, but I draw attention to the confining nature of such language for people like Marta.

After Marta's comment, Tina, the youngest woman in the Oakland group at age 24, said:

> When I was living in Austin for a few months I wrote something for this Latina group, and they rejected it because I'm mixed race. They said I talked too much about how I grew up with my mom, who is White, and that wasn't empowering.

Tina named this experience as ultimately "troubling to [her] identity work." After Tina shared that story, Marta, in a continuing effort to provide validation to others said, "It always cracks me up when Latin people say, I'm pura [pure] Latina or I'm pura [pure] Chicana. It's like the whole thing about being Latin is that we're all mixed." The history of Latina/o culture is one of a mixture of European, Indian, and African peoples as a result of colonization (Anzaldúa, 1987). For some,

Latina/o pride requires a rejection of Whiteness, the symbol of the European colonizer. Tina's explicit naming of her Whiteness was not welcomed by the Latina group, and she was rejected. This experience begs the question, what is lost in instances such as this where someone who is mixed race is excluded from connecting to others with their heritage of color because she names a mixed race positionality? This is a question of significance not only for individuals like Tina but also for the larger system of racial politics.

Ana also felt an identity shift as she matured. She explained:

For a long time I would just say that I'm half Filipino because it's just assumed that the other half is White. At some point, and partly it was because I felt I needed to declare, "You know there's something different about me so let's just cut to the chase. This is what's different about me: It's that I'm not all White." But then at some point when my feminism started kicking in, I realized I was kind of denying my mother and that's not cool. She's always been there for me, you know? So now I'm usually pretty clear, "I'm half Filipino and I'm half British." And actually I always say British because British is White but there is this rich culture that comes with that. And I feel very British in a number of ways. And sometimes I still say, "I'm half Filipino." It kind of depends on the situation. But I can say it now without feeling guilty about denying my mother.

Once again gender politics influence ethnic positionality; Ana's connection to feminism and her White mother made her more consciously acknowledge and claim her British identity in addition to her Filipina identity.

Bobbi also talked about shifting positionalities in different contexts. She said:

Well I used to identify as Somali and White, but I think it always depends on what community I'm in. Like when I'm around Black people I say, "Oh, I'm half White." And if I'm around White people I say, "Oh, I'm half Somali." I used to say, "I'm Somali and White" but no one knew what that meant, so I kind of switched to Black and White. But I also thought that, like, if I say I'm Somali and White it was like I'm trying to say that I'm not Black.

Bobbi then explained that because she had to confront racism often in her life, by the time she was 18 race became important, and she felt the need to "kind of define that and like name that and like say, 'Hey, this is who I am.'"

However, naming her identity was complicated as she found that others didn't often know how to interpret her claims, and she feared that claiming to be mixed Black *and* White might be perceived as a denial of Blackness, something she did not want to imply. But, as exemplified by her statement below, she continued to struggle with how to situate herself, wondering about the intersections of culture, race, and politics and her position within them. She explained:

But now, I don't know. Maybe it's just because the country [Somalia] is so fucked up and out of control, I don't really feel like, I don't know, I just kind of think of myself as like cultures and locations. I don't only think of myself as races so much.

Bobbi explained that Somalia is no longer a place she felt "proud to be associated with because we've been at war since 1982." As a child she was raised around African nationalism and learned that outside sources caused the problems in Africa, so the civil wars where people were hurting their own made it hard for her to maintain pride in her country. Then she added:

I mean if I tell somebody that I'm Somali, that tells very little about me because I grew up in the barrio [in Phoenix]. And what does it mean to be Somali? Like my dad was a goat herder, but then my dad was an engineer, but then the only Somalis I've hung out with are refugees in farming communities. So I just kind of think that like I don't really see people racially as much as I relate to people who are from similar backgrounds.

Bobbi exemplifies how traditional notions of "identity" are inadequate to explain her experience. Her descriptions can be viewed as stories of translocational positionality. As she clearly stated, who she is with (and their racial/ethnic identity and socioeconomic status – named in this case through employment) and where she is located have a big impact on how she views herself, on her positionality.

Bobbi is one of only two people in the group that at times claimed an identity completely separate from her "biological" racial/ethnic background. She said that when she was a little kid she used to lie and say that she was Puerto Rican. Rather than try to explain to others why she looked so different from her sister, who had much darker skin and stronger Somali features, she created a fantasy family. Bobbi knew other mixed Somali/White kids who looked similar to her; she took and brought their pictures to school, describing them as her Puerto Rican cousins. Bobbi was often taken to be Latina and grew up in Phoenix in a community with Latina/os. Claiming a Puerto Rican identity sheltered her from needing to defend her positionality.

Another participant also temporarily claimed a positionality unrelated to her "biological" racial/ethnic heritage. Linda had a Japanese mother and a White father, but was raised primarily by her mom and her Black stepfather, whom she called her "dad." Like so many of the other participants, her identity changed from one context to another and in many places she felt "different." Before identifying as hapa and as a person of color, she went through a time of identifying as Black. She said:

Like how I move in spaces changes then moves, you know, depending on the situation. And it changed before I was even really conscious of what my identity was around shit. I would get shit; I knew that I was different. I was different from this family, or I was different from that family, for sure. Plus my dad's [stepfather's] family was Black. I don't look like anyone. And in my mom's family I'm the tallest person. So recognizing my difference and not being able to name it, and then kind of being able to name it, and then naming it incorrectly. I thought it was Black because of where I rolled, you know – my neighborhood, my friends, my dad. So I was like, "Yeah, I must be Black; I'm different, right?" But like finally I was able to name it, and yet so much changes all the time.

I asked her, "When you say you were able to name it, what does that mean?" She responded with, "Being mixed, being hapa specifically." She explained, "Growing up in Bayview, which is predominately African American, and my dad was Black and my mom was Japanese, I thought I was Black in high school." She even attended Black Student Union (BSU) meetings with her friends until her mom challenged her.

My mom called me out one day. She was like, "Oh, you're not going to be home until late?" And I was like, "Yeah, how did you know?" And she said, "Oh, you're wearing all-black so you must be going to a BSU meeting." I was, like, "Oh my gosh." It kind of dawned on me around that time, "Oh yeah, I'm not Black," and I know that. That was sophomore year, so I was 14 or 15.

Linda explained that even though she recognized then that she wasn't Black and shouldn't be going to BSU meetings, that her "identity politics came a lot later," in college. Going to college, reading Gloria Anzaldúa[18], and meeting other mixed people helped her form her identity politics. Even though only two participants took on such identities, the writings by mixed race people (see Camper, 1994; Creef, 1990) show that it is not altogether unusual for mixed race people to claim an identity unrelated to their biological heritages, especially one for which they are often mistaken. Peer groups have a strong influence in both stories, but Linda's story also raises the question of how stepparents' racial backgrounds might influence mixed race people's positionalities.

Maria has light skin and wasn't raised speaking Spanish, but her name and circumstances helped her feel solid in her Brown identity. She said that as a result of growing up in a Chicano neighborhood, "I just kind of grew up knowing that I was Brown, and people around me were Brown. My name is Brown." Her Spanish last name (given to her by her Mexican dad), her Spanish-pronounced first name, and her early entrenchment in a Chicano community shielded her from challenges to her Latina identity. She said, "I have a Brown name. I don't know what my life would be like if I had gone through with a different name and having to explain myself in a different way. Nobody asked me to explain." Still, she experienced significant shifts in race and gender identity related to experiences in school.

Maria, who was always thin and petite, explained that there were "two big shocks" for her that she experienced among her peers in school.

One was entering into seventh grade, walking into the junior high and feeling like all my friends were women. I remember having seen [my friend] Dora in May in sixth grade. And then seeing her in seventh grade, when school started, and she had super-high chola[19] hair, and was in these tight jeans, and her hair was all big, and she had on all this makeup. And I was still like this little girl who left the sixth grade three months ago, and these were young women who were now in seventh grade. I remember that being one of the biggest things for me. And I remember everybody else being taller, everybody had big boobs, everybody was talking about their periods. And I just felt like I was in some other world. It was crazy. I was like, "Wait, these are all people I knew!" There were five or six schools that fed into my junior high so there were a lot of new people too. I just wasn't prepared for that.

Maria was raised without any television, and she expressed anger that no one warned her of the impending change from elementary school to junior high. She said:

There's a part of me that's like, nobody even said, "You know, it's going to be different, and it doesn't need to be scary, but it's going to be different *mija*,[20]" you know? "There's going to be more kids there. Boys and girls are going to be growing at different rates now, so there are going to be boys and girls who are bigger than you," or whatever.

She said that she remembers feeling like she didn't belong and added:

But I don't know how much of that was race stuff and how much of that was just me feeling like I did not belong. And the other thing too, is that I was placed in gifted classes so I was always, there was always some sort of separation.

Being in gifted classes separated her both from her peers in the neighborhood, many of whom were not in those classes, and from other girls because she became a "schoolgirl," the '80s term for a nerd.

I felt separated in that way. And it was always an issue, like, "You're really smart, huh?" Like, "You're a smart girl." That was a term in the '80s, right, schoolgirl. They were like, "Well, she's a schoolgirl." And that's what I got called. And yet, at the same time, a lot of people left me alone. Like I really didn't get picked on too much, like it was just kind of like, "Oh, she's a schoolgirl."

So, for Maria, the first "shock" was moving from elementary to junior high and not being prepared for the new gender dynamics. Racialized tracking and being placed in gifted classes exacerbated this. Through Maria's descriptions of the chola and the schoolgirl we can see intertwined race, class, sexuality and gender dynamics impacting her shifting sense of self.

Part of what she feels like saved her from being teased was her ability to dance and her wide range of musical tastes. At her school, the White kids listened to "Van Halen and all that." The "Brown" kids were into "break dancing" and Michael Jackson. Maria explained, "So the differences around race were also really defined by music too. I kind of listened to everything and anything. Like I knew songs on both sides, and also stuff that nobody liked, like Duran Duran." She was thankful that her parents let her go to school dances, which she believed also "saved" her from harassment. She said that by attending the dances,

> At least people got to see me out. And I always felt like I was faking it, but actually would hear from people that they thought I was good dancer. And I think that that just kind of like was something. Like, I could be a schoolgirl but at least I could dance, does that make sense?

When she posed that question I could and did reply honestly that it made perfect sense to me because I had, in many ways, a similar experience. I had two groups of friends – White friends and friends of color – who listened to two completely different kinds of music, and, like Maria, I listened to it all. Although my school was predominately White, my ability to dance saved me in spaces with other people of color, which, for me, were roller-skating rinks, and under-21 clubs. I may have been smart, I may have been light skinned, I may even have lived in a White town, but at least I could dance. My mother did discuss with me the changes I would go through as a female in adolescence, thus I did not have the same kind of gender-norm shocks that Maria experienced, but my identification as Colombian/Latina was challenged. However, having been taught to dance at a young age by my Latina mom and my *tías*, gave me particular dancing abilities that provided me the social capital to, at times, resist challenges to my Brownness.

The second big shock for Maria occurred when she transitioned from public school to a private high school.

> My second thing was high school. Because then I went to Catholic high school in another part of town. My junior high was like four blocks from my house, but now I had to take a city bus and I was in a whole other place. So now I'm not even in my neighborhood. And that was probably the next really big shock.

Maria explained that attending private high school had nothing to do with religion. Her parents felt it was important to have a good education, so they sent her and her three siblings to private high schools. The only choice she was given was which of the two local private schools she wanted to attend. She chose the school that was closer and less wealthy. The new school was predominately White and a culture shock. There was an upside but a larger downside.

> Here it was like now it was okay for me to get good grades, it was okay for me to want to excel in that way. But the standards of beauty at that school and the culture there were radically different than where I had come from, right? Because the girls I thought were pretty from my neighborhood weren't the girls that were at that school. So all of a sudden, it's like White girls were pretty. And that's the first time when I got it. I was like, "Oh." So if you think about it, I was outside of media, and I thought Brown girls were pretty because the boys always liked the Brown girls because that's what was there. And so now I'm like, "Oh wait, they like White girls." And, "Oh wait, White girls are what they see."

Maria, who was, "definitely read as Latina, or Mexican" by her classmates, did not fit the new standards of beauty. Given these early life experiences, college did not have as large an impact on her as it did on other people because she had already experienced two "really big culture shocks." Once again, we see that the intersections of gender, race, class, geographical location, and sexuality politics intertwine to affect positionality. Maria's geographical move to a wealthier school (class) had an impact on notions of beauty (related to gender and race) and dating choices and options (sexuality).

Other participants discussed major shifts in identity that related to gender and sexuality, as well as race. Alana, for example, talked about how when she was younger "femininity was so much about White womanhood," and she really tried "to perform a White femininity." But now, she says, "I don't feel like I am performing that." This is related to several factors including a change in her choices of whom to date based on their positionalities; Alana shifted from White men to men of color and later from dating men to dating women. Naming a connection between gender performativity and sexuality, she stated, "I never really came into my femme identity until I started to identify as a queer person." Linda similarly talked about feeling different as a teen from her peers as a queer girl. When she was a freshman in high school there was a group of junior and senior boys who took interest in her friends, but she was "exempt" from that attention. I wondered why, as Linda struck me as quite attractive. Surprised, I asked her, "You were exempt?" She replied, "Yeah, I was, I don't know, gay at an early age. I don't know. Gawky and awkward, I don't know. Yeah, no, no one was interested in me. I'm really glad though, because it was high drama, high drama." Before she came into her gay identity, her sexuality was rendered, for all intents and purposes, nonexistent.

Two people who did not describe major shifts in identity were Brittney and Elizabeth. They were the only two participants who reflected on their mixed race identity as almost exclusively positive. Brittney, whose mom is White and dad is

Black, started her individual interview and her group interview saying she "loves" to be mixed because she can "see the view of two different people" and because "combining races is beautiful" to her. Throughout her interviews her reflections on her life as a mixed race person were overwhelmingly positive. Although she had encountered some racial discrimination, she tended not to internalize it and, rather, viewed it as "their problem." There were a few instances where she was called the "n-word." She shared stories of the sister of a boyfriend and an ex-girlfriend of a boyfriend calling her "nigger." She shrugged it off.

> You know I just think they didn't have anything else to say. So they couldn't say anything else, so they had to use that. It's like "Okay, you know, pull out your race card or whatever." It's like, "You don't have anything else to put me down for. If you're calling me a nigger to put me down that's not putting me down. You're just ignorant." I mean that's an awful thing to say to somebody, but it's not directed towards me, I feel. I feel like it's just you being dumb. I mean that's not something I can change, nor would I want to. So if you're calling me nigger to like put me down, that's not putting me down. Really. You know? I'm not getting offended by you calling me that; I'm offended by you using that word, you know? If that's the only thing you can say to me to insult me then I really don't feel that bad. 'Cause I don't feel bad about my race. I love my race. So if that's what you're using to like… if that's what you have against me, then you really don't have anything against me.

Rather than focus on the insult of the word itself, Brittney chose to dismiss the name-calling and claim her pride in being Black, as evident in her statement, "I love my race."

Brittney was one of the youngest participants, age 26, and was the only person in the study who had not attended college. I wondered how her perceptions of racism might shift in the future. I could already see the beginning of a shift in consciousness as we reached the end of the Albuquerque group interview when she said:

> These interviews have opened up my eyes a lot. I notice things more I think. It makes me look at people and notice things more, whereas before I was just kind of like, I never noticed that. I never noticed any racism or anything; maybe I just didn't want to notice, so I didn't see it. But now I think I'm going to notice it more, and be more aware of what's going on.

She didn't seem bothered by her new awareness. Instead she seemed curious about this new consciousness, and it prompted in her to want to learn more about her family history. At the beginning of the second individual interview, after she had participated in the group interview and heard the stories of other mixed women, she said, "Like I want to research my ancestors more. I think that'd be awesome. And I never really thought about it before, but I want to know."

As I listened to Brittney's stories I couldn't help but wonder how much of her overwhelmingly positive experiences with others were influenced by the fact that she was a beautiful, conventionally feminine, straight woman. The word that comes to mind when I think of how to describe her is "adorable." She was always dressed with cute clothes, high heels, a perfect manicure, full make-up, and ponytail hairpieces that were so well blended you would never know (except that she showed me her extensive hairpiece collection) that it wasn't her natural hair. Although she could never pass for White, she definitely fit into conventional norms of sexuality and gender and, to some extent, beauty (when considering non-White mainstream images of beauty). She showed me a picture of her and three mixed race friends, one of whom was a professional model, and the photo looked like it could be an advertisement in a fashion magazine. Thus it was not surprising that, in many ways, her experiences with others were often positive. However, I do not want to minimize the fact that Brittney also had a very warm, sweet personality, a genuine openness to others, and a generally positive outlook on life. She was outgoing and social and told several stories of reaching out to make new friends. All of these factors likely played a role in her positive experiences living as a mixed race female.

Elizabeth, whose mom was Filipina and dad was White, also described her experiences as mostly positive. She was quiet for much of the group interview. At one point I checked in with her and asked her if she had anything to add, and she said:

> I guess I feel almost out of place [a] little bit. You know? In our individual interviews I just kept stressing how much I love being mixed race. It's been such a positive experience for me. I don't have a lot of issues, I guess, about being mixed race. I don't have a lot of angst about it.

Elizabeth had described to me in her individual interviews that within Filipina/o culture, mixed race people, known as *mestiza/o*, are generally thought of positively. Elizabeth explained that "being mixed race is regarded highly" and that most of the movie stars are mixed race, "partially White." She revealed that she had a darker skinned cousin, whom she was very close to, and relatives would make comments about how dark she was and tell her not to go out in the sun. She and her cousin would manage the differential treatment by joking about it. She said, "[My cousin] and I used to, in a fourth grade way, we'd joke about race. She'd be like, 'You whitey, you cracker.' We were absolutely aware of the privilege that I enjoyed." As a revered mestiza she said, "I don't feel troubled."

Mindy, the other mixed Filipina woman in the group, struggled considerably with her identity, and in the group interview she often talked about the difficulties of being mixed. This shocked Elizabeth who assumed that other mixed Filipinos would have similarly positive experiences. Elizabeth, age 31, had always viewed her experiences as overwhelmingly positive. She could pass for White, and acknowledged her White privilege, which she felt added to her positive experiences. She said, "I pass so much for White, I don't encounter much of anything." Her revered Whiteness didn't trouble her.

Although all of the women had positive things to say about being mixed race, all but Brittney and Elizabeth talked about the struggles of being mixed. As can be derived from the stories shared thus far, there were often moments of angst and suffering in relation to identity formation. What most of the women had in common were shifting and changing self-identifications and accompanying wide ranging feelings related to their mixed race identities, which were influenced by life experiences, situational contexts, and intersecting social identities (such as gender, class, and sexuality).

INFLUENCES ON IDENTITY FORMATION/POSITIONALITIES

These stories of translocational positionalities point to the intersections among race, class, sexuality, and gender. Race/ethnic identification is intricately intertwined with other social positionalities. Although it is impossible to document all the intricacies of each woman's story, upon review of all the data, it is clear that how the women identified was impacted by myriad factors. As each of these women struggled to formulate their racial and ethnic identities, they were constantly faced with constricting external structures and personal challenges from family and peers. Some of the factors that influenced racial/ethnic identities include: language (as in Maria's story of having a Spanish name solidifying her Brownness), home culture (as in Tina's story of feeling Mexican), relationships to each parent (as in Ana's story of more consciously claiming her British side to acknowledge her relationship to her mom), where someone grew up (as in Diana's story of growing up in a historically Black neighborhood), appearance (as in Mindy's story of not feeling she can claim space as a person of color because she looks White), school (as in Maria's story of culture shocks), and friends (as in Janet's story of feeling White because she had White friends). Because the main marker in the social construction of race is skin color, one might assume that skin color would be the primary factor in racial identification; that was not the case in this group.

Even though my parents never talked to me about my mixed race identity, one of the most shocking findings for me was that almost no one's parents talked to them about their racial identities. I asked each participant at some point, "Did you talk about race at home," or "Did your parents talk to you about race?" Although in some households there were discussions about race related politics, there were only two participants, Joanna and Katherine (who were siblings), who remembered having distinct conversations about *their racial identities* with their parents. Katherine recalled:

About being mixed ... the first time I remember talking about it in my family was really young. I remember my mother, in my mind, she worried about it a lot. And it was her job to teach us what it was to be a person of color, what it was to be Black. My dad was not involved in that.

She said that at first she "didn't get it" but eventually she had experiences that helped her to understand why her mom worked to educate her. Unfortunately, at the time of the study, she did not have a close personal relationship with her mom anymore, and she didn't talk with her mom about her experiences. Ruth, whose dad was African American, remembered that for "the little bit that he was around" (she described in her interviews how he was a mostly absent father) they, "talked about racism a lot, and [she] think[s] he did a pretty good job of preparing [her] for the real world." For everyone else issues of racial identity were unspoken, assumed, and insinuated.

Given the lack of discussion in their homes about racial identity, many of the women had no idea how their parents perceived them. In response to a question on this issue, I received responses like, "You know, I really don't know. I wish I did. I know they really are proud of me. I know they love me" (Alana) or "I really didn't talk to my parents a lot about identity and about being mixed race. It's still not something that my family really talks about, but I don't think it's so much that they're trying to hide it in some way" (Janet). As young people, they were overwhelmingly left to construct their own identities, often with no role models because there were no mixed race adults around them.

At the end of the group interview in Boston, I asked if there were any messages they wanted to pass along to readers. Mindy spoke up with a message for parents who have mixed race children. She said, "Know that your children's experiences are very different from how you grew up. My father grew up in a White community, my mom in the Philippines. How we grew up had nothing remotely connected, it was much more of a tri-cultural mix." Mindy demonstrated a thirst for greater understanding and acknowledgement of mixed race identity. The two who did have a parent who talked to them explicitly about being mixed race appreciated that their mom tried to make them comfortable with their identities. However, Katherine explained that she was "traumatized" learning about slavery when she was "too young to see it" and that even though she "had a sense of what race meant in the world" she "never experienced it." She believes that her mom did the best she could, but her mom didn't realize that her experience as a Black woman raised during civil rights would be different than the experiences of her biracial children during different times. Still Katherine, and her sister Joanna, seemed grateful to have been given tools to deal with racism.

In the 'Mixed Race' Studies Reader, Ifekwunigwe (2004) delineates three "ages" of mixed race identity: the age of pathology, the age of celebration, and the age of critique. The "age of pathology" refers to the time period from the beginning of colonialism in the U.S. to the 1980s. During this time "hybrid" forms, including mixed race people, were viewed as degenerate. Hybrids stood at the center of eugenics debates, and anti-miscegenation laws were passed in hopes of discouraging the production of mixed race offspring. Mixed race people were viewed as threats. Then in the 1990s a new set of writings emerged in which the authors, many of whom were mixed race, acknowledged and worked to reverse the damaging perspectives about mixed race people. The writers often celebrated mixed race people and legitimized mixed race as a social category, marking the beginning of a new mixed race canon. Ifekwunigwe referred to that shift as the beginning of the "age of celebration." It wasn't long before more critical works accompanied these celebratory writings. In the mid 1990s, there began an "age of critique" in which

> scholars continue to grapple with unresolved tensions between identification and categorization and structure and agency, i.e., the tangle of census terminology or the political limitations of a "Multiracial Movement" (Aspinal 1997, Colker 1996, Cose 1997, Morning 2003, Nobles 2002). (Ifekwunigwe, 2004, p. 8)

The narratives by the women in this book reflect all of the "ages" Ifekwunigwe describes. Because identity formation is constantly in flux and constantly shifting, people can occupy various identity positions. For these women, mixed race identity was simultaneously painful and joyful. We continue to face pathologizing of our identities, we celebrate our identities, and we critique our identities and are critiqued by others for our mixed race identities. Our journeys of racial and ethnic translocational positionalities are, at times, empowering and, at other times, deflating. What is apparent, however, is that our (perceived) identities are constantly up for speculation and determination by others. This begins early in school when we are forced to identify our race for standardized tests – an issue raised specifically by five participants.

Why is it that so many people feel they have the right to challenge and name our identities for us? Why is it that we are expected to prove ourselves? What do we gain from engaging in that power struggle? Is it possible for us to avoid it? How do we find a home in a structure that makes no place for us? The women's stories raise these questions. They are hard questions to answer given that race is a social and political construct (Omi & Winant, 1994), therefore its meaning can never easily be captured or described. Williams (1997) raised important questions about what determines race and culture in her essay, "Race-ing and Being Raced." She asked:

> How do we determine authentic membership into a racial group: by birth? blood ties? kinship organization? geographic upbringing? cultural socialization? presence or absence of one parent's heritage? phenotypical resemblance? a combination of these variables? and moreover, who determines racial and ethnic authenticity? (p. 63)

When it comes to being mixed race, it often feels that everyone claims the right to determine our racial authenticity. We experience challenges to our identities by both White people and people of color, who are often searching for an answer from us that expresses a fixed identity. In addition, we are expected to back up our "choices" with evidence – in the form of life experiences, languages, skin color, etc. – that support our spoken identifications.

The participants' stories reveal that it is possible to hold multiple racial identifications simultaneously; all of the women do so. For example, almost all of the women identified simultaneously as women of color, mixed race, and Latina, Black, or Japanese, etc. These stories demonstrate that there are a plethora of factors influencing racial/ethnic identity, of which skin color is only a small part. The narratives illuminate intricate webs of social positionalities. We learn that racial identification cannot be extricated from other social identity factors such as class, gender, and sexuality. Furthermore, peers, location, upbringing, appearance, and myriad other cultural and structural influences impact positionalities. Mixed race identity is described as simultaneously painful and powerful. These women both celebrated and critiqued their positionalities, and they were both celebrated and critiqued by others.

Amidst a fair amount of joking about how "we are beautiful" within the individual and group interviews, there was a simultaneous desire to claim our beauty without essentializing it. Also, as evidenced by the unanimous rejection of a solely White identity and the overwhelming choice to identify as women of color, these women recognized the political importance of claiming identities outside of the dominant White norm. In the introduction to her Mixed Race Women anthology, *Miscegenation Blues*, Carol Camper (1994) wrote that she refused to include submissions written from a "colonized point of view."

> One such place is the idea that racial mixing would be the so called 'future' of race relations and the future of humanity. One or two contributors do mention it, briefly, without necessarily agreeing with it. I strongly disagree with this position. It is naïve. It leaves the race work up to the mixed people and our entire histories and cultures as if we are obsolete. It is essentially a racist solution.

> For this reason I think it is important for mixed people who have White ancestry to not identify only as mixed but to stress identity with their coloured ancestry. This would be different for those who have no White ancestry, though there can still be oppressor/oppressed history in their lineage which may require examining.

> Our existence is not meant to annihilate. We simply exist. We should not be forced into a 'closet' about White or any other parentage, but we must recognize that our location is as women of colour. (p. xxiii)

Although there were a few instances in which the participants alluded to believing that the mixing of the races was the answer to racial segregation and racism, for the most part, they were thoughtful and critical of their positions within this debate, and all of them recognized the importance of maintaining their cultures and racialized identities.

The narratives in this chapter only scratch the surface of racial positionalities for us as mixed race women. The stories and analysis shared in the next two chapters reveal further intricacies of racial identifications as mixed race women by examining the structure of outsider/insider positionalities in Chapter 4 and how women take agency in the production of fluid identities in Chapter 5.

CHAPTER 4

OUTSIDER/INSIDER

The Constraints of Negotiating Institutional Structures and Identity Challenges

I guess the drawback of being mixed race is only rarely feeling completely comfortable. Like it's great to feel partially comfortable in so many different settings, but it's a really narrow spot where I feel like absolutely, "I'm like you." Maybe it's with other mixed race people, or it's with other children of immigrants, no matter what race or background. Maybe it's with other Asian Americans who are several generations of American. But yeah, it's hard to be – I can't just get my Filipino family who are immigrants, we are just not alike. And it's hard for me to be around my dad's family, because they're so White, they just don't get stuff. But I think there is a benefit to being only partially comfortable that outweighs the discomfort. I'd rather be partially comfortable with lots of different people, but only be super comfortable with this one group, you know? – Elizabeth

Well yeah, it's the comfort of, I know I can fit in this group but I'm not really being myself, you know? I know I can feel comfortable enough, and these people do not think I'm a threat or whatever, but it's never like I really reveal my entire personality, or my entire self. – Joanna

My oldest cousin, when she got married, her husband came to me and was really serious. He said, "Linda can I ask you a question? I don't want you to be offended or anything, but it's really important, and if you want to talk about it I'd really love to. If you don't, that's okay too. But what was it like for you growing up mixed?" I told him that it's hard. And that I didn't feel like I fit in, the outsider stuff, that I didn't feel like I fit in anywhere, that the Asian kids didn't really identify me as Asian, and the White kids saw me as something kind of different, you know? – Linda

The women in my study shared many stories of being simultaneous insiders and outsiders, of feeling a mixture of comfort and discomfort in all areas of their lives as mixed race women. Often these feelings of belonging and disconnection occurred concurrently. There was no escape from identity challenges. They occurred within their families, with friends, at work, at school, and in interactions with strangers. The women's stories demonstrate a sense of struggle to find a place of belonging, a longing for insider positionality, with a simultaneous recognition that outsider status also has its benefits. There was a constant negotiation between the external constraints of structure and the internal ability to claim agency with a betwixt and between situational position.

Sociologist Anthony Giddens (1977, 1984) argued that structure and agency act in concert with each other. There is a dialectical relationship between action and structure (1977, p. 53). Giddens (1977) reminded us that the "reflexive monitoring of action includes the monitoring of *the setting of the interaction*, and not just the behavior of the particular actors taken separately" (p. 57). Thus, to best understand the explanations of why the participants act as they do, it is important to know the settings of the actions and the way that structure, time, and place are impacting the behaviors of individuals. The next two chapters examine structure and agency, specifically insider/outsider positionalities for these mixed race women.

In this chapter I focus on the ways family, school and work structures constrict the agency of the women. However, first I begin with the identity challenges that strangers create for these women. These experiences with strangers, with family, at school and at work constitute much of human life. I emphasize here how the women are positioned into particular categories by external forces. In the next chapter I draw attention to how the women claim positions of strength within their fluid, ambiguous identities. The separation – the emphasis on structure in one chapter and agency in another – is strategic, yet artificial, because structure and agency are always interrelated and directly influence each other. Thus, the stories of both chapters reveal elements of intersecting structure and agency. The purpose of the separation is to remind the readers that structural and external constraints limit self-actualization; at the same time, I aim to minimize any tendencies to pathologize or pity our mixed race experiences by dedicating a distinct chapter to agency and the power of fluid, mixed race identities. Giddens (1977) explained that agentic actions create structures that then both limit and create opportunities for agency. I attempt to situate these women's experiences within this interplay of structure and agency by examining their descriptions of interactions with others, which helps us to understand their habitus (Bourdieu, 1977).

In literature by and/or about mixed race people there has been a tendency to either pathologize (Knox, 1850; Nott & Gliddon, 1854; Rich, 1990) or uncritically celebrate (Root, 1992; Zack, 1993) the mixed race experience. These women dismantle that dichotomy between pathological experiences and universally celebratory experiences by demonstrating the complexity of their lives and the ways in which they occupy concurrent insider and outsider positionalities, locations of simultaneous power and oppression, strength and weakness, possibility and impossibility.

FACING THE "WHAT ARE YOU?" QUESTION

Many mixed race people experience being asked, "What are you?" by a variety of people (Gaskins, 1999). Almost all the women interviewed experienced being asked that question. For some it occurred almost daily, for others it occurred only within certain contexts, when a particular action – how they danced, a word they used, a food they ate – would indicate to others that they might be of a different background than the person originally thought. The participants exhibited a vast range of reactions and feelings in response to that question. At times participants internally debated whether or not they wanted to dedicate energy to a response and deal with the potential subsequent consequences. For some, the question was welcomed as an opportunity to educate or explain themselves, while others felt offended or were simply tired of it. But what seemed to have the most impact on how the participants perceived the question was the assumed intention of the person asking.

In addition to the "What are you?" question, variations and offshoots often felt like direct challenges to identity. In the Boston group interview, a lengthy discussion ensued about such "What are you?" challenges to identity by strangers. Joanna shared an experience of being on a school bus as a sixth grader when a Black girl approached her and said in a threatening voice, "Are you Black or are you White?" Joanna explained her thoughts in that moment, "I was all ready to have to defend my multiracial identity, and be like, 'I'm not going to deny one side or the other,' you know?" But when Joanna responded in a non-threatening voice, "Actually, I'm both," the girl simply said, "Oh, okay" and walked away. Joanna believed that for some, the idea of being mixed "never occurred to them as a possibility. And then when they think about it they're like, 'Okay.'" In Joanna's experience "almost all the people who correctly identify [her] racial background have met other mixed people." She elaborated that people who "grew up in fairly diverse areas" knew she was "something other than White" but weren't sure what she was. She has only "ever only known White people" who "assume [she's] White or Jewish." Joanna's experience resonated with the other women.

For most of the participants, it was primarily White people who assumed they were White. For example, Elizabeth said, "I feel like it's easy for White people to see you as the same as them." Participants found that when they defined themselves as mixed race or as women of color, White people often became defensive. In the group interview, Diana began a story emphasizing this point to which three other women added on.

Diana: I've been taken for White so much in my life that sometimes I don't say anything. It doesn't mean I'm trying to pass; it's just that I don't feel like getting into it with somebody. I had a coworker, a White man, he stormed my desk. He came up to my desk hit his fist on the table, and said, "Why do you go around saying that you're Black?"

Joanna: Yeah.

Mindy: Yeah it's like they're offended that you claim something other than...

Diana: Than being White.

Mindy: Yeah.

Diana: That you don't want to be White.

Mindy: Yeah.

Susan: That's the key.

Mindy: That's been all of my negative experiences with White people. When they find out that the identity is something that's mixed.

Joanna: Yeah but you would get your ass kicked by whatever community of color you're a part of if you say that you're White.

Diana: The thing is that there are a lot of White people in America who are not White. There've always been people that have been passing and crossing over from all these different ethnicities, you know? And White people are so oblivious to that. Look at somebody, and they're so dark, and their hair is so kinky, and you're like, this is a White person? And yet to them, they're a White person.

This reflective exchange is indicative of participants' encounters with White ignorance and the desire by White people, sometimes consciously other times unconsciously, to suppress mixed race identities. Most of the women expressed anger at these challenges and acknowledged that it was White entitlement that allowed people to feel justified in making the challenges.

Initially Susan argued against assigning intent to the question of one's racial positionality. She explained that the question she always has to field when she tells people that she is Latina and White is, "How did that happen?" Susan argued that some people just do not have the life experiences around racial issues to understand that their question is offensive. Joanna, however, was incredulous and exclaimed, "But that's rude. How could you not even know that that's rude?" Susan maintained that some people are "really clueless" and "just don't understand."[21] Mindy chimed in on the conversation and argued:

But going back to intent. I think... I know it is hard to determine the intent of every question, but a lot of times I feel like because my issues have usually been with White people, I always felt that some of these questions were just coming from a place of entitlement.

Ruth immediately backed her up adding, "Yes, definitely." To which Mindy added, "All these questions are very invasive and very personal. So it's like, why do you feel like you can ask these questions? You don't know me." When I asked Ruth to explain her emphatic reaction she illuminated the undo burden of having to constantly deal with White people's entitlement. She said:

I don't know why I had such a reaction to that. I think one of my biggest issues with people is attitudes of entitlement. I really can't stand that. And I feel like I have to point that out more than I should. I think that a lot of people who feel entitled have no idea that they act that way. And it gets tiresome to have to show that. Because I feel like, how many other people have the nerve, or whatever, to hold a mirror to these people who act entitled? And I'm one of those people who believes that if somebody's being out of line, you tell them exactly how they're being out of line. So maybe they'll learn something. Because I think sometimes people can be told, "Hey, you're being out of line." And they're like, "Oh, I'm really sorry," and they'll adjust. But there are other people who, you know, have been told they're jerks all their lives and they still don't make any attempt to change. But I think I have some resentment about having to correct so many people, you know? It's 2006 and we're still not anywhere near where I'd like to be.

In response, Joanna said:

It's funny. There's only one phase of my life where I had resentment about these questions. Usually I actually enjoy those questions as long as they're not downright rude, even if they're a little bit rough around the edges. Because I take it as a chance to educate these people and to share my experience. Which is always interesting to me and to them, you know? But when I was in college I had a department full of rednecks, and I became like a department hippie, *the* diversity. So I was constantly having to combat them, day in and day out, I had to stand up because I was the only person who had a conscience about it. And at that point in my life I definitely resented having to constantly put on a Black hat, or the feminist hat, or the whatever.

Mindy, responding to Joanna's story, said, "They don't understand that they're making you a representative."

In response to the "What are you?" related questions, while participants resented the need to endure the challenges and the defensiveness of others at times, they welcomed the opportunity to educate in hopes that people could better understand their lives and perspectives as mixed race women. Joanna's description of using the questions to educate people demonstrates agency. Diana's opening comment that sometimes she doesn't say anything because she "doesn't feel like getting into it" is also a form of agency. Yet, as demonstrated in the following example, the context dictates agentic opportunity.

At times, the "What are you?" identity challenges are clear exertions of White power, as evidenced in this story by Diana:

> I remember this time that I was driving to this gas station to get gas. And this was in South Carolina and the guy pumping the gas order puts his head into the driver's window and says, "We see you here all the time, what are you?" I didn't say anything, so he said, "You're Spanish?" I said, "No." So he went around the car and then he came back and he said, "Injun." I said, "No." He had this whole list of everything, so finally he said, "I give up. What are you?" I said, "I'm Black." So he starts shouting to this other man inside the office, "Joe, Joe come out here!" So he tells me, "Get out of the car and turn around so we can look at you." He says to Joe, "This girl says she's Black!" And I said, "If you don't get out of the way I'm just going to run your foot right over." And I took off. I couldn't believe it.

Not only was Diana questioned about her identity, but she was subsequently denied the right to define herself and expected, like an animal, to parade herself for approval by the racist White man who challenged her racial identity and demanded her sexuality.

In the Albuquerque group interview there was also a discussion about challenges to identity by strangers. Brittney, concurring with the Boston group's discussions of how difficult it can be dealing with confrontations by White people, said, "It seems like you could talk more open with people who aren't White." Brittney felt that being asked the "What are you?" question by other mixed race people was "safe" because in that context, the question is about making connections. But, taking the discussion in a distinct direction from that of the Boston group interview, which focused on challenges by White people, she raised the issue of being challenged by Black people who aren't mixed. Brittney began the discussion and Maria finished it.

> Brittney: Yeah, but when like a Black person who's completely Black asks me, it's kind of like, "Oh, well you're not…"

> Maria: (interrupting) Like they are testing you. For me it's more like how it's being asked not necessarily who's asking. I've totally been offended by people of color who have asked. And I think there is an assumption too that all people of color have some analysis around racism, and I don't think that's true.

Although not necessarily in relation to the "What are you?" question, other mixed Black women in the study talked about feeling dismissed by Black women. Alana said, "Like I always thought that Black women hate me. Even to this day it's hard for me to connect and to be intimate with Black women." Brittney also later brought the topic up by explaining:

You know, I'm half Black and half White. I don't hang around that much with just Black people, just African American, or whatever 'cause they kind of separate themselves from me. I've noticed that I get a little like, for me, I think Black women that are fully against, or more against mixed races. Like, they don't like when a Black man dates a White woman. They get territorial, and they get offended. I think that's stupid. I have a couple, like, full African American friends, but not that many. They kind of stick to themselves, it seems like that to me.

Joanna also said, "I'm always on guard in a group of Black people." Ruth, age 34, explained that although now she has several Black friends, as a youth she was a complete outcast in her "99 percent Black" school. Diana, who grew up two decades earlier in a predominately Black neighborhood and moved in circles comprised mainly of Black people, was an exception to this experience; she never raised the issue of being dismissed or rejected by Black people. One particular aspect of the women's stories that I think is worth highlighting is the interplay between race and gender that consistently emerges. Alana and Brittney emphasized that it was Black *women* who didn't like them; Brittney connected this to women being territorial about Black men but the layers seem thicker than that, especially given that Alana dates women. Systems of internalized racism and sexism are at play in these interactions.

The problem with focusing exclusively on the "What are you?" questions that mixed race people often face, as often happens in discussions of the mixed race experience, is that it only begins to scratch the surface of identity challenges and external constraints on self-identification. For many of these women, identity challenges even occurred within their own families.

EVEN FAMILY MEMBERS POSE CHALLENGES

Although it is difficult to face constant questioning of identity by strangers, it can be even more difficult to face identity challenges from family members, both immediate and extended. Maria explained:

I think my biggest challenges have probably come from my family. In terms of like, I mean like my mom not really acknowledging, and my dad at times really struggling when I started really identifying as Chicana and got involved with MEChA[22]. My dad was saying something around like, "Oh aren't you going to join, like, a German group?" I was just like, "That's stupid." Like, it didn't even make sense. It was really bizarre, and so I think that sometimes even my parents don't really know me, our experiences and how we identify and why, right?

Ana also talked about separation from her mom around her identity. She said:

I know there were times that my mom didn't really relate to me because she's White, and I'm Brown. A few years ago I told my mom that I was a part of this organization for women of color, and she said to me, "Do you think of yourself as a woman of color?" And I was like, "Yeah, hello?" And it was just like this dawning on her mind like "Oh, what? I think that I know my daughter's Brown," but like [loudly] "OH, she knows she's Brown too!"

As mentioned in the previous chapter, for almost all of the women, mixed race identity was not discussed in their homes, and as a result many of the participants did not know how their parents perceived them.

Susan similarly named challenges to her identity by her White mom. Often this manifested as her mom trying to control Susan's appearance and squelch parts of her identity that made her stand out as different from her White mother. For example, her mom always wanted her to straighten her hair. She told this story:

My mom is the White one, and one thing that this made me think of is that she was always trying to make me look more White. My hair is very frizzy and curly; I have this big bush on my head. I just got it cut [lots of laughter from the group because her hair looked really straight]. I have this really wiry kind of, whatever, and when I would come home from college, she would pick me up at the airport the first thing she would say is, "When are you going to straighten your hair?" And I remember just, like, being really upset, and I would complain to my little brother about it. And he would be like, "You so made that up! There's no way," you know? "That's ridiculous." And I said, "Okay. The next time, you come to the airport." And he came to the airport, and it happened, and his jaw dropped. Because as the boy, there was enough separation, I guess. The gender offers enough separation. My mom really saw me as an extension of her, and what wasn't White about me she really felt she had to address, she had to change.

Maria, Ana, and Susan all felt a separation from their White moms because they identified as women of color. Demonstrating the confluence of gender and race, sometimes the challenges or dismissive remarks that their White moms made were around issues of appearance or beauty – White beauty – as in the story above in which Susan's mom wants her to straighten her hair. Susan felt that her mom's extra attention to her appearance was because they shared womanhood, connection as women; however, it may also be that Susan's mom put a greater emphasis on wanting her daughter to conform to dominant culture beauty norms because within dominant culture, beauty is considered a much more important trait for women than men.

Maria also shared stories that revealed ways her mom made her feel ugly. She cried as she recalled, "Then there was my mom who was like, well... I was like, 'Do you think I'm pretty?' And she would be like, 'Well you're interesting looking.'" Although Maria currently has fairly light skin, when she was younger she was darker (she showed me photos and there was an amazing difference in skin color), and her features resembled the Mexican women on her dad's side of her family, not her White mother. Maria's mom was an artist, and she remembered that, when she was little, her mom began a painting of her, but became frustrated with it. Maria recalled, "She just kept saying, 'Why can't I get your face right?' And I remember getting it. And I was like 'Oh, it's because I'm so ugly, she can't paint me.'" Her mom never finished the painting.

Personally, I would describe Maria as beautiful – high cheekbones, a beautiful smile with full lips, soft long curly hair, and petite – so it honestly surprised me that she received negative messages about her appearance growing up. I asked her, "You don't remember your mom telling you that you were pretty ever?" She replied:

> No, and it doesn't mean she didn't, so I don't want to just create this. But I distinctly remember the messages I got when I wasn't. Clearly those outweighed whatever else she may or may not have said. So kind of like, in some ways it doesn't really matter.

Knowing that she looked nothing like her mom, Maria's feelings of inadequacy were exacerbated by the continual attention her dad gave her mom for her conventional White beauty. Maria said that her mom looked like a beauty queen, and that her dad remarked daily on her mom's looks.

> What does it mean to hear that your mom is beautiful when you don't look like your mom? I remember seeing those shows sometimes, those like pageant shows, the mother-daughter ones. They look the same almost, and it's this whole thing. I was just like, "Oh yeah, that's so not me."

She appreciated the fact that her mom and dad were still in love, and she expressed the desire to be with someone who, like her dad did with her mom, would tell her daily that she is beautiful. Although she felt that her dad told her she was beautiful, it was never to the extent that he admired her mom's White beauty. Given that Maria looked nothing like her mom, she felt she could never live up to that standard of beauty. This affected her self-esteem; she was angry about the negative messages she received from her mom and remarked, "I'm fucking 34, and I don't think I'm beautiful. Like, when the fuck is that going to happen? And let me tell you, she didn't do much to help me get there, you know?" Thankfully, for Maria, she had extended family members whom she resembled and admired, her *tata*[23] and her *tía*[24], both of whom told her she was beautiful.

Similarly Janet, who also had a White mom and a Mexican dad, received some messages from her mother about not looking beautiful, although it wasn't as clearly linked to race. However, her sense of not feeling beautiful overall was impacted by race dynamics because she was raised mostly in an all-White community with White standards of beauty. She explained that, "The women that had more value were definitely blond and blue eyed, and looked just like this kind of Barbie girl."

> I definitely feel like the boys when I was growing up definitely thought that the girls with the blond hair and the blue eyes were the prettiest. And I remember going through a phase where I wanted to be like them. I remember thinking, "I wish I had blond hair and I wish I had blue eyes," and you know not really being happy with the way I looked.

I asked her if she talked to her mom about her feelings and experiences. She said:

> I do remember talking to my mom about not being happy with the way I looked, but the only one thing I remember specifically, is saying that I was real unhappy with my nose, and that when I was older wanting a nose job. And I remember my mom just kind of looking at me and rather than saying what I think she would say, like "You don't need that," or "No way." You know? I think I remember her saying like, "Maybe when you're older and we have enough money, you can get one."

Again, I was surprised to hear her story. Janet is also someone who I think would most likely be described by many people as beautiful.

Alana, who also had a White mom, talked about a sense of separation as well, although it wasn't connected to standards of beauty. Alana explained that she often tried to educate her White mom around issues of race in hopes of helping her to understand her experience as a mixed race Black woman. However, these challenges often felt threatening to her mom. This feeling was exacerbated when Alana came out to her mom as queer. Alana recalled:

> In the summer, I came out to her as a queer person. And we got into this huge fight, I remember, down near the beach. We were around all these White moms and White daughters walking along the beach. And my mom and I were standing kind of far away. Then she started screaming at me, "We are never going to be close because you are queer and Black. We are never ever going to be close. And what am I supposed to do?" I completely lost it. I started screaming and crying, and our relationship has never been the same ever since then.

Instead of reaching out to her, Alana's mom got caught up in her own sense of dissonance from her daughter and added to it by focusing on their differences rather than connecting with Alana, as her mom, in a time when her daughter was searching for support. Alana's intersecting positionalities as queer and Black, distinct from her mom's straight and White identity, made her mom feel that they could not connect. In the way this story was told, Alana was perceived to be at fault; Alana's mom placed the blame on Alana's identifications with the phrase "you are queer and Black" versus stating, for example, "We have different skin colors/races and sexual orientations." In contrast, Joanna and Katherine, the siblings whose Black mom talked to them frequently about race, received clear, distinct messages from their mother that they were beautiful mixed race women.

Mindy, whose dad was White, felt a connection to her Filipina mother, but her mother at times dismissed a connection to her daughter, whom she perceived primarily as White; this is part of the reason why Mindy felt like she could not claim a "woman of color" identity. She shared, "It's hard when your own mother says, 'You're your father's daughter' based on skin. And then you don't really feel a connection to your father, it's just one more thing, you know?" She added, "Even though I feel somewhat closer to my mother, there's still like a distance that gets created because it's like nothing of her is recognized in yourself." Mindy struggled significantly with her identity because she was most often assumed to be White by strangers, her mother, and her extended Filipina/o family, yet she felt more of a connection to her Filipina mom and Filipina identity than she did to her White dad and White identity. This conflict created a sense of "social homelessness" which is experienced by people "who upon first glance, should be wholly accepted in one or more social categories. However, the individual is unable to fully participate in the life of the social group because of competing identities" (Harrison, 2010, p. 202).

Differences between the mixed race participants and their monoracial parents often came to the fore when participants were not recognized as their parent's kids, sometimes in very painful ways. Marta shared this story about one time when her dad came to her house to repair a door that didn't work. She said:

> And he had taken the door off and he was in the yard with the door, and this guy who lives downstairs came running out, and he ran over to me. And said "There is this guy in the yard and I don't know what he's doing. I don't know if he's trying to break in." And I just looked at him and I said, "That's my father." And he just looked like he wanted to die. And he just said, "Oh, I'm so sorry" and ran away.

Although Marta has very similar features to her Peruvian father, people were often unable to recognize the similarities between them because of their different skin tones, her dad's being brown and hers being white. In this situation, racism likely played into the interpretation.

Bobbi also had experiences in which she wasn't recognized as her mother's daughter. She added:

> I think that happens to me all the time, because my sister looks a lot different. My mom is a very fair, blond, blue eyed, White woman. But the time it sticks out the most is when we were in, my sister married a Bahamian man, and we were in the Bahamas. And we were in this place where all the women make these cool doodads out of straw; it was this marketplace. And the tourists there treat the locals like shit. And this tourist lady asked my mom, "Where did you get your purse?" because she had just gotten it from the

straw people. And my mom was like, "I don't know." And I was like, "Oh, she got it over there," like I'm telling her where my mom got it. And the lady just looked right through me. And the place was so packed that she was right here [indicates a space only inches away]. And I was like, "Oh, she got it right there," and she thought I was trying to hustle her. She's basically treating me like the locals, and I was trying to tell my mom, "That bitch." And I was like, "Oh, I guess you don't hear me then," you know? I told my mom and she was just like, she totally couldn't even recognize that something like that would be happening. It's so frustrating when you're like, "There's somebody who is really fucking with me and treating me like shit right now." And your mom is just like [silence]. You know, like, it's weird.

This instance began as a dismissal of identity by a stranger but, in the end, it illuminated the distinct and disparate positions between Bobbi and her mom. Her mom was unable to understand or validate Bobbi's experience with racism, which positioned Bobbi as an outsider in relation to her mom.

Maria, Ana, Mindy, and Janet also told stories of not being recognized as their parents' kids. I too have had that experience. I remember people asking my mom if I was adopted. It happened so often that it was not until I was 10 and my sister, who looks just like me, was born that I was sure I was indeed my mother's child. These instances are reminders to us of outsider positionalities even within our own families.

At the same time, some of the women also recognized the ways their parents went out of their way to make connections. Ana said:

When I think about my mom and me, there are lots of things that I've experienced that she never has experienced. But she has worked really hard to try to stay connected to me, to learn about the things that are important to me.

Bobbi, who told the story of frustration with her mom above, also spoke very highly of her mom, stating that her White mom "speaks really good Somali" and emphasizing how her mom taught her Somali culture. Even Maria recognized that her mom tried to protect her from her grandfather's racist jokes. She said, "So I know my mom really tried, where she got it [meaning where she understood racism], to say stuff like that. I know that she did [try]." Again, gender role expectations seem to be at play in these interactions; dominant culture generally dictates that it is the mother's responsibility to teach and protect her children.

Although participants shared several stories of being accepted by extended family members, some of the women were made to feel like outsiders by extended family. Eight of the women described stories of their White grandparents not accepting their parents' relationship. After Brittney shared a story of how a friend of hers told her that he couldn't date her because she was Black, she stated that the negative things her friends or other people said didn't really bother her. Then she added, "The thing that affected me was my mom telling me about my grandma and how she was like that before. But I never noticed it because she never treated me different." Brittney's story is indicative of several of the women's experiences in which they learned later that their White grandparents disapproved of their parents' marriage. Oftentimes they, as the mixed race children, were accepted, but sometimes their parents severed contact with their extended families as a result of the disapproval of the interracial marriage and the women never got to know their grandparents. Mindy shared, "For a while there we had really limited contact with my grandmother because, you know, her attitude towards the marriage and everything was so negative."

Most of the women had a sense of being different within some or all extended family situations. Elizabeth talked about going to a recently immigrated aunt's house and feeling very different from the rest of the group. She said, "They treated me different. They gave me special food. My own special American food. I couldn't understand their language ... I felt so different." Mindy, who lived in Boston, talked about feeling disconnected from her Filipina/o family by language and culture and distance. Most of her Filipina/o family lived on the West Coast or in the Philippines. Mindy's mom made traditional Filipina/o food at home, which became "comfort food" for Mindy, but there was still a language barrier and a cultural barrier. Mindy felt that she was seen by her Filipina/o family as "the American daughter" that her mother had. Mindy also perceived the White side of her family to be very different; interactions with her grandmother always "set [her] on edge." Janet similarly recalled going to her dad's side of the family for Christmas and feeling out of place. She said:

> And I have these memories of when I was younger going to my father's side of the family, with like second and third cousins who are all Brown, and I remember Spanish, and I remember like it being Christmas, and them making tamales in the kitchen, and I remember just feeling like, kind of like an outsider then too, because I didn't really know even who these people were. And so I feel like that whole side of my family has always been kind of very far away.

Some, like Ruth and Linda, had virtually no contact with extended family.

Other times being with extended family, especially extended family of color, allowed participants to create closer connections to their cultures. For example, both Tina and Susan discussed how their Mexican grandmothers reminded them that they were Mexican. Susan said that identification with Mexican culture came more from her grandmother than her father. When she went to California to visit her family, she spent time cooking with her grandmother while her brothers went off "doing whatever." During those times, Susan said:

> My grandma used to very, very specifically say to me, in so many words, like exactly, "You are a Chicana. If somebody asks you, your answer is, 'I am a Chicana.' That's what you are. You are mine. You belong to me." That was her thing.

Tina similarly remembered spending time with her grandmother and the large influence it had on her positionality as a Latina.

> I would say when I was little, up until fifth grade, I really identified as Mexican. That's what I was. I spent all kinds of time with my dad's side of the family. My great grandma, I spent a lot of time with her. She didn't speak a word of English, and so I spent tons of time trying to communicate with her. It was very rare for me to eat hamburgers and hot dogs. I was just really eating tortillas and rice and beans all the time.

For Tina and Susan, spending time with their Mexican grandmothers solidified their Latina identities.

Often, home and family are thought of as places of belonging. As exemplified above, these women also had experiences as outsiders, even within family contexts. With constant identity challenges outside of the home, often these women were left with no safe space. As Janet said, "I think it's hard, because sometimes I feel like I don't really have a place. Where do I belong? That really comes up." It mattered, however, that some found particular family members that helped them to feel like they belonged. It also appeared to make a difference when their parents made an effort to understand their experiences, especially the White parent, with whom most of the participants felt most distant. Ana shared this 2001 journal entry she wrote that names this complex dynamic of wanting to be understood but appreciating the love that is displayed, even if there isn't always understanding.

> Mom asks if I see myself as a woman of color and I think about how my white mother cannot understand her brown children's lives, how I count brown faces when I walk into a room, but she does know what it means to be an outsider, to be different than those around the table, maybe she does know what it's like to look the same as the others around the table but to be different, her British whiteness at a table of Americans like my half-Filipino pan-brownness at a table of Latinas, I can fake it okay but it doesn't resonate or hum, I feel white to their brown, butch to their femme, bourgie to their ghetto, and yet I fit enough, am accepted enough, my mother does not understand me, my brownness, my queerness, but we love each other and it is enough.

Other women may not say that love is enough, but what Ana's mom did, that not all parents did, was make a continual concerted effort to understand and support her daughter. For example, her mom took college courses on sexual orientation and identity when Ana came out to her, and even though she was surprised when she heard Ana claim an identity as a woman of color, she didn't challenge it; she accepted it.

The women occupied insider and outsider positionalities in relationship to their family members. Maria, Susan, Ana, Alana, Janet, and Bobbi all felt some level of distance, disconnect, or discord with their White moms as mixed race daughters. Sometimes their moms emphasized their differences, and sometimes outsiders pointed out their differences. Mindy also felt distanced from her Filipina mom because her mom perceived Mindy to be White and, thus, more connected to her White father. Moreover, extended families of color at times similarly viewed the participants as outsiders. For some, racist White family members created outsiderness. Conversely, for some of the women, extended family members provided a sense of belonging and identity as evidenced in the relationships between Susan and Tina with their grandmothers. Overall the stories centered much more on the women in their lives – moms and grandmothers – than other family members.

SCHOOL AND FRIENDS

Some of the women found refuge with their friends, but for the most part identity challenges and outsider positioning extended to school and peer networks. These started in grade school and extended all the way through college. There were several stories of switching schools, desiring to drop out, and/or studying abroad to escape the school atmosphere. In addition, this was a highly educated group of women who were generally very successful in school; most of them were in gifted classes, which also created outsider positionalities.

Gifted Classes

All of the women did well in school overall, particularly when they weren't faced with overwhelmingly direct challenges by friends, teachers, or unrelated negative outside circumstances. Eleven of the 16 women – Maria, Ana, Linda, Marta, Diana, Ruth, Joanna, Elizabeth, Susan, Bobbi, and Mindy – talked about being in upper level and/or gifted classes. Although others did not discuss gifted classes, per se, all of the other participants explicitly stated that they were "smart" and/or that they did well in school. For many, not only did they do well, but they were at the top of their class and were afforded special privileges. For example, Maria and Ruth were both valedictorians; Ruth skipped the first grade; Elizabeth spent her senior year of high school at a university; and Diana was known as "the smart kid" in the neighborhood and got 100% on the Howard University entrance exam. As I was conducting interviews, I was struck by the overwhelming success these women experienced in school. They were highly formally educated. However, being academically gifted/successful often placed them in predominately White spaces, separating them from other people of color. For example Maria, Ana, Linda, and Joanna talked about how even though their schools were racially diverse, their classes weren't. Maria said, "I was placed in gifted classes so I was always, there was always some sort of separation." Diana and Ruth both attended predominately Black high schools but their honors classes were comprised of almost all White students.

Challenges by Teachers and the Institution

Even though they were all self-proclaimed "smart" women and overall did very well in school, they also faced several challenges. Some of these challenges came from the teachers and the institutions of school. For example, upon starting school Maria and Marta were both placed in inappropriate classes because of their Spanish surnames. In first grade Marta was "tracked into a slower reading group because her last name is Rodriguez." Maria had a similar experience. She said, "I was put in an ESL class in kindergarten because I was actually really quiet and they thought that that must mean that I didn't speak English." Bobbi explained that racist teachers "put [her] in all remedial classes." She believed their decisions were based on assumptions about her because of the neighborhood she was from. Brittney, of all the women, appeared to struggle most in school. She was held back in the third grade and was placed in special education during high school. She moved to a more diverse high school, tested again, and was found not to need special education. Her senior year she had a "3.7 or 3.8" grade point average.

Diana experienced her greatest challenges to excelling as a student from the administrators in the institution of school. Although she was in gifted classes and recognized as smart, she was not aided by any teachers to apply for college. Diana did not know anyone who went to college, and her family did not posses the cultural capital to encourage her to apply. She recognized her senior year that all the White Jewish kids around her were applying for college so she decided to visit the guidance counselor to ask how to apply. However, she explained, she received no support.

> I went to the guidance counselor and told her I wanted to know about going to college, and she said to me, "Oh no, Diana. Colored kids don't go to college." She starts writing and gave me this slip of paper and she said, "This is the vocational school. You can go there and take up sewing. That's what you should do." I instantly knew this was wrong, because in the eighth grade we had to take sewing and that was the only class I ever had in my life where I had less than an A or B. I got a D in sewing, and I was completely humiliated at having to wear this homemade dress in a fashion show on the school stage.

Fortunately, the "lady next door" came by and told her and her mom about a test at Howard University that weekend. She went and took the test, scoring 100% and earning a full scholarship.

Many of the women also discussed the limitations related to how they were allowed to identify on school forms. They were frustrated by the fact that they were forced to choose only one identity. These institutional challenges were compounded by harassment by peers, both White peers and peers of color.

Suffocating in Predominately White Schools and Harassment by Peers of Color

For many of these women, experiences in K through 12 schools included many challenges by peers to their identities as mixed race females. Several women shared stories of feeling out of place in predominately White spaces. Two of the women – Janet, and Bobbi – actually changed schools to escape their predominately White peers. Janet explained:

> One of the little things I forgot to bring up is that…well, it's kind of a big thing, because it was another transition growing up, but most of the people that I went to grade school with, we all ended up going to the same high school, and it was just right up the street from where my parents lived and still live. And again it was mostly White teenagers and I was there for two years, and I just couldn't take it anymore. Like I think part of that is like the comments that were made to me, like people calling me the Mexican girl, and part of that just being that it was also a lot of…and this is Catholic school too. So that's another thing. So I went to Catholic school growing up from K through 12. So you know there's like White, Christian, rich teens there, and so there is a lot of privilege going on and I just, yeah, I just couldn't really, I couldn't handle the way that people were treating other people… Just like mean things that people would do to each other. So I convinced my parents to let me go to a different high school, because I had already started hanging out with people at this other Catholic high school, and there were a lot of White students, but I'd say about a third of the students were Latinos, because it was just in a different neighborhood where there were just more Brown people living around there. And it wasn't so far deep into the suburbs, so it was definitely just more mixed. And I definitely felt more comfortable there. And there were still like the cliques going on but people were definitely just more laid back, and I think about that kind of environment, when you get all these people together that are so alike, and they look so alike, then you have a few different people in there, it creates a very like fearful and like hateful environment I think. And also what people are going through at that age too, like combined with that kind of environment where everyone looks the same. And so I think that was part of that, and so I definitely felt more comfortable when I went to this other school even though it was also like Catholic, and it

was also co-ed. It was just a 15 minute drive away; it was just so different because of the people who made up the school.

Janet described that time as "the hardest time in [her] life." Bobbi similarly chose to attend a different school and leave her predominately White school. Her school was "racist" so she "went a little bit more central where it was more diverse."

Ruth, Maria, and Alana all had the desire to do so but never actually changed schools. As described in Chapter 3, Maria had a very difficult time when she moved from her predominately Brown public school to a predominately White Catholic school. Drinking became her form of escape, and she sought validation from men. She explained:

> I drank so much in high school. Because I would get really drunk, and then I would make out with someone, just crazy. I mean I have crazy stories where I would be like, "Who the fuck drank my bottle of vodka?" and people would be like, "You did." So I think I had a lot going on. I don't think I had the language to process it, so that was what I did. Because there was always processing. It was just a sense of just never feeling, again it was race, it was body, it was uhm [silence]. I think I was really good at just being able to look like I belonged to this other group and not feeling inside that I really did. Which I'm sure everybody has that feeling, we're all trying to fake it.

Maria referred to trying to fit in. She had the capacity to make herself look like she belonged to a group but she never wholly felt it. Alcohol became a way for her to fit in and forget.

Alana also struggled significantly in her all White high school and similarly turned to alcohol as escape and men for validation. She explained:

> Well, I did well in school until I got into high school. I started to do poorly my sophomore year. I went to class high every day. So I think that was definitely key, but I really think it just has to do with just incredibly low self-esteem, you know? It really plummeted when I got into high school. I just had horrible self-esteem. I really think a lot of it had to do with just feeling really inferior like around Whiteness, in Whiteness. It makes so much sense to me now where that was coming from all of a sudden. And why, in high school I think that you really do come into your identity around then, and how I wasn't coming into that White identity and wasn't receiving that privilege in the way that all my friends were, you know, in terms of the counselors in school. Even though I had access – I could've taken the Kaplan review, I could've had all those resources that a lot of my friends did. For whatever reason I had low self-esteem, and at that point I was having really severe anxiety issues. I have intense school anxiety. Actually in terms of what we been talking about in terms of mixed identity, I really think that I

was traumatized by being in a White school. I just had horrible self-esteem. I really think a lot of it had to do with just feeling really inferior like around Whiteness, in Whiteness.

There were a few people of color that Alana could have tried to befriend in school, but internalized racism prevented her from doing so. When I asked her why she didn't want to associate with people of color in her school, with shame, she explained:

It wasn't conscious. It was just internalized stuff. It was about me not wanting to be associated with people of color, you know? And me wanting to be really associated with White folk. God, I'm like so embarrassed to talk about the stuff. But I really think that I was embarrassed to be associated with anything around Black culture or Blackness specifically because of my own association with it, you know? Feeling like Black people were ugly and this, that, and the other thing, and I didn't want White people to associate me with that. I feel like, especially a lot of White folks said racist things, you know, growing up. And me always knowing that I would be associated with that. And at that point because I was mixed, and because I lived in a liberal space, then I could choose if I wanted to hang out with all White people, and I chose to do that. And there were definitely a handful of mixed people like myself who also chose that. I became more open to it when I was in my senior year in high school.

Instead of identifying with her Black peers, Alana kept trying to fit in with her White peers and consequently struggled with her femininity and sense of beauty as a Black woman in an all White space.

To prove herself, she constantly sought validation from White men.

I would say that my sexuality was pretty much based on getting affirmation from White men. So with all these men I dated, I don't think I ever really enjoyed having sex with men, I think it was really about getting affirmation from them...I dated mostly men who were 10 to 15 years older than me. So it's very much about being sort of young exotic pretty thing that they could take out and buy stuff for, and do that.

Often, once she had sex, she was "treated like shit" by the men she dated.

In addition, Alana also suffered from much sexual harassment. Besides feeling isolated as a Black mixed race woman in an all-White space, another reason why she began to do poorly in high school is because she was assaulted by a White man her freshman year. She remembered:

You know what? There is something. I guess my freshman year in high school I was accosted and molested by a man that I babysat for for two years. But um, yeah, then I think I just felt profoundly isolated. I started to have a lot of emotional issues and my friends didn't know how to deal. It's hard, you know, I was 16. So I pretty much just medicated and went numb until I graduated. I barely graduated.

Unfortunately, this was one of many negative experiences she had with men; she was sexualized and harassed repeatedly from a young age. She explained:

It started when I was really young. I remember just being followed home when I was walking to school and walking to my house. It became so normal for me, and it started when I was probably like in seventh grade, like maybe like 12. And I know that other women deal with this, but I think there's something specific about being a light skinned Black woman, and also looking Latina as well. And it wasn't just White men. It was like Latino men and it was Black men, but it was mostly White men just because I lived in [a predominately White city] and it was mostly White men there. They would say things. I mean like really derogatory shit about blowjobs. I've had men jack off in front of me. That was pretty normal. Like, I was solicited a lot for prostitution especially when I was walking from high school to my house, which is a few blocks away. The section of the street that I lived on at the time was where Black women were who were sex workers; they were on that strip. I would be wearing a hoody and jeans and my backpack. It was very obvious that I was a high school student coming home from school, and they would follow me home and asked me if I wanted to trick. And it became so normalized.

After hearing that story I said, "That's intense. That's not most people's experiences." Alana responded:

Maybe, I just assumed it was. But the thing is that it wasn't for all of my White Jewish friends, none of them got that attention. And I also got a lot of attention from my friends' dads and their brothers. It was just always something that like I was very aware of from a very young age, that I was viewed as a sexual object. My White friends were coming into puberty as well and they weren't getting that same kind of attention. It was something very specific about being a Brown woman that I was getting that attention, you know?

Although young women can experience harassment in any town and any school, Alana experienced a very specific racialized form of sexual harassment from strangers as well as acquaintances. Her double subordinate positionality as a Brown woman made her vulnerable to continual harassment by White men. That harassment, coupled with the sense of inferiority she already felt as a mixed Black person in a predominately White space, made her schooling experience hardly bearable. To cope, she "medicated and went numb."

Another reason there was a large shift in her experience of school from grade school to high school is because she shifted from attending an alternative school to a regular public school. Alana harbored anger at her mother for removing her from her alternative school, "one of the free schools" that was part of the free school movement. While the school served students in K through 12, her mom removed her from it and sent her to public school. Although her alternative school was predominately White and middle class, she did not feel isolated like she did in public school. This is how she described the freedom school:

I think it was kind of a thing that happened in the '70s, '60s, you know where they start all these alternative schools that deviate from traditional education; students were more empowered through, like they had more freedom in the classroom I guess. I don't know if it came from a Freirian approach to education, but I feel like they kind of got that, definitely more of a personalized relationship with teachers and faculty. I called all my teachers by their first names. Small school; we went to their houses on the weekends. There was definitely a much stronger emphasis in heart than in academics and, we weren't punished and surveyed in the ways traditional schools are. We would have more dialogue, I guess. And it was started by Jane Fonda and some other hippies.

Moving from that school where it was personalized and there were no grades, only evaluations, to another school in which there were many rules, restrictions, and guidelines was "traumatic." For myriad reasons – changing from an alternative school to a public school, being a Brown girl in a predominately White space, being unable to live up to ideals of White feminine beauty, and being repeatedly harassed – Alana was positioned as an outsider in school and among her peers.

Maria also had stories of sexual harassment interspersed in her stories of growing up. Only one other woman talked specifically about sexual harassment: Brittney, who was raped in seventh grade and ended up in the hospital after a subsequent suicide attempt. However, I did not ask about sexual harassment specifically, so the numbers may be much higher. Regardless, the impact of sexual harassment cannot be underestimated, and we must recognize that these stories of sexual harassment are completely intertwined with dynamics of racism in ways that are unique to their experiences of belonging and being hyper sexualized and exoticized as mixed race *women*.

Ruth was also physically harassed in school. Her experience was distinct in that the majority of her harassment came from Black people. She explained that grade school was "kind of living hell." In her predominately Black school most of the other kids did not accept her; her only friends were other students who were "outcasts … the White girl, the fat girl, and the burn-fire-survivor." Ruth's White mom worked in the school and her "teachers liked [her]," but her classmates refused to accept her. She explained that in high school she had a "really hard time." Although Ruth has dark brown skin and looks Black, she said, "I got teased a lot about not being Black enough – I talk like I'm White." I asked Ruth to explain more, and she said they weren't used to "punk rocker Black girls" and elaborated that she had White, Filipina/o, and Asian friends and friends "with Mohawks and combat boots." She had no Black friends and "didn't listen to the right music;" she listened to The Cure. In addition, she said, "Hair was a big deal," and she refused to straighten hers. Consequently, "Everybody was telling [her], 'You need to relax your hair. You need to do something with that mess.'" But Ruth never gave in. She said, "My thought was, 'Who in the hell are you? Mind your own damn business. I can handle it.'" The worst incident of harassment was in high school. Ruth explained, "This group of people decided to throw me on the ground. I was just walking, here are these people, and then all of a sudden I'm on my stomach with my arms in front of me and my books sort of spread all the way down the hall." Ruth, however, did what she could to claim agency in that situation.

> I jumped up and I chased whatever guy I could – I just chased this guy, chased him all the way up to the top floor of the school, and I grabbed him by the shirt and he turned around. I thought I knew who it was, and I looked at him and I thought, "I've never seen you in my life. I don't even know you." I think I said, "I don't even know you." I just let him go and I just went back downstairs and I took my books, and I went outside to the car. I started crying because I just didn't understand how people could have such hatred for... these people even weren't recognizable to me, but I was obviously recognizable to them and worthy of... to me, I saw it as a violent thing.

She decided to exercise her right to stay in school. She stated, "It was really bad. Really bad. I thought about transferring but I stayed because I didn't want to let them win. So I stayed and I got through it, but it was really difficult."

Unlike Alana and Maria, Ruth did not turn to drugs, and she did not try to conform. In fact, at the end of the second interview, when I asked her if there was anything she wanted to add in relation to school she said, "I'm proud that I stayed true to myself the whole time. I didn't try to do anything to fit better. Instead I thought, 'They're stupid.' I never turned it on myself as far as I was doing something wrong." I asked her what helped her keep that perspective and she replied, "I don't know." Even her mom said to her that she wished she could be as strong as her.

Ruth made it seem like she was born with the instinct to fight for herself. She started that way from the time she was born being in spaces where people didn't necessarily want her. She explained that her mom didn't know she was pregnant until Ruth was born. One day her mom collapsed at work, and they took her to the hospital. The doctors told her she was pregnant, and "they had to induce labor right then and [Ruth] was born like two pounds, like two and a half pounds and two months early." Her parents didn't know what to do with her. Her father expected her mom to raise her. Her mom didn't know what to do; she gave Ruth to the neighbors for a month before deciding to take her back and raise her.

Thus, Ruth had a history of fighting for her life and experiencing displacement from the moment she was born. However, she also had teachers who encouraged and supported her. She explained that teachers liked her and encouraged her to do well. It was not until college that she encountered teachers who were not supportive. She said:

> I hated undergrad; it was a racist institution. The professors had low expectations. They assumed I got there on a sports scholarship and asked, "How did you get here?" I applied. Professors weren't good to me.

She finally found a place where she felt at home when she went to graduate school at another university. "For the first time in my life I didn't have to think about race," she said. The student body was diverse with a lot of foreign-born students who were working adults. The classes were small and students were friends with the professors.

Like Ruth, in school Susan also suffered from peer harassment, but she described her teachers as "wonderful." Susan explained that since grade school she felt like an outsider among her blond peers in suburban Minnesota. Although quite fair skinned, she had dark hair and brown eyes. She said:

> I grew up in Minnesota. And it was, and it was so, I was really dark, like it was so blond. It wasn't just like White people, it's just blond people. So I used to have kids come up to me on the playground and say, "Why are you so dark? Are you Black?" That kind of thing, because it was that blond! So, it was like living in Norway, you know?

Even though peers challenged and questioned her, she was "happy" and "loved school" because she was "favored by teachers." She stated, "We happen to be quite an intelligent family, and we excelled, and we had a lot of encouragement." Susan explained that there were no other Latinos in her town so it was as if there was no opportunity yet for the teachers to create bias. Although there was bussing in her school, there were no students of color in her accelerated classes. Susan did well with her peers until freshman year when they unexpectedly turned on her, spouting racist remarks.

> We [Susan and her brother] sort of all of a sudden became spics. So you know people ever since you were little, but all of a sudden they think it matters. So all of a sudden my group – not even people in the hall passing, like people in my group of friends, all of a sudden they would just call me spic. Like that was it. And I just wasn't their friend anymore.

Luckily, her best friend was a 6 foot 4 inch tall guy who told her harassers to leave her alone, so they did. Still Susan remained distant from all but that one friend from that day on and didn't trust the majority of her peers. To cope with the growing racism among her classmates, she removed herself from the institution, spent her senior year in Turkey and became immersed in an entirely different culture. In Turkey, Susan was often mistaken to be Turkish and, ironically, experienced a greater sense of acceptance and insider positionality there than within her high school in the United States.

Tina, while very fair skinned, identified strongly with her Mexican heritage and culture as a young child. However, she also experienced rejection by her peers. Like Ruth, she was rejected by students of color, the Mexican kids in her elementary school. As touched on in an earlier chapter, she said:

> When I was younger, I felt like I looked a lot like my family members. So that made me feel like I was identifying more as Mexican. I was always around Spanish speakers, but I don't know any Spanish. When I was growing up, I felt like that was my culture. That's how I grew to know myself and identify.

But when she went to school she tried to hang out with the Mexican kids and was shunned. She said:

> Yeah, so when I got into fifth and sixth grade I starting realizing that, "Wow, I can't hang out with the Mexican kids." I really wanted to. They reminded me of my family and my cousins. "I'm really one of you." It didn't work really. So... I was friends with them sometimes, but especially when I got into high school, barriers got dropped, but I think they thought I was trying too hard. They really like, I felt like I constantly had to validate myself. [I would say,] "My family's from Mexico. I know what it's like." You know? I don't know. It was sort of silly.

Since Tina had difficulty connecting with people based on race, she began to find new ways to identify and bond with people. She said:

> So I think after I was, from probably fifth grade on up to end of high school, I started thinking of other ways that I identified. I was a roller-skater for a while. And that was like it – I was a roller-skater. And then in high school I became really political and a feminist. And that was me – I was a feminist, and I was political.

Her strategy to cope with her outsider racial status was to create non race-based social positionalities. However, since leaving high school she has been involved in a process of continually examining her identity as a mixed race Mexican woman. She said, "Not a day goes by that I don't think about what it means to be biracial."

NEGOTIATING STRUCTURES AND IDENTITY

Latinas and Language

Tina felt that not speaking Spanish was the largest barrier to not being accepted by her Mexican peers. She explained that "colonialism" and "racism" were influencing factors as to why she did not speak the language because when her grandparents moved to California they were told outright that their children could not speak Spanish in school. Wanting to help their children succeed, they stopped speaking their native language at home, and as a result Tina's dad and his siblings didn't learn Spanish. She said:

> I always wonder what it would have been like for me if, if the Fremont school district wasn't so racist and they allowed kids to speak Spanish. What would that have been like for my family? I always have this nagging part of me that says, "You're biracial sure, but you're also Mexican and that's something you really should really invest your identity in. It's the part of you that you grew up with, and that's who you are."

Latina participants felt that Spanish language abilities, or lack thereof, contributed greatly to their inclusion or exclusion in the wider Latina/o community.

Maria harbored anger about her ongoing struggles to learn Spanish throughout her life. Her Mexican dad became a victim of racist, colonialist practices and was forced to attend "Americanization" schools as a child, where he was not allowed to speak Spanish. Maria understood why, after that experience, he chose not to teach her Spanish at home. However, Maria's White mom was also fluent in Spanish, and Maria resented her mom's choice not to share that skill with her. Recognizing the importance of her family's language, Maria has worked to learn Spanish in various ways on her own, yet it is a continual struggle.

Marta, who was never taught Spanish, felt that speaking Spanish was often the key to being accepted within Latina/o communities. She remarked:

> I just had so many issues about being light skinned and not speaking Spanish, 'cause one of the litmus tests I think for being Latina, the first question is, "Do you speak Spanish? You don't speak Spanish!" Even if you slightly speak Spanish, it's okay. But if you don't speak Spanish, it's like, you know, who raised you? You know, forget it. So it's always been a little bit problematic for me to find Latino community.

Like other Latina participants, Janet dealt with challenges resulting from not knowing Spanish. Janet exclaimed that she had "Learn Spanish" at the top of her list of things to do. Although their Spanish language skills were not very strong, both Janet and Marta happened to be working on independent projects that involved creating films in Spanish; they were finding ways to centralize Spanish in aspects of their lives. Maria similarly took on work projects that involved using Spanish language skills, challenging herself to learn by doing and using what she knew to reach out to the Spanish language-speaking communities.

Susan also attempted to learn Spanish at times throughout her life, although she said, "Right now it's in horrible disrepair." Even though Spanish was her grandparents' first language, similar to other Latina participants' stories, her grandparents spoke only English to their kids believing it was necessary to "give their kids an advantage." Consequently, her dad doesn't speak Spanish. Susan studied Spanish in high school and college, spent some time in Spain and in Mexico. She has extra difficulty maintaining language, however, because while living in Turkey she was hit by a car and suffered brain damage that's "very localized, just with language."

It is striking to note how all five of the Latina participants discussed the importance of the Spanish language in relation to their lived mixed race positionalities. None of them were taught Spanish at home and many specifically identified the root of the problem to be racist, colonialist, government imposed practices that vilified the use of Spanish during their parents' upbringing.

Outsider Positionalities

As evidenced by all these stories, virtually everyone experienced challenges at school related to their racial positionalities. Ana was the only person in the group who did not discuss negative experiences in school related to race. She attended a magnet school and had a diverse group of friends, including friends who were mixed race. Her best friend was Filipino "so there was a nice reinforcement of that culture." She said:

> It was fun. My friends were there. I did well in school. I got to do extra stuff in school because I finished that unit. I had teachers who were of color and who weren't of color … It had multicultural stuff. I remember we weren't all White. We did an identity unit in eleventh grade, "Who am I?" We had to reflect on who we were. Racially, it was fine. Sexual orientation and being a girl, there were memories around that.

Because of the diversity among the students and staff, and because Ana did well in school, race was not much of an issue. Instead, for Ana, the bigger deal was "sexual orientation and being a girl." She was a tomboy and came out her sophomore year in college. Others – Marta, Mindy, and Joanna – also had challenges as tomboys. These stories of conflict experienced by participants related to gender performance remind us that social positionality is created in many ways, some of which take prominence over others depending on the context. Like Ana, Mindy also attended a diverse school and discussions of racial challenges were notably minimal. At several points in the interviews she specifically mentioned that she felt grateful for having been raised in a community of diverse people. She said, "If I grew up in Needham [the all White community her dad was from] it would have been more damaging. I don't understand how I look, but I didn't turn that in on me."

For many of these women, these racial identity challenges continued in college as they struggled to find community, insert themselves in communities of color, battle predominately White spaces, and deal with racist professors and institutions. As the women battled challenges to identity by peers and racism from teachers, they employed a variety of coping mechanisms, some positive, some negative. Amazingly, despite the challenges they faced, all but one of the participants succeeded in graduating from college and many went on to graduate school. Brittney, the only woman without her bachelor's degree, had attended "beauty school" but dropped out when she was only a few credits shy of graduating; she was sexually harassed and felt she needed to leave. Here again, we are reminded that the participants navigate more than their racial positionalities, other positionalities of gender, sexuality, and class come into play. In this instance, Brittney was battling discrimination as a woman, as a woman of color, as a young woman of color, and as a student who was unable to obtain help in her schooling institution. Although Brittney did not have a degree at the time of her interview, at age 26, Brittney remained relatively young, and still maintained a desire to complete school.

Overall, these women displayed amazing resilience in the face of barriers to claiming space within educational institutions. Unfortunately, upon leaving school, many of the women continued to face challenges to their identities within the work world.

WORK

The women struggled with outsider positionalities at work and faced challenges to their identities, although there were fewer stories of identity struggles at jobs than at school. Work struggles often related to dealing with racism in the workplace. Ruth, for example stated, "Even as an adult I was accused of stealing twice at a job that I had at a hospital and it was just unbelievable to me. I was accused of stealing a video camera, which, to me, is horrible. I would never." In the end, Ruth was found innocent, but the accusation itself, with its racist overtones, was damaging.

Jobs also sometimes provided opportunities for the women to explore issues of racial identity. Linda, for example, recalled how activities she was asked to engage in at her non-profit job allowed her to think more deeply about her identity as a mixed race woman. She worked for an educational reform non-profit that had professional development programs on Fridays. One of the activities focused on equity. In the first exercise they were told, "I want the White people to talk for five minutes and I want the people of color to talk for 10 minutes." However, as Linda recalled, "Of course that did not happen." White people took up more time. Several activities required participants to share their own stories. In one meeting, people were instructed to "draw a representation of [their] life in art form. What does the roadmap to life look like?" and then explain how their racial identity was formed and what influenced it. Linda described this as a turning point.

> That was the first time that I really articulated stuff like the BSU [Black Student Union] and having the Black dad and growing up in Bayview and stuff like my relationship with my dad, and maybe even potentially hating my own Whiteness, my own self-hatred, and all that stuff, for the first time. So that, I think, was really key in my identity formation or articulating my identity.

At the time of the interview, Linda had since left that organization and was working for a non-profit created by and for people of color. Linda admitted that she had some trepidation about taking the job as a mixed race woman. Before accepting the position, Linda asked her potential employers how they felt about hiring her since she was "part White." They informed her that it was fine because she identified herself as a person of color. Linda's mixed race woman of color positionality makes her very conscious of the ways that she "takes up space" at work. She explained:

> When I first started at my job I was really ultra hypersensitive to the fact that I'm usually the first person to talk. We do things in a collective so at all of our meetings you would say what you think about this issue. And I would say, "Well I think blah, blah, blah." Then I started to be super conscious about it. I was like, why am I always the first person to talk? Is that my White privilege? Why am I always the first person to talk? I'm really wanting to work that shit out.

Although she enjoys her job and appreciates the opportunity she is given, Linda realizes that she needs to make an extra effort to make sure that her potential White cultural ways of being are not impeding others.

Ana discussed her varied experiences of opportunistically being both identified and dismissed by employers and colleagues as a person of color. She tells this story of her experiences at a few workplaces:

> Well, like I work for this organization where every so often we have to turn in a chart to show how many people color we have in the organization and I know they count me, as I would want them to. But I think that in our day-to-day interactions they would forget that I'm a person of color....It's a very Black and White world there, and it was a mostly White organization. I remember when we were hiring, people [colleagues] would be like, "Why can't we find qualified Black candidates who want to take the job?" And at some point it occurred to me that we were looking for somebody who has a particular skin color but thinks the same way as everybody else in the organization. And that's why you can't find a fit, because people want to be

able to come in and be all of themselves and have their opinions valued, [which requires] creating a space [for that] within the organization. And I don't know if, I mean I just kind of felt like I was treated like any other White employee. Which in terms of, if I think about being treated with respect and dignity like everybody else in the organization that's great, and I don't think for me there was denial about my culture, but I don't think there was that much interest in my culture. We have another Asian woman who's all Japanese, [who shared] an experience she had with one of my colleagues that I was really close with. I was close with both of them. And this White colleague made some off-the-cuff joke about someone else's name, "Soh," which is a Japanese name. And she made some comment about that person being so-so in a certain area or something. And I just remember being really shocked, because I was like, "Oh I love this person like my surrogate mom," and we've talked about a lot of different kinds of stuff, like my family not accepting the gay relationship and all that, and yet she would say something like that. She totally forgot that there's an Asian person at the table. If I had been in the room would she have totally forgotten? I didn't say anything because I wasn't a part of the whole conversation. I can't remember whether or not my friend spoke up.

In this story, it is clear that Ana, as a mixed race Asian woman, was positioned differently than her Asian colleague who was not mixed. Ana is naming institutional racist politics that she, as a mixed woman, was able to mostly evade. It is implied in this story that she was able to fit in due to her cultural Whiteness, yet she served the interests of the organization in that they could claim her as a person of color. Other people of color, who were unable to "fit in" in the same way, were either not hired, not willing to work in an organization where they could not be fully themselves, or hired and unwittingly belittled.

Diana similarly explained that there are specific cultural ways of being that are expected at work.

You have a professional façade, your public façade, and your real self. And you have to know which hat to put on in different situations if you're going to survive, like in the business world. There is a certain culture where you work, how you're supposed to behave. You need to pick up those clues and get with it if you want to work here. If you can't, you know, get with it, you need to move on. Because no matter what validity you have in your response, in your way of delivering information for your research, whatever it is, if it isn't the White way, it isn't right. You are incompetent.

Diana found that in order to be successful at work, she needed to cater to and behave within the inherent White institutional expectations and norms. This story matches Ana's assessment of her workplace in which there were White dominant unspoken rules for behavior.

Maria shared a similar particular positionality as a mixed race woman in her workplace to that of Ana's, being both an asset and overlooked simultaneously. Maria explained that she conducts presentations in Spanish for her job. However, when her agency needed someone to read something in Spanish for a video that was being created by coworkers, they did not approach her. No one else at her work had the ability to present in Spanish, yet given her location in Albuquerque, and Maria's mindfulness to reach out to the Latino/a communities, people requested Spanish-language presentations, and it would have served the agency for her to fulfill those requests. One can only speculate as to why she was not considered, or perhaps considered yet not found to be good enough, not Latina enough, to read for the video.

Highlighted here are stories of both constraint and opportunity. We see how the women's access to White cultural ways of being assisted them in being successful at work, yet their abilities and identities were sometimes dismissed. Thus, work became a place of both opportunity and challenge in relation to their mixed race positionalities.

CONCLUSION

Although throughout the stories in this chapter we see continual glimpses of the women claiming agency, more apparent are dominant culture institutional norms and structural constraints that limited agentic action; interfered with the potential for loving, equitable relationships; and/or caused pain and trauma in the lives of these women. These stories illuminate lives filled with constant challenges related to their mixed race positionalities. For many of these women, people in all areas of their lives positioned them as outsiders. This outsider positioning was related to structures and settings that rejected their existence as biracial individuals.

Strangers

Virtually all of the women had to manage personal questions from strangers about their racial identities. I highlight here important points that can be gleaned from the participants' stories of interactions with strangers. First, it was White people who most often assumed they were White. In addition, we learned from Joanna that White people who have been sheltered from interactions with mixed race people tend to be the least likely to understand the experiences of multiracial individuals. Thus, as we already know from years of research and writing about race politics, their stories confirm that White people who have more diverse experiences are more likely to be more sensitive to the complexity of racial dynamics (Bonilla-Silva, 2006), in this case related to mixed race women. Second, participants encountered White people who wanted to suppress their mixed race identities. Several of the women dealt with defensiveness from White people when they claimed to be "something other than White" (Diana). Participants named two interconnected factors related to this reaction: (White) entitlement and (White) racism. Consequently, it would seem that the more White entitlement and White racism is addressed generally, the more at peace mixed race people will be in the presence of White people. Third, there was a distinct dynamic of fear, judgment, and mistrust between Black/White mixed race participants and Black people who did not consider themselves mixed. All but one of the mixed race Black participants experienced and feared judgment and exclusion by Black people who were not mixed. Diana, the one women who did not share such experiences, was raised in the era of the "one drop rule" so she was considered Black by all those around her, and she considered herself Black, which minimized separation between herself and her Black peers. However, that "one drop rule" is no longer popular; the rules have changed and, along with it, so have racial politics. The opportunity to choose distinct, more complex identities has created divisions between Black people who don't see themselves as mixed and Black people who claim a mixed identity. Due to the ways mixed race racial politics have been used to deny resources to Black people, this animosity and distrust is understandable (for more information see Williams, 2008). Nonetheless, it creates an atmosphere in which it is often difficult for mixed Black women to connect with other Black women. As I probed about what these challenges meant, there was an overarching theme in the responses from the women about what they desired – that others will listen and learn. As Diana emphatically stated in a discussion about White people who don't get it, "They just don't listen and learn!" In response to that comment, Susan recommended a book. She said:

> One of the things that I suggest is that book called *White Like Me*. [25] It's written by this White activist. It's for a White audience. It's about how you benefit from White power. And it breaks it down for you so you have some understanding. And the one thing he says is believe people when they tell you their story, and their experience.

Evident in the dialogues among the women about the impact of White entitlement and racism as they relate to challenges by strangers, we see that institutional structures of White power impacted their lives, even in daily interactions with people they didn't know. Understanding these structures of White supremacy through reading books such as *White Like Me*, as Susan recommended, can assist both people who are mixed and those who wish to better understand and support mixed race people in claiming agency in ways that might shift structural norms, given, as mentioned in the chapter opening, that actions create structures which then impact actions (Giddens, 1977). Two initial commitments that people can make in order to be more sensitive to the needs and experiences of mixed race people include: (a) taking the initiative to educate themselves, and (b) listening openly to the stories and experiences of mixed race people. Ideally, such learning efforts will lead to more caring, equitable actions.

Family

Unfortunately, judgment by strangers often paled in comparison to the effects of challenges to identity that these women experienced within their own families. Stories of insider/outsider positionalities in relation to families illuminate important patterns for examination that reveal race and gender structural norms. First, several of the women had extended family members who were racist. It was painful for them to know, for example, that their grandparents disapproved of their parents' relationships and, consequently, their existence as mixed race individuals. Second, the women were sometimes judged and challenged by their parents about the ways they chose to identify racially, and the race-based groups in which they became involved. Although often the challenges stemmed from parental fear of dismissal (either themselves or their spouses), in essence the disapproval is what created the discord, not the initial involvement in a monoracial organization. Third, painful stories emerged of disconnection from, most specifically, White moms. Two main themes emerged related to this disconnect: (a) the White mother's inability to understand her child's experiences with race issues and racism, and (b) the mother's vocalized disapproval of her daughter's looks, which for the participants was interpreted as directly related to being mixed race rather than monoracially White. Gender factors into these experiences; it is relevant to note that the women did not share stories of feeling disconnected from White dads. More generally, however, some women did indicate that neither parent could understand their mixed race experiences. Stories of exclusion by family members were intertwined with the stories of inclusion, for example in the descriptions Susan and Tina gave of spending time with their Mexican grandmothers and in Ana's appreciation of the ways her White mom made explicit efforts to better get to know and support her. Extended family members, especially family members of color who helped pass along culture, often made a huge impact on these women's lives in helping to positively shape their racial identities and counter feelings of being an outsider.

School and Friends

The dynamics of school and friends were quite complicated. The main theme in the majority of the stories is a sense of alienation. Within the institution of schools, almost all these women experienced alienation, isolation, and rejection. Sometimes the discrimination was clearly linked to school procedures and the ways in which teachers and counselors acted as power agents within the schools, as in the experiences of being placed in remedial reading, ESL classes, or being told not to go to college. Such actions were influenced by racist ideologies and most likely occurred because the participants were identified as people of color. In terms of mixed race identity, many of the greatest pains in school came from rejection and harassment by peers. Participants in predominately White schools felt like they didn't belong. The women shared stories about the ways in which they could not live up to the White standards of beauty and suffered from low self-esteem as a result. This predicament brought up issues of internalized racism and, for some, led to self-destructive behaviors. The one participant (Ruth) who was in a school with mostly people of color (who attended school within this generation) also experienced alienation, this time for not being able to live up to Black standards of beauty and perceived acceptable (Black) ways of being. The participants who fared the best emotionally were in racially diverse schools. Even Joanna, who told two stories of being confronted in a threatening way by Black girls at her school, described school overall as a good experience because it was racially diverse and she found her niche among the "musical kids," the "nerds," and the "hippies." She had a diverse group of friends who were Black, White, Jewish, and multiracial. It is important to note that the two participants who did not discuss any identity challenges related to race at school, Ana and Mindy, not only attended diverse schools but were also both mixed race Asian. Ana, for example, mentioned that the students with her in the magnet school classes were less diverse, but there were Asians. Thus, she was not isolated from other Asian people. Elizabeth, who was Filipina but attended a less diverse, mostly White school, also never discussed any particular identity challenges; however, when she was a teen she began to define herself racially in contrast to White people and "hardly had any White friends." Asians are known as a distinct minority because many Asians have traditionally excelled in school at much higher rates than other students of color (Jo & Rong, 2003). The confluence of these factors – being in diverse schools and being mixed race Asian, a part of the perceived "model minority" group – may be what led to their positive schooling experiences.

These collective stories reveal some important information with implications for school policy. Although the majority of pressures these women felt as students came from their peers, it was the structure of segregated schools that created the atmosphere within which their peers acted to maintain segregation. Even participants who weren't in segregated schools overall were in segregated classes. This is a direct result of tracking policies and procedures. In the wake of the 50th anniversary of Brown v. Board of Education, there has been much debate about the effects of desegregation and the potential benefits of segregated schools (Ladson-Billings, 2004). It has been well documented that segregation has actually been increasing in recent years rather than decreasing (Kozol, 2005). Some scholars of color have demonstrated that many African Americans received better schooling before desegregation (hooks, 1994; Siddle Walker, 1996). In a keynote address given at the North Carolina Law Review Symposium in Chapel Hill, North Carolina, Gloria Ladson-Billings (2007) argued, "If we are unwilling to fully implement Brown, could we at least have Plessy?" (p. 1280), stating that given the increasing segregation of schools, what we need is to strive for more equity of services between schools, paying particular attention to schools that serve predominately students of color.

This argument has merit; however, within the mixed race context, equitable services in segregated schools still will not likely amount to quality schooling experiences in terms of emotional health and development for students who are mixed race. Embedded in this assertion is the idea that successful schooling entails more than high academic achievement. Sociologists have long debated the purpose of schools (Bennett deMarrais & LeCompte, 1999; Childress, 2006; Rothstein & Jacobsen, 2006; Wolk, 2007). Although general rhetoric about schooling "excellence" focuses on high academic achievement for the purpose of obtaining "good jobs," scholars writing about schooling in the context of social justice argue that institutions of education should do more than produce and sort workers. Having quality of life, learning compassion, displaying care, understanding interdependence, and experiencing emotional well-being are all important factors. Within this broader vision of "successful schooling," racial diversity, or lack thereof, was a key factor in the schooling experiences of these women. Although virtually all the women excelled academically, the majority of them in schools lacking diversity suffered emotionally; some of them even changed schools. Among these women, racial and cultural diversity was often named as a key factor related to positive experiences with peer groups. Thus their stories reveal that the current racially segregated structures of most schools and school systems are likely to alienate and marginalize biracial White/of color students and result in negative schooling experiences.

School language policies also impacted the Latina participants' experiences of race and identity alienation, none of whom were taught Spanish in their homes. As Tina astutely pointed out, it was schooling policies that created the situation in which she did not have access to the Spanish language from her Mexican father. All of the Latinas – Janet, Marta, Maria, Susan, and Tina – expressed a desire to learn Spanish and lamented that they were not taught Spanish. Each of them understood, however, that a legacy of racist politics factored into the reasons why they did not learn Spanish at home. Their inability to speak fluent Spanish exacerbated their experiences of alienation with Latina/o peers and within Latina/o communities at large.

Throughout the interviews, the women shared stories of marginalization and/or discrimination based on their racial/ethnic positionalities. Stories surfaced about such experiences among strangers, at home, in school, and, to a lesser extent, in the workplace. Three of the mixed Black/White women – Diana, Ruth, and Brittney – experienced racism at work. Ana and Diana discussed the complexity of being counted as a person of color yet being expected to act White, and Linda struggled with her positionality as a mixed race Japanese/White woman within a women of color organization. Perhaps part of the reason that there were not as many stories of identity challenges at work is because they had more opportunity to choose where they worked. However, as will be discussed further in the chapter on Whiteness, it is important to note that these women, as a whole, possessed the White cultural capital they needed to succeed in the work world. Also, work, in comparison to school and home, is not necessarily a place of primary identity formation.

These stories provide a broad overview of the multiple outsider positionalities these women experienced in a variety of institutions. The focus on the structure of institutions – of family, school, and work – allows us to better understand their actions, and the actions of others, as they are situated within particular settings. The women's narratives reveal pain and trauma. They also provide glimpses into possible actions that others can take – whether family members, policy makers, school administrators and personnel, or employers – to support mixed race people. The next chapter shifts the focus away from the settings and their consequences to more carefully examine the agency these women claimed through particular actions and discourses.

CHAPTER 5

CHAMELEONS

Claiming Agency through Fluid Identities and Learning to Live with Ambiguity

I was in New York a few years ago for a conference, and we went dancing one night at this club. And, you know, in New York there are these huge clubs, like three floors and there's different music on the floors in the different areas. And I swear to God, it was crazy, even my friend was like this was crazy. Because at one part there were these French people who were speaking to me in French, and they were just like, "Well you're French." They just assumed that I was French. Then I would walk 100 feet over and there was this group of Russians who were convinced that I was Russian. And it went like that for the rest of the night. From like, you had your Slavic country, you had your Latino countries, people just assume; there was this whole thing of like trying to almost claim me in some sort of way. I felt like it was this ultimate, ultra mixed race experience, you know? I mean, if you are going to market the mixed race experience, this would be it. – Maria

For me, I love being mixed. It's one of my favorite things in the whole wide world. There's definitely some baggage associated with it, but it also gives me a really, I think, unique perspective that monoracial people don't get. – Joanna

I feel like pretty much everywhere I go, I fit in. I feel like a chameleon. – Bobbi

In the last chapter, I highlighted the stories that demonstrated the ways in which the women experienced *limits* to agentic action as defined through Giddens' (1979, 1984) theory of structuration. However, even with the focus on structural limits, the narratives provided glimpses of agency because structural constraints and agency are always operating in a dialectical relationship. Giddens (1984) argued, "Structure is not to be equated with constraint but is always both constraining and enabling" (p. 25). In this chapter, I shift the emphasis from the constraining aspects of structure to the enabling aspects, and I highlight the strengths and possibilities for *agentic options* related to being mixed race. The women's narratives reveal a constant tension between the challenges and the benefits of being mixed.

103

Many described a consistent outsider status coupled with a contrasting sense of belonging in a broad range of contexts. Despite the multiple challenges and constraints to their mixed race lived experience, many shared joys and benefits related to being mixed race women.

I LOVE BEING MIXED

Although all of the women at some point claimed agency through their mixed race identities and named positive benefits of being biracial, only three of the 16 women described being mixed as an overwhelmingly positive experience – Elizabeth, Joanna, and Brittney. Elizabeth emphasized throughout her interviews how much she enjoys being mixed race. She recognized her anomalous situation, as she listened to others in the Boston group interview and said:

> I feel really comfortable being mixed race… because my mom was so positive about me being mixed race. Because I feel being half Asian and half White is not fraught like being half Black and half White. It's like people are really willing to see you. If you're part Black then it's not okay. But if you're part Asian, they're very willing to see you as White. For me it's not been a problem. I haven't had people say weird stuff to me because they assume I'm White. I haven't had people expose their inner racism to me.

Elizabeth recognized that her overwhelmingly positive experiences probably had a lot to do with her mother's positive attitude about her mixedness, her ability to pass as White, and her Asian ethnicity.

Although the other two women who perceived their experiences as primarily positive were mixed Black and White, and some Asian women in the group did not perceive their situation as so positive, there was further discussion about the implications of being mixed Asian versus mixed Black. Joanna, who is mixed Black and White and was also very positive about her identity, concurred with Elizabeth's analysis stating, "I think that Asian is such a different type of minority." Mindy, who, like Elizabeth, is also Filipina and White, has struggled tremendously with her identity. Nonetheless, she acknowledged Joanna's statement saying, "It's the whole model minority thing." Mindy added that "in the Philippines there's more of a history of mestizo" in which mestizos, people who are mixed part White, are looked upon and treated very favorably. Although Mindy described this general ideology, the descriptions of her experiences as a mixed White-Filipina individual were fraught with more angst than joy.

Although Joanna had experienced some discomfort with being "*the* diversity" in her cohort in college, she said, "I love being mixed. It's one of my favorite things in the whole world." In her interviews she discussed being mixed as an overwhelmingly positive experience. For example, most of the time she welcomed the "What are you?" question because she liked to talk about her life, and she felt that her mixed race experiences gave her a unique perspective on the world. The duality of her identity, she said, allowed her to move within a variety of circles. As a self-described "social butterfly," Joanna liked the "fluidity of floating in and out of different groups." However, Joanna had some discriminatory confrontations with others that prevented her from uncritically celebrating her mixed race identity. Upon going to college, she experienced "a major culture shock" and a "racial coming of age" as a result of moving from a racially diverse neighborhood and high school to a place where "suddenly everyone was White and had never met people of color before." Joanna explained:

> I knew I was a person of color. I knew I was a minority but it didn't mean anything, because where I was from, it didn't affect, as far as I could see, my life in school, or how my school treated me. And then all of a sudden I went to college and I was like, "Why do they have all these organizations for minority students, like do we still need this?" And then after a month, I was like, "Oh right, I get it."

After being in her all-White college community for only a month, she realized the difficulty of dealing with prejudiced White people. In her stories, she both celebrated her identity and acknowledged the struggles she faced.

Brittney, who, like Joanna, is also mixed Black and White, framed her mixed race experience as overwhelmingly positive as well. Brittney was the first person to speak in the group interview when I asked, "Tell me what it's like to be mixed," responding, "I love it because I see the view of two different people, and combining races is beautiful to me." In her first individual interview, Brittney emphasized how great she thought it was to be mixed race. Her narratives mirror the writings of the era that Ifekwunigwe (2004) would describe as the "age of celebration." Brittney was uncritical of her experiences and stated that she "didn't ever get treated any different." Yet upon examination of her narratives as a whole, it is evident that she was discriminated against, for example in her story from the previous chapter of being called a nigger. By the end of the group interview, however, she was beginning to view the totality of her experiences in a new light. She shared:

> It [participating in the project] has opened up my eyes a lot. It makes me look at people and notice things more, whereas before I was just kind of like, I never noticed that. I never noticed any racism or anything. Maybe I just didn't want to notice, so I didn't see it. But now I think I'm going to notice it more, and be more aware of what's going on.

Brittney's critical consciousness was changing as a result of participating in this project, and she was beginning to reflect on her experiences in new ways. Still, I do not want to imply that her previous view was incorrect; there was a sweetness about Brittney and a way in which she was able to refrain from internalizing the ignorant remarks made to her by others. In addition, overall, she did have positive experiences. As mentioned in the last chapter, Brittney was particularly attractive and had a conventionally beautiful group of friends; I wonder, again, how much beauty played into her overwhelmingly positive experiences.

The stories the women in this project tell, with the exception of the three women above, are not overwhelmingly positive, yet all the women appreciated their mixed race identities and many did emphasize several benefits of being mixed. These stories add greater depth to the previously uncritical celebratory stories of "the mixed race experience." Joanna's narrative, for example, demonstrates that context is a huge factor in her mixed race experience; the environment and interactions with others create the conditions for joy or struggle regarding being mixed. Of course the dichotomy of joy and struggle is false; experiences are multifaceted. The interplay of structure and agency weaves in and out of harmony and discord. In this chapter, I highlight positive experiences but also expose the sometimes accompanying challenges. The most common thread I found in the described benefits of being mixed was related to having fluid identities that created possibilities for being accepted among wide ranges of people.

FLUIDITY: MOVING BETWEEN MULTIPLE WORLDS AND CONNECTING TO VARIETIES OF PEOPLE

In her group interview, Ana, the participant who stood out as least challenged in the last chapter, highlighted the value of being mixed race.

> It's walking in two worlds, or three, or four, so therefore getting comfortable walking in lots of different worlds, crossing boundaries a lot. I think it's just being able to flow in and out of different kinds of groups. For me, it would be flowing in and out of Asian groups and White groups. But also as part of me exploring my mixed race identity and spending time with other groups of people of color, I feel like I have more comfort now with lots of different types of groups.

Brittney concurred with Ana's statement responding, "I feel that way too." Yet a few minutes later, Ana reminded us of the tensions between agency and structure:

> I feel like a strength is that I feel like I can go lots of places in the world, but the challenge is: What if other people will try and keep us down? What do I do if I personally don't feel equipped to do the analysis? Because some days I feel sharp and some days it's like I'm British – I'm mad, but I just stuff it. I don't have any words to say anything about it. It's hard if I'm the only person of color in the room, or if I'm the only Asian person in the room.

Although Ana appreciated the capacity to walk in different worlds and feel comfortable with a variety of people, doing so also made her vulnerable to attacks and other people's ignorance, and she didn't always feel prepared to deal with the discrimination she might face. Nonetheless, her identity and experiences as a mixed race woman provided her with the fluidity to "walk in different worlds" and feel comfortable with a variety of people. This acknowledgement of fluidity as part of the mixed race experience was prevalent in many of the women's narratives.

Joanna, for example, said in her group interview:

Something that I kept saying in my individual interview, for me it always came back to fluidity and always being able to go wherever I want, and fit in any group. Part of it happens to be that I look racially ambiguous; I don't stick out in any group. But also that translated into my personality and my social interactions. And now it's one of my favorite parts of my personality, that I can get along with virtually anyone, you know? Even if they're not my favorite person, and I'm not their favorite person, I can find some way to relate to them. Because ever since I've been growing up I've been having to move between worlds. And that has been extremely positive.

As Joanna shared those thoughts, others in the group interview exclaimed, "Exactly!" or "Yes!" throughout her dialogue, acknowledging that they could relate to what she was saying. The group conversation about fluidity continued as others responded to what Joanna said. Elizabeth chimed in first:

I think it's what she said, the flexibility of the ability to identify, to be almost chameleon-like I guess. And yet it depends on how, how people see you, definitely. Like whether or not you can slip in and out of different communities.

As the participants acknowledged their fluidity, many recognized that within US culture, their mobility is highly influenced by being specifically part White. Katherine named this explicitly in response to Elizabeth's comment when she said:

We are all White, too, regardless of what we look like or how we believe we may or may not have White privilege. You're talking about fluidity and being mixed. I think it's probably a very different thing when you can move between different groups, but none of those groups are White.

As I will describe in greater detail in an ensuing chapter, many of these women had a heightened awareness of the privilege associated with Whiteness. Katherine directly named this privilege in the statement above. These collective stories reveal that they perceived their cultural fluidity to be based, in large part, on skin color and being part White.

Alana, who could not pass as White in terms of skin color, nonetheless acknowledged her cultural Whiteness as an asset to moving in a White dominant world. She said:

I'm never going to be White...but it's the cultural Whiteness that I really identify with...I don't feel safe in White spaces anymore, but I know how to negotiate with them...and I know how to like communicate with White folk, and I know how to like go in and out of their spaces.

Ruth, who is a dark skinned, mixed Black woman said:

I don't feel like I have as much fluidity as maybe some other mixed race people do, but I feel like I can get along with everybody pretty well. But I also feel like, I don't know, more so in Boston, that there are parts that I have to, that other people make me very aware of. I don't know if it's about slang, or just my neck definitely. I feel like Boston for some reason isn't the most welcoming for Black people.

In this instance Ruth acknowledged that like Joanna, she can get along with everyone, and she implied that having a mixed race experience makes it easier to get along with a wide range of people. However, as she explained, that fluidity is limited by skin color; she would always be recognized as (at least part) Black and places exist, like Boston, where Black people and Black ways of being are not always accepted, even in mixed people. Earlier in the group interview, Joanna had talked about how for Black women "as soon as your neck starts moving, [White] people stop listening." When she said this all the mixed Black women in the room nodded their heads in agreement. Thus, it was clear that when they acted in ways culturally associated with Blackness, their fluidity diminished, and in some instances, when they were identified as Black based on skin color or appearance, the capacity for fluid mobility disappeared.

Nonetheless, the women shared several stories of cultural fluidity. Bobbi, for example said, "I don't know if it's because I'm mixed, but I think it's just because there are so many different people in my family. If anybody comes at me from another culture I feel able to talk to them." The women articulated personal fluidity in their abilities to feel comfortable interacting with people from a variety of backgrounds. Yet that fluidity was at times halted by racism. During the Boston group interview, a discussion took place regarding Boston's long history of White racism against Black people that is still palpable today in interracial interactions and visible in the prevalence of segregated neighborhoods. Ruth found herself on the receiving end of anger from both White people, who perceived her as Black, and Black people, who perceived her as mixed. She felt hostility in the air in Boston in ways she did not experience in Chicago. In addition, throughout her interviews, she shared stories of being discriminated against based on race. These experiences occurred with strangers, with coworkers, and with college professors. She added, "It's interesting because my experience with racism as an adult, I really feel it's more because society perceives me as a Black person. It's not mixed racism. It's racism as a Black person." Although she experienced a fair amount of racism, she also described an amazing ability to get along with a wide range of people. Ruth, it seems, experienced racism as a perceived Black person and fluidity as a mixed race person.

At times, the experiences of fluidity stemmed from assumptions by people with whom they interacted that they were of the same ethnic/racial background, which created a sense of connection, albeit at times ungrounded. Susan, for example, had a similar experience to that of Maria as described in the opening quote. Maria, in a New York nightclub, was assumed to be the same ethnicity of whichever group she found herself in. Susan similarly shared that often, no matter where she was, people assumed that she shared their background. She said, "When I was in Turkey no one actually knew I wasn't Turkish until I opened my mouth." Marta similarly said:

> I feel like I'm a chameleon in some ways, like if I'm in a Latin city I definitely get taken as Latin and I think Latin people look beyond skin color. And I definitely have Latin features if you look, but a lot of people don't look. Um, a lot of White people assume I'm White you know, and then tell me their really deepest racist thoughts, which is always a pleasure. And if I'm with a group of Jews, I actually get taken as Jewish.

Diana similarly stated that Black people identified her as Black while White people often perceived her to be White. There were numerous stories by virtually all the women about feeling a fluidity that allowed them access to acceptance in a variety of racial and ethnic communities. At times this fluidity was conferred when others made assumptions about their backgrounds, other times it was something they consciously strove for as they worked to gain acceptance in various communities.

LEARNING FLUIDITY

In the Albuquerque group interview, I asked the question, "How do you navigate moving in and out of different cultures?" Ana responded first, stating:

> I said in one of my individual interviews that because I often felt like I didn't quite know what was going on in the first place within my own cultures, I would observe a lot, just kind of get a sense of how things worked and what was cool and what wasn't. And I think that's something that I bring with me wherever I go now, just to listen a lot, get a feel for the place before I start interacting with folks. Because I don't want to do anything stupid, you know? I don't want to get kicked out of the space.

Maria added to what Ana said, stating:

> Well, yeah I think I told you, like for me, doing stuff within my family is where it is all learned. This is how this side of the family is, and this is how *this* side of the family is, you know? I mean if you grow up with it, then you just kind of like know it. It's just like how you know language or not. It's like

a language right? Like all communication. But then if it's groups I'm not a part of – yeah, I actually would say it's more like observing. I just think like traveling too, like when I went to Tunisia and then Caracas for delegation work, we had a lot of conversations around like, "Okay so we're a whole group of people color, and we're American, so like don't take up space." You know? We did a lot [of work] around not being loud, not taking up space.

Both Ana and Maria emphasized the importance of observing others to learn their cultural norms.

In Ana's individual interviews, she explained that she learned different ways of being as she spent time with each side of her extended family because the cultural norms were very different. Early in life, she learned to pay close attention to how others acted to know how to act in acceptable ways within each group. This observation skill is something she takes with her in all unfamiliar groups of people that she enters. Maria shared similar experiences of learning young that different groups of people have distinct habits of being. She too emphasized the importance of observation and being cautious to not take up too much space.

At that point in the group discussion, there was a moment of silence. I waited a bit and then asked if there were other comments. Maria spoke up, making an important point, "I guess it's just like being yourself still in those spaces." She said, "I mean I don't think it's, like, about taking on a different persona." Maria cautioned that sometimes people feel like they need to act a certain way or use a certain language, but she argued, how one acts when learning new cultural codes should be genuine and stem from respect and not co-opt others' ways of being. She explained:

Certainly there might be pieces of that [learning how to act differently in different spaces] that might work but I think there is a lot that goes on around this. I feel like people can co-opt culture in being with certain groups, you know, from like how people address each other.

As was common in the engaging group interviews, Brittney, eager to enter the conversation, chimed in with her thoughts:

For me it's not like a group of race, it's just like how different people get thrown together, not maybe by race, but maybe by type of music they listen to, or what they like to do. It's not really like, with different groups I hang around with I act different with each one of them kind of because we do different things. There's different things that we, you know, we have different interests, so it's not really a race thing. It's just we have different things in common.

Thus, Brittney changed the direction of Maria's point arguing that she would act differently in different groups by virtue of being connected around distinct activities not necessarily because of race. Maria again emphasized her original point saying to Brittney, "But you're still yourself. You're not like all of a sudden some other person."

Then, however, Maria recalled what it was like for her to navigate academia and how she had to learn "what people wear and how people talked." She acknowledged that she had to alter her ways of being to fit in and be successful. This occurred when she switched from public school to private school as well. She explained:

I know especially for me at that age, it was very much about not standing out too much because I already had shit going on, so I didn't need anything else. But, I don't know, I think that navigating academia is like a whole other culture too.

Maria recognized that there are situations in which she takes on different ways of being in different spaces, but she had to in order to be successful, as she did in her school culture, for example. In an effort to validate her experience as someone who has also had to learn how to navigate academia, I shared some of my thoughts on this topic:

But I think it gets complicated, that you might act in different ways in different spaces. I mean it's all me, it's just that different parts of myself get accentuated. I think that I have really different ways of being, and part of that comes from having two different cultures. They're both me, but different things get accentuated. Like even my language, my language changes from one space to another and how my name is pronounced. Or physical space, like how much physical space I have with other people, that changes from one space to another. The humor I use changes from one space to another. There are some things that some people can accept that others can't. So I think that if somebody watched me they might say that I act different, and if they didn't know me they would think that I'm not being myself. But I feel like different parts of myself get accentuated in different places, and they're all parts of me.

Brittney said, "I agree," and stated that there are different things she can say and do with different groups of friends but then added, "I don't know if that has to do with race, but it's like who you're with."

Ana continued the conversation; she removed the focus from a personal desire to fit in and emphasized a desire to gain understanding of and respect for difference:

The thing about kind of scoping out the new culture and trying to figure out about fitting in is that I don't know if I'm actually fitting in or not fitting in. But I think for me in these spaces, a lot of the observing comes from trying to understand and respect where this culture is coming from. Because sometimes it can be really different from where I'm coming from, so maybe I'm partly looking for common ground, partly just if something happens, just trying to find a way to explain it, just trying to make sense of this in the culture that I'm within.

Brittney then added that she too watches people to understand different races. The ideas discussed in this exchange resonated with me. My mother and father have quite distinct ways of being, but the understanding of multiple worldviews was solidified for me when at age seven I moved from Massachusetts, where my Dad's family lived, to Bogotá, where my Mom's family resided. I learned quickly and at a young age to observe, listen – to non-verbal cues as well as words, because at first I did not speak the language – and figure out new ways of being me in order to navigate distinct cultural norms.

The discussion between Maria, Ana, and Brittney provides some valuable insights into how fluidity is learned. The stories reveal that the fluidity experienced when navigating diverse cultures stems from a combination of three main factors. The first is learning from a young age that different people have different ways of being and, to be accepted in a group, one must learn the customary ways of being and avoid actions that might be perceived as disrespectful. The second is the importance of careful observation coupled with active listening. We know that we must pay attention to the distinct cultural codes present in each group. The third is genuineness. This means that even as we learn new ways of being, we must still find ways to be ourselves. Like Brittney, Ana, and Maria, Alana also discussed the importance of listening more than talking and striving to create space for others. She said:

> And really what I'm learning too is just to be more silent and not talk so much and to really listen to folks. Because I feel like we learn from listening. And I think I've learned a lot from really just like trying to be more, like I said, just more aware about not taking up so much space.

Susan shared a similar sense of fluidity; she had traveled to a variety of countries and often found that she could easily adapt to the cultures. She explained:

> I think you're just able to read cues over a lifetime…of going back and forth where you have different rules. You never have an idea that there's one way the world works. So you don't go into some place just flabbergasted that people aren't doing things the way you do them, or resistant to them, because you're used to switching between [different] ways of doing things, or ways of speaking even, or ways of body language. I found in Turkey that I was able to really get the Turkish body language down and that was another reason why I could really fit in a crowd.

Mindy discussed how she learned about middle class White culture from her White dad's mother. Although at first she had little contact with her White grandmother, who disapproved of her parents' interracial marriage, eventually her grandmother spent time with Mindy and her sister. Mindy stated:

Despite the difficulty, my grandmother gave me some really positive things. When we were kids she would take us up to Boston and bring us to museums and the symphony and just all these cultural things that I don't think – if it weren't for her we would never have gotten that, which is important. It's funny, I think now where we grew up and who we were, maybe she was afraid we were, I don't know, just so not cultural. I don't know.

Mindy was raised working class. Her parents ran a souvenir shop, and Mindy worked much of her childhood. Her grandmother literally provided her with cultural capital by teaching her aspects of middle class, White culture.

Although for some of the women, fluidity was accessed at least in part to due to ambiguous physical appearances, there were also distinct ways that we learned how to move between various cultural and ethnic groups by being exposed to cultural differences through our family members. In these stories we see the influence of translocational positionality and performativity. Shifting place (translocation) – including culture (of a particular family, for example) and geography with its political history (Boston, for example) – impacted cultural norms, which we respected through particular culturally appropriate performativities of identity, which in turn influenced fluidity and acceptance.

CLAIMING SPACES IN MONORACIAL GROUPS

There were a variety of ways that the participants took risks throughout their lives to claim space in communities, cultures, and situations in which they were originally either cast out or too afraid to approach. Many of these women had to learn to claim space, for example, within their respective ethnic and racial communities of color.

Alana, for instance, talked about how she "did not grow up with Black women at all" and thus "did not feel comfortable in Black spaces at all." However, as an adult, she has been consciously claiming Black spaces. As a result, she said:

Now it's like I actually really appreciate being in Black spaces, like I definitely feel a camaraderie and a community. I don't feel weird about speaking, and I don't feel like people judge me in the way that I always thought that they did.

In fact, at the time of the study, Alana's community was composed primarily of people of color. She had chosen to live with people of color and was only interested in dating people of color. She found that being around folks of color provided a place of refuge from the discrimination she encountered from her predominately White graduate school classmates who perceived her as "the angry Black woman." "I know that people hate me in my classes," she said. "I'm okay with that; I don't care. That doesn't really bother me so much. I mean it bothers me that there is a stereotype." The reason why she didn't let her classmates' racism bother her greatly was because she recognized that while she was oppressed in that space, she simultaneously earned privilege in other spaces as a *light skinned* Black woman with access to White cultural ways of being. She and her darker skinned friends noticed that she gets "more attention in queer spaces" from both White women and women of color because, "even though there may be mixed race, Black dynamics, even with other people of color, they're still there because we live in a White supremacist culture and everyone is indoctrinated within that, you know?" So, for Alana, "It's always like well you're thin, and you're light skinned, shit is really different for you." In other words, she is accepted to a greater extent by White people and, because of internalized racism, at times Black people favor her as well. It's notable also that she mentions being thin, alluding to accepted forms of dominant culture's beauty standards.

As Alana claimed her space within Black communities, she strove to learn from challenges posed by Black women about the societal privileges she holds. She was learning to listen yet remain in Black spaces instead of automatically assuming that others didn't want her there. In fact, she welcomed the challenges and simultaneously found strength in the comfort of shared ways of being. She said:

> That's really why I choose to live with people of color too, because I feel like I'm going to be challenged, and I'm going to be checked in a lot of ways, and it will force me to deal with a lot of things that with White people I know I won't have to deal with. But mainly it's around the safety issue because they [White people] get so angry sometimes, and I feel I need the space to cry and vent and feel very vulnerable.

Alana was claiming space simultaneously in Black spaces and White [academic] spaces; in both locations she often was not immediately accepted. Within people of color spaces, as a mixed Black and White person, Alana occupied a unique position of simultaneously finding refuge from White racism and experiencing challenges regarding her White privilege.

Katherine, who was also mixed Black and White, did grow up with Black friends, yet she often felt out of place in spaces exclusively for Black people. She said she thought about joining a group for Black students in high school, but she didn't try to do so because she knew she would be uncomfortable. In college she gravitated towards groups for mixed people, but after college she consciously participated in a focus group for Black women. She said, "I knew I was going to be uncomfortable" but "nobody there made me feel uncomfortable." At the time of the interview, Katherine was preparing to begin graduate school. She said that she wanted to get involved in the multicultural group, but added:

> I am also thinking about the Black organizations, and I want to be involved in that. But I think my main motivation for being involved is so that I get over my discomfort with it. You know, we're talking about graduate students,

nobody is going to make me feel uncomfortable there. If I feel uncomfortable, then it's me.

Katherine was slowly moving towards taking the risk of inserting herself in spaces for Black people. Doing so felt less threatening in a space in which she knew she would have some form of common ground: in this case, graduate school.

Janet and Tina, who like Alana grew up in predominately White circles, also talked about claiming space within people of color circles. Although Janet viewed herself as more White than Latina as a youth, after being exposed to more Brown people in high school and her later geographical move to Albuquerque, Janet began to insert herself more into spaces for women of color. She got involved in a local group for young women of color and said:

I definitely feel that the couple times I've been with the group and that I've kind of hung out with them, I felt very comfortable. They're very inviting and warm, and very easy to get along with, and the women are going through all sorts of things, you know? Body image issues, dealing with things in their past, and I feel like it's a very comfortable space for me. But it's hard too, because I feel that then it comes back to my background, and the fact that I don't know enough about my family history, and just about history in general, and then also being mixed race, too. I'm always constantly questioning how people are perceiving me.

Janet was still in the process of learning to feel comfortable in women of color spaces. Similar to Katherine, she recognized that there may be points of connection that move beyond race. However, she noticed through interactions with the group that she lacked knowledge about her family background, which sparked in her a desire to learn more about her culture and history.

Like Janet, Tina had also recently begun to insert herself in women of color spaces. She found a new interest in her Mexican family history when she began college and started consciously exploring her mixed race identity. She first began asking her Portuguese coworker questions about his cultural background. Then, she said, "I started asking my grandma these same questions, and I would spend a lot of time at my grandma's when I was in community college and really just trying to probe her about family history." Tina, who naturally has light brown hair, dyed her hair black. She said, "I really like black. That's like one of the only physical traits I can actually change to like help myself put a point to that biraciality. I like having that little marker." She had been dyeing her hair for about four and a half years. I asked her if there was anything going on at that time that prompted her to dye it black. She said, "I was applying for the [Latino] scholarship. It was a very hard thing for me to sort of be validating my cultural background. Maybe it was around the same time, I don't really remember." At age 19, while at San Francisco State, a mixed race friend gave her a flier about a scholarship for people of color interested in doing research on mental health. The funds were specifically for people of color. Tina applied and was awarded a three-year scholarship. She utilized that time to study race issues and as a result, she said:

> I really started to transition myself from calling myself Mexican to someone of biracial heritage. And then you know, I started reading about those mestizas. I started, you know, from there, I'm multiracial! So I just started a process of trying to shape my identity.

The scholarship gave her the opportunity to claim her biracial identity, but it also challenged her because up until that point she considered herself Mexican. However, she found it difficult to solely claim her Mexican identity in the face of other scholarship recipients who challenged her authenticity. She elaborated:

> Those next couple of years in the scholarship I really started to realize that I was mixed race because it was a national well-known scholarship that was given to students of color. We would go to this conference once a year, and I would get these looks like, "What the heck are you doing here?" It would drive me crazy.

Tina, who to most people "looks White" and doesn't speak Spanish, said she had to constantly "out" herself as Mexican year after year. During that time she began to embrace her mixed race identity, but she still questioned whether or not she should be in people of color spaces. At age 24, Tina continued to insert herself in Latina/Chicana spaces and questioned her legitimacy.

> I joined the Chicana club where I go now [as a master's student]. And I get these emails and I'm like, "This is not me." I would feel like I would take up resources if I applied to scholarships. I don't know. And I get really nervous when I think about, you know, thinking about my last name. My name is so, you know, Mexican, it's Tina Torres. And you know I worry, does my name privilege me in applications? Is there a racial quota? I get really nervous about stuff like that. And then I've had times when I've gone to caucuses, and I've emailed people that are setting them up, and I'm like "I'd like to contribute" and whatever. They'll meet me and they're like, "Oh, wow. You're Tina Torres? Oh, ok."

Another time she went to a Chicana caucus and when she arrived they said, "Oh your Tina Torres. That's weird." Thus, Tina had instances of being included and excluded as a Latina. Although it still caused her to question her identity and legitimacy, she felt more comfortable claiming a biracial identity and argued, "Biraciality seems to be a new emerging identity. It takes people time to learn. It's a new form of unlearning racism we need to do, stop questioning people's physical attributes of color. That's how I feel about it."

Susan attended her college campus group for Latinas a few times. Like Tina, she also had the experience of being "looked at very suspiciously" in the Latina group meetings. However, at the time of the interviews, at age 36, Susan said she had come to a place where she no longer worried about how others identified her and what they thought.

The women shared many stories of claiming space within communities of their ethnic groups and within communities of color. In addition, as evidenced in the last chapter, there were many ways in which the participants claimed space in work and school institutions that were predominately White. With the many conscious attempts by the women to insert themselves in non-White monoracial spaces, their comfort level with their identities shifted. These stories exemplify continuing practices of learning fluidity. In addition to understanding from a young age that multiple cultural norms exist and recognizing the importance of active listening coupled with careful observation, we see in these stories other strategies, as well as perceived barriers, to fluidity. Rejection, and sometimes merely fears of rejection, at times prevented these women from continuing to claim space. Common among these stories is a fear of entering monoracial spaces for people of the same ethnic background of color; for example, for mixed Black women entering spaces with only Black people and for mixed Latinas going to groups for Latinas/os. However, we also see shifts, along a continuum of varying degrees of comfort, in overcoming such fears with time. Strategies shared include searching for other points of connection, accepting challenges (particularly by people of color) as learning experiences, deliberately learning more about one's cultural heritage, and simply not worrying so much about what others think. Fluidity, the ability to move in and out of various social spaces, was connected to learning to live with ambiguity.

LEARNING TO LIVE WITH AMBIGUITY

For a number of these women, a large part of the mixed race experience was learning to live with ambiguity in the sense of uncertainty, vagueness, and sometimes even contradictions. The topic of "ambiguity" was raised in all three group interviews. Although only four women used the actual word "ambiguity," they all described experiences of dealing with the ambiguity of their mixed race identities. Ana, for example, talked in her individual interviews about ambiguity in her life and then raised the topic again during an Albuquerque group discussion about having children. She said:

> I think I spoke at my earlier interview about being comfortable with ambiguity, and how, with no clear answers, it gets complicated sometimes. And sometimes it just is what it is. So I think there's some sadness about what shade of brown my son is, and there's some incredible joy about how incredibly beautiful he is; it's all simultaneously true.

Ana had a son whom she described as "ambiguously beige." Although she too had self-described "ambiguously beige" skin, she worried about how her son might choose to racially/ethnically identify himself in the future because, based on skin color, he could pass for White.

Mindy, in an entirely separate group interview in Boston, also invoked ambiguity. She said:

I think being mixed is also about ambiguity, you know, learning to live with that. Learning to live with your own questions about who you are and how your identity changes in each setting. You know, like dealing with how people see you in trying to shift.

Susan spoke next, saying:

I think that dealing with ambiguity is a personal process as you grow up, as you age; I think it's interesting how that's a very personal individual process. It seems that no matter what you're doing internally about ambiguity you always come right up against the same thing externally. So it seems like you struggle internally to get a comfort level with ambiguity and then find that you're constantly being called on your ambiguity externally so you go through this double process of finding a comfort with yourself but having to be constantly challenged at the same time in trying to develop a comfort. You know? You have to be comfortable with yourself but also comfortable with portraying yourself. You know, there's a strange internal and external portion of it.

Mindy interrupted Susan to emphasize that ambiguity is about "constantly dealing with people's expectations" that are "especially based on how you look, not necessarily what you also know culturally." Throughout her interviews, Mindy described never-ending struggles with being identified by others as White yet not feeling White culturally. Mindy explained that whereas mixed race people have an ambiguous identity based on "two sets of knowledge," monoracial people "have a more holistic path that they can access because their family histories are more, more one." Although issues with ambiguity arise due to people's expectations (external pressures), dealing with ambiguity is an internal process, as described by Susan.

Later in the interview, Ruth, who cannot pass for White, added her thoughts, arguing that not being able to pass as White makes a significant difference in experience related to ambiguity. She said:

I feel like I don't fit in the so ambiguous category, but I felt like I can relate to some of the things. And during this conversation I've realized that my experience as a mixed race person has been good, but my experience as a Black person has not been good.

The accounts given by Mindy, Susan and Ruth exemplify the constant interplay between agency and structure. Racial politics played into their abilities to claim agency. For each of them it caused conflict, although those conflicts played out in entirely different ways.

Halfway through the Oakland group interview, upon listening to others in the group, Alana said, "We talked about the tolerance for cultural ambiguity in the borderlands. I could go read us a quote." In reality, no one in that group interview had previously used the phrase "tolerance for cultural ambiguity" but many of the stories shared by the participants exemplified a tolerance or a need for tolerance for ambiguity. The Oakland group interview was held at Alana's house so she had access to her books and left the room to retrieve the reading. It wasn't until almost the end of the interview that Alana found her opportunity to reintroduce the quote. The conversation had been intense and at times emotionally charged as people discussed dealing with Whiteness, racism, and the need to educate ignorant people. Wondering how to wrap up, I said, "It's heavy in here. I can feel the weight, and it's also been two hours and one minute (I had promised the interview would be no longer than two hours)." It was at that moment that Alana asked the group if she could read her quote. She pulled out the book *Borderlands/La Frontera,* by Gloria Anzaldúa (1999), and read:

> The new mestiza copes by developing a tolerance for contradictions, a tolerance for ambiguity. She learns to be an Indian in Mexican culture, to be Mexican from an Anglo point of view. She learns to juggle cultures. She has a plural personality, she operates in a pluralistic mode – nothing is thrust out, the good, the bad and the ugly; nothing rejected, nothing abandoned. Not only does she sustain contradictions, she turns the ambivalence into something else. (p. 101)

Immediately Linda said, "I love that book." I shared that I did as well; for me, reading Anzaldúa had been a turning point because, up until then, the concept of claiming a mixed identity had not even occurred to me.

Although the group interview could have ended at that moment on a positive note, it would not have been true to the overwhelmingly heavy sentiment and critical thought present throughout most of the interviews. Linda spoke up about her inability to live up to Anzaldúa's description of the powers of "the new mestiza" and confessed:

> I'm really struggling with this. I just feel really negative. It's just the downward spiral of feeling bad about stuff. I don't feel like I can sustain contradictions or turn inner hurts into something else. I can't even hold those. I don't. And I am always choosing one. I'm always going to be identifying as a person of color. I'm never like, "I'm White." That's what I'm struggling with right now, is learning to acknowledge, to be in the contradiction and embrace it, and all that. Sustaining the contradictions, to turn the ambivalence into something else. I don't feel like that's even a comfortable place for me to be, to be in both. I love thinking that, yes it makes me pluralistic, it makes

me, you know think differently, and it does. But, every day I'm making choices about how I'm presenting my gender, how I'm presenting my sexuality, and how I'm being White or not, and I'm never being White. I'm never choosing White. I don't think that I've ever chosen White in my life because, because that's how the world views me in a lot of ways. I'm sure it's different a lot of times, but a lot of times I pass, too. And I'm in the space of then of not even choosing it. I'm not saying I'm going to pass as White, and this is what feels good for me, you know? I don't know if I'm holding the contradictions.

When Linda finished talking, Tina asked her, "What do you think it would take for you to hold those contradictions?" Linda responded, "Being more comfortable with being White." This topic of dealing with Whiteness was ever present and clouded a tolerance for ambiguity. As evident in the descriptions of racial identity formation discussed in Chapter 1, none of these women wanted to claim their Whiteness; there was not much tolerance for the ambiguity of being part *White*.

This is not to say that the women did not hold a tolerance for ambiguity, but the juggling of cultures was not as easily navigated as Anzaldúa might make it seem. These stories reveal the complexity of maintaining a tolerance for ambiguity, as well as how a perceived ambiguous identity might contribute to experiences of fluidity. Susan made a distinction between internal processes of embracing ambiguity and external pressures to discard ambiguity, particularly in the form of pressures by others to claim an unambiguous identity. However, Ruth, who could not pass as White, highlighted that for her, fluidity was limited by being perceived most often as Black, rather than mixed or as ambiguously ethnic. The women often discussed the interplay of a tolerance for ambiguity, ambiguous ethnic appearance, and related practices of fluidity as an asset, despite the fact that maintaining a tolerance for ambiguity was difficult at times and even rejected by some people with whom these women interacted. Another benefit of being mixed described by several participants was that their experiences helped them to have a more open-minded and consciously critical perspective on things.

OPEN-MINDED, CRITICAL THINKING

As the participants strove to claim agency they continually faced structural, institutional, and political barriers. However, the women also acknowledged benefits to being mixed. Several of the women claimed that being biracial contributed to their critical thinking skills. Tina, for example, said:

I guess for me it's about helping me to be more critical about very important issues about identity, not just only the political, societal level, but being critical about race, class, and heteronormative behaviors. And the way that people stereotype each other; it's helped me realize what those boundaries are and how we learn, how my response is to that. And it's also helped me think really critically about who I am and what my role is, and how to, I guess, how to identify. Because I don't think I would ever really be thinking this critically about race and things like that if I weren't mixed.

Since Tina was able to pass as White and grew up with a White mom and primarily White friends, she understood that many White people had the capacity to be raised in homogeneous communities and never had to think critically about race. She too could have had that experience had she not been Mexican and not been close to her extended Mexican family.

Even Linda, who spoke about her struggle to hold contradictions and emphasized her positionality as an outsider, conceded that her outsider perspective was "a position of power" that allowed her insights into distinct cultures. Marta concurred, admitting that no matter what group she was in, she often felt "different, for whatever reason." But, she added:

> The good part is that I do feel like there's some strength or power in this fusion. I feel like it's expanding my way of thinking. That I just don't think of things in boxes, or like what you are saying, so I'm always looking for new ways to do things. And I feel like there's a way it has enhanced my creativity. Because I feel like I'm always trying to look at things from different points of view. And in some of my art I'll bring in both sides.

Marta is an artist. She shared with me pictures of her amazing art and there was often a fusion of Latin and Jewish influence. Thus, her creative thinking translated into the creativity of her art. Alana also shared that she too felt her experiences as a mixed race woman helped her to think from multiple perspectives and make connections with a variety of people of color. She said:

> I think that definitely in terms of what you are saying, in terms of not thinking in boxes, I really relate to that. I'm able to think more fluidly about a lot of things, for me, because I'm Black and White, and because in this country we tend to only talk about race within a Black/White binary, it's really enabled me to connect. I feel like I connect more to the collective, as people of color from like multiple different national and racial identities. There's a link of solidarity in being colonized subjects. And so I feel like being mixed has enabled me to break outside of that binary and really connect with a lot of different types of people of color. So I really do appreciate that.

In addition to feeling that her open-minded thinking enhanced her ability to connect with a wide range of people, Alana also felt that her mixed race identity helped her to better come to terms with both her queer identity and her gender identity as a femme[26].

And also coming into my queer identity as a mixed person sort of really enabled me to think about my own gender identity and my own identity as a femme person. Which is something that like, because when I was growing up I only thought about my identity or my femme identity as something that was connected to a White femme identity very specifically. And I never really felt feminine because of that. And I always was a tomboy and always kicked it with a lot of guys, and had a couple girlfriends that I had crushes on. But more recently now that I'm mostly in queer spaces of color, my femme identity is something very different for me. It's not just about assimilating or trying to be, or aspiring to this White femme identity. I think that also has enabled me to think about gender variance in different ways because of the fluidity of my racial identity.

Although it was Alana's mixed race identity – being a mixed Brown person in a predominately White world – that made her understanding of her femme identity problematic, it was also her mixed race identity that enabled her to embrace her "gender variance." She implied that her tolerance for racial ambiguity translated into a tolerance for gender performance ambiguity.

Bobbi also shared that being the product of an interracial couple helped her to be more open-minded. Linda added to her statement.

Bobbi: Like me and my sister always say that we know what our parents are going to say, and it's because our parents are different people. I think there's a very Somali attitude toward something and there's also a very White people attitude, you know? And we can think like both those people, so there's something about that. Maybe we're more open-minded.

Linda: We're able to negotiate. [lots of mm-mms from the rest of the group]

Bobbi: I think it's good for us.

Thus there was an overall sentiment within the Oakland group that being mixed helped create more open-minded, thoughtfully critical perspectives on issues even though it can also create a sense of isolation. Yet, there were also concerns expressed among the participants about this idea of mixed race people *automatically* having critical, open-minded perspectives as a result of being multiracial. Maria, for example, when I mentioned this idea that being mixed aids us in communicating with diverse people, argued:

Do you think there is even a whole myth even around that though? Around like, somehow if there is an all-Latino group that somehow we're all, they are all the same. I mean maybe because we're all mixed and that kind of breaks things up to begin with, but even in all-Black spaces it's not that people are all the same, you know? I think that we have to be really careful around that because again, are we perpetuating stereotypes too, around ideas of sameness? I mean I think that something that I'm realizing that, like, you know, there's all kinds of people and so, even if that's how I'm identifying, and I'm not identifying as mixed in a certain space, I don't necessarily feel like that necessarily means like I'm not Latina either. Because there are all kinds of ways that people identify, and have some sort of experience around that. You know being like tenth generation Black versus being an immigrant and versus Jamaican descent, and all that. And the U.S. is like, "Oh, that's Black," versus someone that is like of Ethiopian descent, you know what I mean? I just feel like when you start looking at Blackness, or any sort of group, there is no sameness.

Maria's perspective provided a critical reminder that if we believe ourselves to be models of understanding differences, then we can inadvertently dismiss the diversity that exists within all groups of people; we risk essentializing experience.

Linda also had a critical perspective on this idea that she shared in the Oakland group interview. She said:

I wish. I wish that were true. There was something that somebody said, I forgot already, but it was something about how we are more tolerant, that yes we have this ability to see outside of the box. But just like any other group or any category, or people who are really narrow-minded, there are people who are really fucked up and racist or whatever. I wish it would be true that yes, we are going to be clear because we have fluidity in our face, so we're going to have fluid gender, and yes we're going to be open to non-gender conformity, but I don't think it's true. I think it's about who we're around. I think it's about how we're raised. But it's also about what we choose to expose ourselves to.

Bobbi disagreed, countering, "But I think that if you have one parent from one culture and another parent that's from another culture, even if you were raised with one culture, you have to think like them." Linda argued back, stating that especially if you were raised with only one culture, you won't necessarily have an understanding of two cultures. An important part of the context necessary to understand this exchange is that Bobbi was raised primarily with her White mom, thus in a way she was speaking about herself. Bobbi felt she had two perspectives. However, Bobbi did not have a strictly monocultural experience because she didn't grow up exclusively in the United States. She was raised part of her life in Somalia, thus she had an experience of living in two different countries and cultures. Alana, acknowledging Linda's point about the importance of who you hang out with, said:

I'm kind of curious, because I feel like the way, the reason that I think critically and the reason that I have this consciousness around mixed race identity is because I'm around radical folk. I think it's because I'm around queer spaces. I really don't want to romanticize it.

Alana said that it was being around politicized people that contributed most to her consciousness. She felt that under different circumstances she would have identified as mixed race but "wouldn't have cared at all." Alana then said that she had always thought part of the consciousness came from not passing as White, but she had met several mixed people who pass who had a critical consciousness and she wondered why. That led, once again, into another conversation on the politics of Whiteness.

Thus in the end, several of the women wanted to claim that they were critical, open-minded thinkers because of their bicultural, mixed race experiences. However, at the same time there was a growing critique of that perspective and a caution about romanticizing "the mixed race experience." Although there was some dissention at times in the group interviews, for the most part there were many points of connection. In addition, the individual interviews revealed many overlapping experiences. Having a tolerance for ambiguity, learning and practicing fluidity, and engaging in open-minded, critical thinking thus can all be linked to the participants' positionalities as mixed race women and that connection can also be simultaneously troubled. Returning to the concept of agency, for many of these women, claiming agency included finding solidarity with other mixed race women.

CREATING MIXED RACE COMMUNITY

The stories of agency also included stories of isolation. As told in the last chapter, there were countless stories of feeling like outsiders and being excluded by others. However, virtually all of the women articulated that they felt a sense of community and connection with other mixed race people. Some women stated that they felt the most solidarity with other mixed people of the same racial/ethnic backgrounds, but one determining factor of solidarity appeared to be embodying a mixture that was both White and of color. Alana elaborated:

And I think it's important to have these categories because they create these links of solidarity, these links where we can create communities and sort of re-imagine what it means to be mixed. And it doesn't mean that we're all going to have the same experience identically. I mean just look at this group, we're all coming from totally different places, but I think there is definitely something to having one parent of color and having a White parent. I mean I can't speak from outside this country but just even within the history of our culture there are so many different ways you can talk about it. Whether it be blood quantum, whether it be among indigenous folks, or the one-drop rule, or within the way the racial hierarchies were established within the U.S. through slavery, which has impacted all people of color. And then all these anti-miscegenation laws, eugenics. I mean, there are so many different ways to talk about the idea of White cultural purity trying to be, like, created within this country to create a supreme Master race, right? All of us are really challenging and being able to, like, have some sort of analysis of Whiteness but also to be people of color. And I think that because of that history there's definitely, there is definitely a commonality in common experience that I think that we all probably share on multiple levels. So yeah, definitely. But then also there is definitely room for differences in that.

Thus, Alana argued that mixed people who have one parent of color and one White parent have a connection by virtue of being caught in the middle of a history of racism and White supremacy. Creating solidarity with other mixed people could allow us, she said, to "re-imagine what it means to be mixed."

Two of the participants had started groups for mixed race women. I too helped found groups for mixed race people, one in college and one particularly for women after college when I moved to Albuquerque and was in search of a mixed race community. In 1981, Marta founded a group for mixed race people that she participated in for several years. Linda had helped start get-togethers a couple years back that she called "mixed race mixers" for (primarily queer) mixed race folks. Although there had only been two or three gatherings, she said:

It's funny. Whenever I run into people that I don't see very frequently who are also mixed, it's like "Oh, when are you going to have another mixed mixer?" But it's kind of amazing, once we started doing it, we realized how many mixed people we knew.

Two important points can be gleaned from that statement. The first is that mixed race people are expressing a desire to congregate with other multiracial individuals. The second is that often when we are in the presence of other mixed race folks, we are unaware of it consciously, thus we don't always connect as mixed race people.

Most of the women affirmed either a strong connection to other mixed race people or a desire to connect with other mixed race people at some point. Clearly, from the stories above, Marta, Alana and Linda desired connection with other mixed race folks. Joanna stated:

Generally I feel more comfortable around a mixed group of people. Because I feel inherently we have something in common... I feel mixed people have an understanding to not fit neatly in the box and move in two different worlds.

Katherine declared that she felt most comfortable "with other mixed Black and White women" but also felt "very comfortable around mixed people in general." Mindy and Elizabeth both said that they felt most comfortable around bicultural people.

Many of the women had a core group of mixed race friends. Brittney, for example, said:

I have a lot of friends that are half Black and half White, and it's weird that we all come together. And there is like maybe eight or nine of us that hang out, and we're half Black and half White. And it's like, we are all different, but somehow it's just because of us being of two different races, we come together, because we're not really accepted in the Black, just all Black, groups.

Susan said, "All my friends are mixed race." Maria's closest friends were mixed race, some Latina and White, but not all. Ana too had mixed race friends and a light skinned Black partner who could relate to many mixed race issues and experiences. Her best friend growing up was mixed race, and they are still close. Among my closest friends, the majority are mixed Latina and White. Thus, for most of us, a large part of claiming agency and creating community involved developing friendships with other mixed race people, especially people who were mixed White and of color.

However, trying to create that community was scary for some. Linda admitted:

There was this hapa conference and I couldn't go. I was terrified to be in a community where, I don't know, where I would see people who look like me and I wouldn't be able to position myself as an outsider. It was too much to actually find somewhere that I might actually belong.

Marta understood that fear and said:

I had a similar issue. And my lover was like, "Are you afraid it could be good?" And I was like, "I'm afraid it could be good, and I'm afraid it could be bad." Sometimes they're just things. You expect them to be really good and then they just suck. But then if I didn't go I could hold out the hope that there's something out there, that there is community that I could find some day. But if I went, and it was bad, then there is no hope. And I think that's just hard for me.

Nonetheless, both Linda and Marta, at different points in their lives initiated groups for mixed race people. Thus, the desire to connect with other multiracial folks was greater than the fear of not finding community.

Throughout all the women's stories, there was an expressed desire to connect with other mixed race people in order to find validation and a sense of belonging. Some of the women, including myself, founded groups for women who are mixed, and most of the women cultivated significant friendships with other mixed race women. The women demonstrated a conscientious effort to create mixed race community. Those who did not have significant community and/or individual friendships with other mixed women appeared to be longing to find communion with other biracial women.

COMFORTABLE SPACES

In the course of the interviews I asked each participant, "Are there spaces in which you feel more comfortable or spaces where you feel less comfortable?" Because of the nature of the interview, the women understood that this question related to race, but they were also told that their responses could be broader. All of the women at some point talked about feeling comfortable in spaces with other mixed race people, as described in the previous section. In addition, many of the participants – Susan, Katherine, Joanna, and Marta – described diverse or eclectic groups as places of comfort. Joanna, for example, said:

> A big part to me is never fully feeling I belong to a group unless the group is already eclectic, certainly racially. The group I feel most comfortable with is a group that is racially diverse and has similar race politics.

As exemplified in the quote by Elizabeth in the opening of the previous chapter, many of the women found refuge with others who are bicultural, whether mixed race, raised in a community in which they were different, born in another country, or children of immigrants. Mindy said, "I find myself connecting more with people who were bicultural in some way. Like I had one friend who was Palestinian and she grew up in Britain." Bobbi similarly said, "I like being around people from different countries." Linda claimed that she wanted to "be with people that have a shared sense of what it is like to grow up and not really fit with others." Many of the women explicitly stated that they were not comfortable in all-White groups. Joanna said, "I feel 99% of the time out of place in a group of White people." Others similarly remarked that they were not comfortable in any kind of homogeneous group. Elizabeth said:

> I feel less comfortable with anyone who is way, way, way the stereotype of whatever that race is, or perform their race obviously. Like in BC, they were so White. They dressed so White, and it was uncomfortable. I just felt like I could not be accepted by those people. I feel uncomfortable if I'm with Black people, and I'm the only person there who's not Black, if they talk about cultural things that I don't know anything about.

Several of them added other non race-related attributes that they appreciated in others including: "progressive" (Joanna, Katherine), "open-minded" (Bobbi, Joanna), "Democrat" or "not Republican" or "liberal" (Joanna, Katherine, Ruth), "college educated" (Ruth, Joanna, Diana), "creative" (Ruth), and "queer" (Ruth, Joanna, Marta, Maria, Alana). Most of these attributes imply an acceptance or understanding of difference. A common denominator in the majority of these comfortable spaces is that they imply either an eclectic, diverse group – some kind of mixture, either embodied or as a collective group – or, as Linda described, people that have a shared sense of what it means to not fit in with others.

CONCLUSION

The interplay between insider and outsider status for these mixed race women is complex. Although it is important to acknowledge structural constraints to gaining insider status and internal trepidations about belonging, it is equally important to recognize the benefits and agency these women found in being mixed race. Mixed race experience is set in a sordid history of White supremacy and racism that has included widespread degradation of miscegenation and a simultaneous exoticizing of mixed race bodies and lives.

Anti-miscegenation laws were not repealed in several states until 1967, either shortly before or shortly after these women were born. A long history of colonization in the United States has created a general mistrust of White people by people of color that continues today (Willinsky, 1998). One of the ways that people of color have been able to sustain themselves and achieve success in a White dominated society is to unite and demand equity through programs such as affirmative action (Williams, 2008). Often people of color have created safe spaces with other folks of color. Most people with a critical analysis of race relations understand the need and benefit for spaces exclusively for people of color.

However, this division between White people and people of color places mixed race people who have one White parent and one parent who is a person of color in precarious positions among many groups of people, for they can be perceived as a threat in many circles. As discussed in the literature review, the history of racism includes a vilification of mixed race people (Knox, 1850). Although rarely discussed openly, one need only do an Internet search for White supremacist groups[27] to realize that hate groups continue to actively name multiracial people as the demise of society and the ultimate sin. Without much effort one can find a plethora of racist propaganda that maligns mixed race people who are mixed White and of color. Some civil rights advocates distrust mixed race people who claim mixed identities; they fear that multiracial people will deny their heritage of color and argue that affirmative action is no longer necessary (Williams, 2008).

To counteract this hatred and distrust of multiracial people, over the past 20 years there has been a growing body of writings that celebrate the mixed race experience. Mixed race people are speaking, and being spoken for, in many positive ways (Anzaldúa, 1999; Camper, 1994; O'Hearn, 1998; Root, 1992, 1996). Within these writings there have been some authors (Root, 1992; Trueba, 2004) who have exalted mixed race people as the answer to great racial divides, romanticizing the mixed race experience and dismissing the power in the politics of racism. Mixed race people are often caught in a trap of being either pathologized or romanticized, neither of which allows us to be understood as complex, multifaceted human beings. The participants' stories in these chapters on structure and agency break down the binaries of pathology and celebration while demonstrating how maintaining such binaries creates struggles in the lives of mixed race people.

In order to understand the participants' stories, they must be considered in the context of these ongoing race wars and hybridity discourse. Many of the women in the study were highly educated, politicized, and racialized. They were thus cautious about adding to the romanticization of mixed race people and conscious of why some people of color may not accept them. This context helps explain why so few of the women would say unconditionally, "I love being mixed race!" It also explains why some of them centered themselves in communities of color, while others struggled to claim space within their own communities of color and simultaneously dealt with barriers in White-dominated institutions. Nonetheless, these women did, and continued to, claim space for themselves and were learning to live with the ambiguity of their multiracial existence.

Anzaldúa's book, *Borderlands/La Frontera* (1999), is a powerful reference for understanding these women's experiences of living in the borderlands. Alana invoked a quotation from that book about the mestiza's ability to tolerate ambiguity and contradictions. Linda admitted that this tolerance was something with which she still struggled. However, the struggle did not negate her personal power. Like the stories these women tell, Anzaldúa's writing is also about both the power of the mestiza consciousness and the struggle inherent in being mestiza. She wrote:

> Being tricultural, monolingual, bilingual, or multilingual, speaking a patois, and in a state of perpetual transition, the mestiza faces the dilemma of the mixed breed: which collectivity does the daughter of a dark skinned mother listen to?... Cradled in one culture, sandwiched between two cultures, straddling all three cultures and their value systems, la mestiza undergoes a struggle of flesh, a struggle of borders, an inner war. (p. 100)

Linda's concern about not having a tolerance for ambiguity is a part of the mestiza experience as Anzaldúa defines it. Linda, as the daughter of a dark skinned mother, faced the dilemma of determining which collectivity to listen to. Anzaldúa is arguing that mestizas will better be able to cope when they develop a tolerance for contradictions; Linda knows this and she is actively working to increase her tolerance for that which she rejects – her Whiteness. It takes work. Anzaldúa argued:

> The work of the mestiza consciousness is to break down the subject-object duality that keeps her a prisoner and to show in the flesh and through the images in her work how duality is transcended. (1999, p. 102)

Linda's narrative and Anzaldúa's quote highlight the unique experience of embodying hybridity. As mentioned in the first chapter, something is lost in disembodied, abstract discussions (Grossberg, 1993; McLaren, 1997) of so-called "hybrid" experiences.

In the heart of these stories of exclusion, there were also multiple stories of transcending racial divides as these women learned and cultivated the ability to move fluidly between people of various races and ethnicities. These forays created links between cultural divides. We cannot be sure of exactly what created their abilities to effectively communicate and integrate across lines of difference, but we can learn from what their stories tell us. As an educator, I have found that one of the most difficult tasks in helping people to understand the politics of power, privilege, and difference is helping them to see that their current worldview may not be the only, or the best, worldview. These women's stories remind us that there are multiple worldviews that can coexist and that one worldview is not necessarily better than another.

Perhaps one of the most important messages throughout all the stories is the power to learn through active listening. Although several of the women gained access to fluidity by virtue of having ambiguous physical features, adapting to distinct cultural groups was not innate for these women. They learned it through powers of observation. Through their stories, the participants tell us that they were able to move between various cultural groups, in part, because they would take the time to respectfully observe others, actively listen to what others had to say, and then take care to act in ways that did not impose their own cultural habits and would not offend people's cultural ways of being. At the same time, some of the women cautioned that this observation and adaptation must not be used to co-opt culture and that the key to successful mobility between cultures is to remain genuine. Genuineness is a tricky concept because it implies some form of authentic behavior. Yet, as explained in Chapter 2, ways of being are created through performativity – repetitions of particular performances. Race, gender, and class, for example – as performed and perceived – are constructed socially through actions that reinforce or resist dominant norms (Bettie, 2003; Lorber, 2001; Omi & Winant, 1994). Thus, I do not want to reinforce the myth that there is some "real" concept of a "genuine" behavior. It seems to me that here the concept of genuine, as Maria was describing it, entails a conscious effort to learn cultural ways of being in order to be respectful of others. This stands in contrast to those who, upon learning about others' cultural ways of being, either use what they learn for their own gain (for example, co-opting and commodifying aspects of Native culture and spirituality) or to degrade others (Deyhle, 2009).

Navigating ambiguity, however, does point to the importance of translocational positionality (described in Chapter 2). We see, through the narratives, how the women strive to define themselves and understand their experiences through the social categories of gender, ethnicity/race, class, and sexuality in various ways depending upon the context – the time and space – they are in. They reinforce and/or downplay particular positionalities depending on the situations they are attempting to navigate. These performances reveal nuances not only of their own lives as mixed race women, but also about the intricate webs of power related to privilege and oppression that interface with the dialectical relationship of structure and agency. Linda's comments perhaps exemplify this best as she described her struggle with sustaining contradictions while being forced to choose. She stated, "But, every day I'm making choices about how I'm presenting my gender, how I'm presenting my sexuality, and how I'm being White or not, and I'm never being White. I'm never choosing White." Yet at times, others nevertheless positioned her as White. Thus she made choices about her performances related to gender, sexuality, and race that were both constrained and broad. Having the ability to not choose White, yet being able to reap the benefits of White privilege creates intertwined experiences of being isolated and accepted, of being constrained by norms and able to claim agency, of being oppressed and privileged, of claiming power and being denied power.

Another self-described attribute that many of these women possessed was open-minded, critical thinking. Some of the women felt that their bicultural experiences led them to think outside of dominant culture norms, understand various perspectives, and be open to differences. They felt their biracial experiences helped them to be more accepting of other ambiguities related to race, gender, and sexuality. However, during group discussions some participants felt cautious about naming a cause and effect relationship between the mixed race experience and open-mindedness or increased critical thinking skills. Some argued that their critical perspectives were a result of the people they chose to have in their lives, "radical folk" for example. Perhaps we cannot say what created their open-minded, critical thinking. Maybe it was the experience of living in the borderlands that drew the participants to be around open-minded, politicized people. Regardless, this is a positive attribute that they could directly link to their mixed race lives.

For educators and parents, perhaps one of the more important points to take from these stories is the validation these women found from creating community with other mixed race people. Having other mixed race people to connect with helped them to better understand their unique biracial experiences and to feel validated. In addition, as was noted in the last chapter, these women often found safety in diverse, eclectic groups and comfort with a variety of bicultural people. Educators and parents can assist mixed race children in creating healthy racial/ethnic identities by providing them access to mixed race role models, cultivating a diverse community, and providing opportunities for connection with other multiracial individuals. However, it is important to allow mixed people to create their own mixed race communities.

In addition, these women found comfort in knowing about their cultural backgrounds. The levels of connection that participants felt to their languages, heritages, personal histories, and cultural ways of being often times influenced their sense of agency. Participants appreciated their connections to family languages, traditions, and cultural foods. As such, parents who make a concerted effort to pass on ethnic culture may be assisting their mixed race children in their abilities to navigate diversity and challenges to identity.

I argue that these women *learned* fluidity; they learned how to navigate distinct cultural groups. However, it is important to note that these women had *access* to learning the skills needed to navigate structural and institutional constraints not only because they were mixed, but specifically because they were mixed part White. Their Whiteness helped to provide them access to enter White spaces and White conversations. This topic of how Whiteness operated in these women's lives will be addressed in the following two chapters.

FORCED "PASSING"

Being Perceived as White

I don't want people to think I'm White… I think as far as passing, I don't know that I really look White, but people think I'm White a lot. But most people don't think I'm Black. I think it's weird, because I think you have to put up with a lot of bullshit…It's kind of a weird position because people will tell you things to your face about your own race. – Bobbi

Some people are going to think I'm White, some people are not. I don't really have control over that. I try to just make that their issue and their problem.
– Marta

And I think ever since I was younger I haven't felt comfortable. But it's kind of like I don't have much of a choice. I pass. So what I do is, I'm an ally.
– Tina

Discussions about Whiteness permeated several of the interviews, in particular, reflections on passing. In the next chapter, I will delve into the complexity of Whiteness in relation to these women's lives and their philosophies of what Whiteness entails and how it is enacted. First, however, I discuss passing. How are these women perceived in relation to Whiteness, and how do they perceive themselves?

Tackling the topic of passing before delving into the participants' deeper discussions on Whiteness is important because of the historical significance and attention placed on passing as White. Many writings about passing have emphasized instances where individuals chose to pass as White (Kroeger, 2003; Larsen, 2003; Pfeiffer, 2003). As a result of this history, many people, both White people and people of color, assume that people who can pass for White would want to do so. As revealed in the earlier chapter on identity formation, the women had various ways they identified themselves, but none of the participants considered themselves, or wanted to be considered, White. Nonetheless, all but three of the participants were at times perceived to be White by others. The women had varying experiences with passing from almost always being labeled as White by others to almost never being assumed to be White.

IMPOSED "PASSING"

The irony of not wanting to be associated with Whiteness is that the majority of us pass for White in terms of skin color, at least in some situations. Thirteen of the 16 participants were identified in some instances by others as White and/or of European descent; I, too, am often identified as White by others. Degrees of passing among us varied. Some women were almost always identified as White, while others were only identified as White in certain situations or by certain groups of people. "Passing" is a loaded term that does not exactly fit in relation to these women in most circumstances. Passing typically refers to purposefully disguising some form of one's identity. Historically the term passing in relation to race typically referred to passing for White. This is exemplified by the title of Sandweiss' (2009) book *Passing Strange*, the story of a White man who chose to pass as Black for a period of his life, something considered unique and unusual. Overall, these women did not and would not *choose* to pass as White in most situations; others identified them as White. Although perceived to be White by others based on skin color and perhaps ways of being, they argued that they did not purposefully try to present themselves as White. Nonetheless, passing – if the definition is expanded from not only presenting as White but also being perceived as White by others – occurred in their lives. To accentuate the distinction, I will put the term "passing" in quotes when it refers to imposed passing rather than chosen passing.

ALMOST ALWAYS ASSUMED TO BE WHITE

Tina, Elizabeth, and Mindy were almost always perceived to be White by others who had not yet gotten to know them. This affected how they identified themselves. In our second individual interview, I asked Tina how she identified and if that changed over time. She said:

> Maybe it depends on what it's for, but mostly I just pick, if it's there, Latino or Chicano. I don't know. I don't know how to explain it. I can't do it very well. It seems like I could stand in for representation, but not a true representation, but an alternate representation. I think if, I don't know how to explain it. I just don't feel like saying "I'm White" is correct, and I don't think Latina is correct either. I just feel like Latina is a more attempting of a more diverse background, at least for me. But sometimes when I pick White, I usually do it because my [Latino] last name's going to be on it, I know that that's going to be a little marker of biraciality. I don't know. It is very, very difficult. I wish people would understand that. I think that's why there needs

to be more education. Not because I'm calling people out to be more PC or anything, just thinking that this is something that truly affects somebody. Just as gender affects people who are trans, or you know, just as the questions of "What is your sexual orientation? Are you gay or are you straight?" and it's like, but that doesn't include everything that anybody could be. It's the same thing. It makes you question your identity, and re-question your identity. And because there's always demographic sheets that say, "Pick only one," it's like you are constantly going through this evaluation of yourself and your identity.

I asked Tina what was so painful about having to choose, and she said:

I think it's just the having to split yourself up like that, [to] halve yourself, and choosing which side of you [that] you want to represent, or which side of you you feel is you, because you can't pick both pieces to make you a whole. Which is, it's so unfair, it's so unfair. I mean, obviously our country is a litany of unfair and unreasonable demands on people who are different. It's just one of those things that you can't expect people to call into question. I don't know. It's just all these things that come into that decision that should be so simple. And that's what's so agonizing about it, because you really have to spend time evaluating yourself. And it just doesn't seem right or fair.

I asked her, "So when you evaluate yourself, what do you find?" She answered:

I don't know. It's different every time. I mean for the most part, it's kind of like, because I appear as White, I can pass for White, I grew up in a mainstream White household, that, there are times when that part, the nagging part in the back of my head says you have to represent this [Latina] side of yourself also because that's what makes you dynamic, that's what makes you you. You have all this White culture and this White appearance, but there are other factors in there that make you the different person that you are. I think the agony is do I really want to shoulder that, represent biraciality? Or do I just want to say whatever, especially when I'm applying to schools or when I did the census, voting. It's how someone perceives you. It's a minute little question that is so loaded. And when they look at it, it's a minute scary generalization and that's it, it's over, there's no conversation.

In the group interview Tina said, "I think that it's really hard for me because I pass as White all the time everywhere, every day, even if I am with my Mexican family. It's also unbearable because I'm a Valley girl, I'm a White girl." Tina spoke with what many would refer to as a "valley girl" accent, which is typically related to White young women and girls. Tina doesn't want to be viewed as *just* White, but that is how others perceive her because of her light skin and because of how she talks. She doesn't feel she has a choice; she said, "And I think ever since I was younger I haven't felt comfortable. But it's kind of like I don't have much of a choice. I pass." Tina struggled with this perceived identity. To cope, she used her perceived Whiteness to be an ally to people of color.

> When I walk into a café, I don't want to represent a stereotypical White, middle class person. I want to represent a biracial woman who grew up in two different households, both of which were working class and both of which had different cultural positions but both of which have combined themselves and made me. And I sympathize and empathize more with the workers in the café. And I'd rather talk to them and spend time with them, than people of privilege that would just class me in their same loop. And it's totally wrong. But at the same time, I don't know if I want to say advocate, but I want to be someone to help, you know? It's kinda like, I don't want to take a top down approach and go in and swoop these workers out of their bad conditions, because I don't even know if they're bad. But I want to be like, I find them to be more interesting and more on my level. They would have conversations that would make more sense to me than people who aren't really conscious of the struggles people go through.

I asked Tina what her vision of being helpful entailed. She explained that, for example, when she bartends, she tells the people (of color) who work in the kitchen that if they break something, or if something goes wrong, that they can blame it on her because she knows that she won't really get in trouble but they will. She said:

> I drop and break glasses all the time; it's no problem for me. I guess just, making friends and making allies with people. I'm using my position of privilege and power, not making boatloads of money and exploiting more laborers or more people but rather siphoning it back into something better.

Tina also spent time tutoring African American and Latina girls in a nearby city and in that role her main goal was to "be a listener, give them a voice and space to talk. And show them that I am an ally, that I'm trying to bridge that connection." Tina "passed" everywhere she went; she was perceived as White. However, she did not primarily identify as White. In fact, in several instances she said that while she considered herself to be primarily Mexican, she recognized that other people did not identify her that way. She took her liminal space as a White-looking, Mexican-identified person and used her White privilege to be an ally to people of color. However, as she did that she also distinguished herself as different from the people of color with whom she interacted, because it was not on an equal level; it was as a person who had a position of power in relation to those around her. So, in her attempt to connect with people of color, she inadvertently separated herself from them. Being a listener is great, but assuming that someone else needs to be "given a voice" disregards the voice they already have.

Like Tina, Mindy is also perceived as White almost all the time. In fact she and Tina were the only two participants who did not identify themselves as people of color because they acknowledged that they tend to be considered White by most people. Mindy, who had a Filipina mom and White dad, did not feel like she was raised with or understood White culture in a way that others expected her to, which placed her in awkward positions. She said:

> I think what's hardest for me, especially since I came here to college, is understanding what Whiteness was. Because I pass for White, and that's what most people expect from me, it's what is normative, is to be White. And the experiences I have are very limited as to what Whiteness was.

Thus Mindy found herself in situations with White people where there was an expectation that she would behave in a certain way or have a shared understanding of something. When she did not meet those expectations, it was disappointing to the White people with whom she was interacting, and to her. Mindy described an experience of being in a film class and everyone had to name a comfort food. She named a traditional Filipina/o dish and people laughed at her. This was hard for her. She said, "When people find that your experiences are so odd or they have some nervous laughter or a reaction, it's like after awhile, you don't want to go out of your way to relate to people." As someone who was more of a loner, she tended to avoid interacting with people, in part for fear that they would have expectations of her that she wouldn't meet. She feared being laughed at again. Instead, as mentioned earlier, she found community online.

Another aspect of being perceived as White that she found distressing includes how her mom and other Filipina/os privilege Whiteness. Mindy was well read in terms of history and politicized around race issues. She understood that favoring Whiteness is tied to a history of colonization and White supremacy. Consequently, it was troubling to her (rather than affirming) that her mom admired her Whiteness:

> It's disturbing to be a white skinned daughter too, you know? Like my mom and Filipinos have this light skinned thing, this color struck thing that is hard to talk about, you know? I remember skin-whitening creams.

However, even as she was admired for her Whiteness, as a brown haired, brown eyed girl she still was not as White looking as her mom hoped she would be. Mindy said, "Like my mom, she was always saying, 'I was always hoping for a blue eyed, blond baby.'" Mindy was caught in this trap of being admired for her Whiteness by her mom and other Filipina/os, while simultaneously being ostracized by White people for not being White enough.

Elizabeth, too, was also almost always assumed to be White by others. Like Mindy, she was also mixed Filipina and White and was situated in a culture that valued Whiteness. Recall that Elizabeth described how both her family and wider

137

Filipina/o culture exalt mixed race people who are mixed with White ancestry. However, Elizabeth did not have the same critical analysis around the racist implications of favoring Whiteness and consequently viewed her experiences of being favored positively.[28] Elizabeth said, "Most White people see me as White." Elizabeth also perceived herself as White until she was about 14 or 15, only then did she start to think more in racial terms. She remembered her mom saying to her not to act like an American student; they were lazy and had no respect. Elizabeth recalled that when she was little she was "really proud of having a mom from the Philippines. Although [she] didn't understand there was a racial component to that." She also did not associate Filipina/os with other Asians.

It was not until Elizabeth reached her teen years that she started to recognize herself as a child of an immigrant, and only then did she identify as Asian. Even then, she defined herself "in contrast" to her predominately White classmates whom she perceived as "lazy Americans." Elizabeth did not have a close relationship with the White side of her family. Given that extended family from the Philippines lived with her, she felt a connection to her Filipina/o culture. Recall that she was one of the few people who described her experiences as a mixed race woman as overwhelmingly positive. One of the contrasting factors between her story and Mindy's is that she perceived both her Whiteness and her Asianness as positive. Mindy found her Whiteness, and its associations to colonialism and White supremacy troubling. This was coupled with the feeling that her Filipina identity made her uncomfortably stand out among Whites. Although both Mindy and Elizabeth stated that there were few Asians in the towns they grew up in, Mindy's Asian ancestry became something that separated her from others, while Elizabeth's Filipina/o background did not make her stand out for the most part. In addition, class factors added to Elizabeth's sense of comfort with her mixed identity. Elizabeth's mom was brought from the Philippines to be a teacher in her working class town because there were no qualified teachers who wanted to teach there. The few "foreigners" in the town were often professionals and revered and appreciated for the services they provided. It placed Elizabeth in a socioeconomic status above most of her classmates, whereas Mindy who was raised working class found herself in situations, for example, with wealthy White people at Smith College in which she felt she did not measure up. Although she never used the words explicitly, there was a sense from Mindy's stories that she was made to feel like she was less than those around her.

The experiences for these women who were most often perceived as White varied greatly. For Elizabeth, it brought a sense of stability and privilege. For Tina, it caused continual angst in thwarting her desire to connect with other Latinos. For Mindy, it caused internal conflict; she was disquieted with the praise she received from Filipina/os for her Whiteness and insecure about the ostracism she experienced at the hands of White people. These stories demonstrate the influence of positionality and the intersectionality of social identities; reactions to race-based perceptions varied among the women in ways that related, for example, to class status.

FREQUENTLY PERCEIVED AS WHITE, BUT NOT ALWAYS

Other participants were assumed to be White/of European descent frequently, but not always. This group included Linda, Marta, Bobbi, Joanna, Ana, and Susan. I would include myself in this group as well. Linda, who was Japanese and White, said:

> I think I pass for White a lot, or if not that way then as the harmless Asian, you know, like Asians are not threatening. So like, I think oftentimes, by strangers on the street, I'm exotified. People are like, "Oh, what are you?" I think that's common.

Her description shows that people sometimes assumed she was White, sometimes not. As will be described further in the next chapter, the frequency with which Linda was assumed to be White forced her to more deeply examine her White privilege.

Bobbi, who was Somali and White, in the group interview said, "In Africa they think I'm a White person." Then later in the interview she added:

> I think as far as passing, I don't know that I really look White, but people think I am White a lot. But most people don't think I'm Black ... To me I never felt culturally White. I don't feel that I physically look White but people do think that. I've never had an African American person tell me I look White, but people think I look White, some White people think I look White, and some Latino people think I look White. It's kind of a weird position because people will tell you things to your face about your own race. Maybe it's because Phoenix is a very racist society. Maybe that doesn't happen out here [in the Bay Area] as much... That was the main thing for me. I don't want people to think I'm White.

Bobbi had the experience of being perceived as White in Africa, but not among African Americans. Whites and Latinos most often assumed she was White. Bobbi's comment speaks to one of the painful aspects of being perceived as White as a mixed race person; it made her vulnerable to hearing racist remarks about "her own race" – about Black people.

It was common among the group for people to have the experience of White people assuming they were White. As mentioned in an earlier chapter, Joanna had this experience; most often it was White people who assumed she was White. Joanna talked about how she was perceived differently by different people. However, because she was often assumed to be White by others, that shaped her self-identity. She felt the desire to be included in Black circles but appreciated her fluidity to move between groups. Growing up she had both White friends and Black friends in her Black/White racially mixed neighborhood and attended a school with large populations of both White and Black students. She explained:

And like there were definitely some racial issues in town but I'd never call it racial tension or anything like that because it was so nonchalant. We would just joke about it all the time. I always got a kick out of it when they included me in it. I have this whole thing in needing to be included and needing to feel like I'm Black. So, I'd love it when they'd make some Black joke and include me in it. I felt really cool. It's something I still kind of struggle with. It goes against so much of what I believe and stand for, to care so much about what other people think. But I can't shake it, you know? Especially for those of us who are fair enough to pass, you know? I was talking to a friend about that after [the mixed race] happy hour. Obviously there were a lot of conversations that came up last night that were interesting. And one of the conversations was about the intersection of how I identify myself with how other people identify me, and that whole topic. And what I was saying [is that] so much of how I identify myself is based on how people perceive me. Because if I were to walk down the street and everyone saw a Black person, I'd have a completely different internal vision of who I was. Because my sister and I, we've had conversations every once in awhile about it, and she calls herself Black. And she talks about being the only Black person in the office. And it always strikes me as funny, but I understand it because she's so much darker than I am. And everyone when you look at her, you think she's Black. You might think she's biracial, but you'd never think she's White. And a lot of people think I'm White. Most people think I'm Jewish, that's what I get all the time, that or Latina. But, you know because I can pass so easily without even trying, it's such a huge shaping factor of how I see myself. Because the world hasn't been constantly telling me I'm a minority, I have the freedom to be more fluid about it, whereas she really doesn't have a choice, because every day the world reminds her. You know?

I asked Joanna how she identified herself, and she responded:

I identify very, very much as mixed, multiracial, biracial. I don't particularly have a strong attachment to any of the words. I use mixed a lot. I call myself a halfie, a hapa, whatever. But that is a very, very big part of who I am. And I get upset when other people try to force some identity on me.

As explained in a previously used quote, because Joanna was close to both sides of her family, she felt strongly about the importance of not denying parts of herself. Joanna's narrative points to the complexity of "passing" only part of the time. Although she was assumed to be White at times, she did not ever consider herself to be only White. Other times she was accepted as Black, but that too did not feel right to her, even though she desired acceptance in the Black community. Thus, although she "passed," her identity was firmly rooted as mixed race, and it was important to her that both she and others recognize the "duality" of her identity, her connection to both parents and both sides of her family. She exclaimed, "I get upset when other people try to force some identity on me."

Joanna, however, talked about passing in relation to another socially constructed category – sexuality – and had a completely different perspective on passing as straight. Joanna said, "But in terms of, when I think of dating women, it's really important for me to date, to have a partner who can also pass for straight, because it's something that I value in my own life." She talked about this in both the group and individual interviews. In the individual interview I asked challenging questions to try to understand why passing as straight was important and passing as White was not. Joanna explained:

I don't care what my partner looks like racially. I don't need a partner that can pass as White. Generally I'm not attracted to White people. But, I think because of the current climate in which we live, in regards to homosexuality, sometimes it's important for people not to know.

Joanna felt discomfort with her own view of wanting to pass and wanting a partner to pass as straight. She even stated, "I offend myself with that statement" and "I think it's horrible of me to think that." Nonetheless, she valued her ability to pass as straight and did not want that to be associated with people assuming that she consequently devalued her sexuality. She elaborated:

Definitely there are things I can see are internalized racism and see how it plays out in my life. But in terms of homophobia, I think I have no problems with the choices I've made in terms of my sexuality. And I think I'm 100% right to do what I think is right and act on it. And I think the people who disagree with me have the right to disagree with me but are wrong if they try to stop me from acting on it. It's like, if someone thinks I'm a bad person because of it, I think they're just wrong. It doesn't make me doubt myself more. But I don't know. I really like being able to pass. It comes in handy.

Thus, although Joanna did not care to pass as White in terms of race, the ability to pass as straight was an important issue in Joanna's life. Her stories imply that encountering homophobia was more dangerous than encountering racism. Joanna emphasized wanting to "choose when to bring it [her sexuality] up and when not to." She was out in some spaces and not in others, whereas with race, she never wanted anyone to make the assumption that she was just White or just Black. It was much more important to her to always be recognized as biracial. There were different levels of risk for her associated with being identified as queer or bisexual versus being identified as Black. In the instance of sexuality, she feared losing power by coming out; she did not have that same fear of losing power by defining her mixed raced identity.

Marta, who was Peruvian and White, also had the experience of sometimes being perceived as White and other times being recognized as "Latin." Like Joanna and Bobbi, she found that it was most often White people who assumed she was White. Marta found inner peace with these false assumptions, and didn't allow them to affect how she perceived herself. She explained that growing up among other mixed people and learning the vocabulary in college to define her experience assisted her in claiming her own identity for herself. She shared:

> I feel like I got the vocabulary in college to make things make sense. I feel like I am my own way. I was in a neighborhood where there were seven kids who were mixed Latin and White and then a mixed race family[29] moved in a couple of houses down. She was my best friend in the neighborhood. And then in high school I was friends with these two Filipino guys and one of them was mixed. So I just feel that I kind of navigated that. Some people are going to think I'm White, some people are not. I don't really have control over that. I try to just make that their issue and their problem.

Marta recognized that she only had control over her response to people's assumptions, not over the assumptions that others would make of her. She decided to not let other's assumptions affect how she viewed herself. However, at the same time, she recognized the White skin privilege she held, and similar to Tina, she felt it was her responsibility to be an ally to darker skinned people who experienced more racism.

Susan, who was Mexican and White, also had the experience of sometimes being perceived as White and other times being assumed to be a person of color, although not always Latina; sometimes she was perceived as other ethnicities such as Turkish, Lebanese, or Pakistani. You may recall her story in the last chapter of being perceived to be the same ethnicity of whatever group of people with whom she associated. Like Marta, she also seemed to find peace with others' assumptions, recognizing that it was others' ignorance, more so than anything about herself, that caused others to make incorrect assumptions about her. Susan claimed a Chicana identity primarily. Chicana works, she said, "because it's very inclusive, it doesn't necessitate any particular racial makeup. You can be mixed and still be Chicana, because of course that's been going on for hundreds of years." She also considered herself to be mixed race.

Ana also had the experience of being perceived as White by White people and being recognized as "something" other than White by other mixed people and people of color. She referred to herself as "ambiguously beige," and said:

> I'm not as obviously racially something. Talking with other folks who are mixed race, we're used to walking into a room and saying, "Oh, I can tell that person is kind of mixed, or light skinned Black or whatever." I think because

I'm not obviously something, folks treat me in a general way they treat other folks, which for the most part was how they would treat White folks. It wasn't quite passing but there is some degree of acceptance or privilege that goes along with that. The more stuff I've had to deal with has been about my age in a professional context or being queer.

Ana wasn't always sure how people perceived her, but she didn't feel that she was treated in ways that were different from those around her, signifying that she may have passed for several races. Given her final remark, once again we see how the relevance of particular positionalities is impacted by context.

I, too, am sometimes presumed to be White and other times perceived as "something" other than White although people don't often know what that "something" is, unless I pronounce a word in Spanish. Similar to the experiences of many participants, it is most often White people who assume that I am White and people of color who recognize that I am "something" other than White. Speaking Spanish and having often worked with Latina/o communities serves as a marker of my Latina identity. However, outside of those contexts, frequently others assume I'm White. I feel most comfortable claiming a biracial identity, but I consider myself Latina as well. It is important to me to connect with other Latinas, and I never consciously desire to pass as White.

Those of us who frequently "pass," but not always, have the experience of visibly straddling racial/ethnic borderlands. None of the participants expressed a desire to pass as White, but Joanna mentioned explicitly that she enjoyed the fluidity of her identity. All the participants but Ana discussed a struggle to understand their ethnic positioning in relation to the assumptions of others. For some people, like Linda, Bobbi, and Joanna, it posed continual challenges to self-identity. For others, like Marta and Susan, they worked to not let others' assumptions affect how they viewed themselves. Some of the stories shared here remind us of the intersectionality of identities as they relate to oppression; we cannot assume that race is or will be the most prominent factor in mixed race women's lives in any given situation.

RARELY, BUT SOMETIMES PERCEIVED TO BE WHITE

Maria, Janet, Diana, and Katherine were sometimes assumed to be White, but rarely. Two of the women were most often identified as their racial/ethnic background of color. Maria was most often recognized as Latina or Mexican. However, sometimes she was mistaken for other ethnicities as well, as she described in the narrative about the nightclub used as the opening for the previous chapter. Diana was most often assumed to be Black. Janet and Katherine were recognized most often as not being White, but most people were not sure about their racial/ethnic backgrounds.

Maria was a fairly light skinned Latina who resembled her Mexican relatives in terms of physical features. She had a Spanish name[30] and given this, as soon as she introduced herself to anyone, they would most likely assume that she was Latina. However, when she did not share her name, there were times, because of her light skin (and people's ignorant assumptions), when others would assume she was White. She recognized that her name was a huge marker of her Latina identity and wondered how her life might be different if she didn't have a Spanish name.

> Like I said earlier, like my name, I have a Brown name. I don't know what my life would be like if I had gone through with a different name and having to explain myself in a different way. Nobody asks me to explain, like there are so many assumptions made around people of color in the U.S. today.

As a result, Maria was firm in her Latina/Chicana/Mexican identity, although she claimed a mixed race identity as well. Nonetheless, as described in earlier chapters, she at times struggled with simultaneous challenges to her Latina identity.

Diana was a light skinned Black woman. At age 56, having been raised in an earlier generation when "one drop of Black blood" made you Black, she had historically claimed a Black identity, although more recently she had begun claiming a mixed identity as well. Although most often people positioned her as a Black woman, sometimes people assumed that she was White. Other times people were not sure what her background was, as her narrative attests in a previous chapter about the incident with the racist gas station attendant. At the time she was interviewed, Diana had dyed her hair blond and found that she was treated differently by White people who then assumed she was White. In the group interview, in response to a comment Mindy had made about White people expecting her to act White, Diana said:

> That's actually happened to me since I've dyed my hair blond. There is this big shift with White people. They all strike up these conversations and they're so embracing of me. Whereas before that didn't happen.

Diana stated that she never desired to pass as White but, as someone who held a high powered business position, she recognized that she was expected to look and act as White as possible in order to succeed in the business world. Later in the group interview she explained why she did not want to pass as White:

> That's exactly why I don't want to be White, because I'm at home in my ethnic culture. I feel a warmth, acceptance. I feel happiness, as opposed to putting on this façade and straightening your hair, and speaking the King's English and having collard greens, or whatever it is. There's so much effort to pretend, that I just want to relax and do what I enjoy with people I like.

Because Diana felt culturally Black and needed to straighten her hair to "appear White" she did not desire to be White; she stated that identifying with Whiteness was a façade. This was especially true for her because she was raised as a Black person, in a Black neighborhood, and attended predominately Black schools in a time where mixed race Black people were considered to be Black. However, reading her story, one might wonder why she refused to straighten her hair yet chose to dye it blond, a hair color associated with White people. This action complicates the degrees to which a mixed person might refuse or adopt White cultural identity markers.

Janet had brown skin but was raised as a young child in a predominately White neighborhood and while growing up she mostly thought of herself as White. Others sometimes knew she was part Mexican, but her identity wasn't always clear to people. She explained:

> And so one of the things I remember from when I was young was my friend saying to me, like always complimenting me on my skin, you know, and wanting to be tan like me. Not necessarily wanting to be a Brown person, but like wanting to be like who they are [White], but tanner, you know? They'd say things like, "How do you stay like that? Like how do you tan so well?"

It was clear to her that her brown skin was only desirable when linked to a White identity. Although Janet thought of herself primarily as White when she was young, her identity had been shifting, and at the time of the study she identified as a woman of color, as Latina, and as mixed race. Throughout her life, most often people wondered what she was and didn't know what to assume. She added later in her interview:

> So yeah, based on that, I think people, I mean strangers, see me in all sorts of different ways. And then I feel like I've had some friends that have seen me as White, too, for sure. I have a White friend, who used to live here, who's definitely one of my best friends, and maybe she's just starting to think about race a little more or something, but she moved back in town recently, and something came up, and she asked me…she was kind of like, like it was just hitting her, she was like, "Wow, you're like a Brown person." Or "You definitely identify yourself as a person of color don't you?" And I said, "Yes."

Because Janet had been White-identified, her friends who had known her when she was younger perceived her as White. However, her changing self-identity began to cause others to perceive her differently.

Janet was one of the participants who frequently got asked, "What are you?" She said, "I remember having to answer that question a lot." She felt that she was at a crossroads in her identity formation. She said:

> I think, I mean, just the more I talk about this and think about how my identity has changed. I really see myself changing a lot in the next few years, and I don't know exactly where I'll go with that. But I definitely feel like

something is rising up in me, and I don't really know like where that's going to go, or what I'm going to do with that, but I think there's just a lot of things that I have to figure out around my identity too. And like also reconciling where I come from too, and like where I lived and the experiences that I've had. It's like I need…I just think there's some way I need to deal with those to kind of like settle them. Not necessarily bury them, but just to make peace with them, and to really think more about who I'm going to become and what I'm going to do with my knowledge, too, you know? I definitely see media being a part of that. And I'm really interested in other people sharing those stories, and that's definitely one thing that I want to do. But I definitely feel this change coming on, and it's, like, slow, but I feel it coming.

Janet's transitions to living in a city with many Brown people and working in an organization with a social justice orientation positioned her in a place in which she was able to critically reflect on her experiences and her ethnic/racial identity. For Janet, it appears as if her immersion in a White community is what contributed to her perceiving herself as White. Because she had brown skin and a Brown last name, in another context she might have never identified as White and passed.

Katherine was perhaps the most racially ambiguous of the participants. She was Joanna's sister and mixed Black and White. Although Joanna said of Katherine, "You'd never think she's White," Katherine herself recognized that there were times when people thought she might be of European descent. I asked Katherine, "How do you think others perceive you?" She responded:

Well, looking at me I don't know, because just judging from the questions people have asked me, a lot of times people ask me what I am. I say they should guess. I've gotten called everything. I get spoken Spanish to a lot. People guess I'm from the Middle East somewhere, Mediterranean, Mexican, things like that, Filipino. I've studied abroad in Japan; I've had people ask me if I'm part Japanese. People have said all kinds of different things in terms of my appearance. Definitely Black people see me as mixed, part Black, although I know Black people who are surprised. In terms of how people see me, my internalized identity, I don't even know.

Thus, Katherine was constantly questioned about her identity and people made myriad assumptions about her ethnic and racial background, putting her in the position of constantly having to identify herself. Her most common response was, "I'm just mixed Black and White." She added, "If the person gives me a bad feeling in the way they ask and I don't want to talk about it much, I might just say, 'I'm mixed.'"

Katherine's best friends in high school were Black, and she identified as Black, but she was still nervous about being accepted by her Black high school friends and often felt she had to "prove" herself. She explained:

I wanted to be accepted by my Black friends. Even though I know they did. In high school they always did at the time. In high school there was a lot of struggles with that. I remember being pretty nervous about that at different times during different conversations, sort of like I had to prove something. Getting really sensitive to little comments. I remember one time one of my friends was dating this boy, and some of [my] other friends were talking about it, about her dating a White boy. And I was like, "It's not right that she's dating a White boy?" And I realized I should be careful of what I do and what does that mean with who I'm around. But I never said anything about it to them.

Katherine, as a result of feeling she needed to prove herself, worked hard to understand and fit in with the culture of the Black girls around her and was cautious about what she shared. Katherine's first boyfriend was White and having heard her friends' thoughts on dating White guys, she didn't want to introduce him because she feared her friends would then perceive her as White. She elaborated:

A lot of times, in terms of dating or what groups I hang out with, I definitely notice I have felt that people see those choices that I make as the choice of my identity. If I date a White person then it's my preference to be White. I don't think I've consciously thought [about it] that much, but that's been a concern that I have.

For Katherine, she was worried that not only would her friends disapprove of her choices but that they would then believe she wanted to be White and thus not accept her in their Black community. She said, "I still feel like I have to prove myself."

Katherine shared this story of being questioned about her identity by a Black woman:

Funny, I was talking to a friend the other day. She's Black. And when we had first met, we were taking the same class for a while before we actually talked to each other. And one of the first times we talked, she asked me what's my ethnic background. The other day we were talking about how there's a lot, quite a number of people who can't interact with me until they know the answer to that question... And she said, yeah, for her, she felt really uncomfortable around me until she knew. And the reason was that she grew up as a Black girl being taught that you present yourself a certain way with White people and you present yourself a certain way with Black people. You're kind of a different person around different people. She didn't know who to be around me because she didn't know who I was, and she didn't know what I would expect of her and what she could say to me.

Although this statement was disturbing to Katherine, she understood it, especially in the context of racism. Black people learn to act a certain way around White people for survival. Katherine admitted that she had learned the same. Although Katherine never tried to pass as White and consciously claimed both Black and biracial identities, she recognized that there were different ways of acting culturally that helped her gain greater acceptance in each community. Her story provides insight into why people might ask about racial and ethnic background – so in turn they know how to act. The implications of this, however, vary greatly based upon the racial/ethnic identity of the asker.

Katherine also traveled to several Asian countries and had a strong appreciation for diversity. She said:

> I definitely feel the need to have a lot of friends of color, and Black friends. What's important for me is that all the friends I have allow me to feel like I feel, closer to myself around all of them.

In other words, it was important for her to find friends with whom she could be herself. Sometimes that was difficult when she battled challenges to her identity. When she was dating a White man, she particularly had trepidation over admitting to her Black friends that she was involved with a White man. Traveling gave her some reprieve from being constantly confronted about her racial identity. She explained that when she was in Japan she "felt relieved." She said, "I didn't need to think about racial identity because I was American." She felt, and was recognized as, "American" above all else, and although that brought challenges, it was a welcome respite from the constant racial identity challenges she faced in the United States.

Thus for Katherine, she was almost never perceived as White by others, but she was rarely recognized as being mixed Black and White. She never desired to "pass" for White; on the contrary she wanted to be recognized as, at least part, Black. One of her biggest obstacles has been constantly facing identity challenges and questions.

Although all these women were rarely assumed to be White, all of them had the experience and thus understanding of what it meant to be treated as White. However, for this group, those moments were often fleeting. Diana's description of the treatment she received by White people as a blond, in contrast to her experiences with White people as a Black woman, begins to provide a glimpse into the distinction between the experiences of White people and people of color, especially in how they are treated by White people. Although these women were rarely perceived as White, three of them – Maria, Janet, Katherine – struggled with how to authenticate their connection to their heritages of color in the face of challenges to their racial identifications. Diana, having been firmly rooted in an all-Black community as a child, did not describe the same challenges to proving her Black identity. She was the only person who shared stories of feeling forced to act and look more White in order to maintain her job.

Thus, all of them constantly faced challenges to their identities and being asked to prove themselves in certain ways.

NEVER ASSUMED TO BE WHITE

Only three participants said they never pass for White – Brittney, Alana, and Ruth. All of them are mixed Black and White and all of them have dark skin. They recognized that they would never pass as White in terms of skin color. Two of them – Alana and Ruth – approached the concept of passing from slightly different angles than the rest of the group. Brittney did not discuss passing at all.

Alana said, "Okay, so growing up, being around my father, it was a blunt reminder to myself and other people that I was Black, even though, you know, I would never pass as White." Yet, Alana felt that having a White mother provided her with a "sort of affirmation" and "a sort of power." It brought her "cultural Whiteness" (as described in Chapter 5) which helped her to navigate culturally White institutions such as academia. Thus although she could never pass for White, she recognized that she still benefitted from White privilege. With shame, Alana admitted that in school, as a result of wanting to fit in and survive in a predominately White space, she tried to do what she could to fit in with her White peers. As discussed in Chapter 4, as a result of internalized racism, she really wanted to be "associated with White folk."

In contrast, Ruth discussed how she has always resisted passing in all forms. Although she did not have the capacity to pass for White, she could pass for straight, and used that as an example of how she resisted passing in general. She said:

Passing in general is something that I really resist. I don't like passing for straight, because I'm not straight, and whenever I start getting male attention I freak out and I have to like, to do something.

She speculated, "And I think if I were lighter, and passed for White, perhaps I would still feel the need to make sure everybody upfront knew [I was mixed]." Ruth had no desire to pass. Ruth, throughout her stories, stood out in her bravery to be herself in whatever situation she was in, even when her ways of being stood in contrast to those around her. Recall, for example, her story of being beat up after school by students who didn't want to accept her, the "punk rocker Black girl."

Alana, Ruth and Brittney all lived in different cities. Although Alana and Ruth could not pass for White, both of them thought critically about the issue of passing in relation to their lives. Brittney never discussed the issue of passing in relation to her life. This could be due, in part, to the fact that passing was not discussed explicitly in the Albuquerque group interview. Passing was discussed in both the Boston and Oakland group interviews. Brittney was also younger and less political than either Ruth or Alana, which are factors that may weigh into thoughts about passing.

CONCLUSION

Stories of passing reveal nuances of privilege and oppression. To understand these, it is helpful to note patterns that emerged. First, none of the women consciously chose to pass as White. It was imposed upon them. The participants chose different ways to identify – sometimes as mixed, sometimes in relation to their heritage of color, sometimes switching between the two – but none of them stated that they wanted to be perceived as White.

Second, the degree to which they were perceived to be White did not necessarily correlate directly with their connection to their heritages of color and their security in their identity. Participants in each category on the continuum of "passing" as White felt secure in their identities – Elizabeth, Marta, Diana and Ruth, for example. There were also women – such as Tina, Linda, Janet and Alana – who struggled with their self-identities in each category. In other words, being perceived as White didn't necessarily make people question their identities of color and/or mixed race identities and being perceived as a person of color didn't necessarily make participants feel secure in their identities as people of color and/or mixed race women. Some of the women internalized others' perceptions and subsequently questioned their identity claims – Tina, Mindy and Janet, for example. Other women, such as Elizabeth, Marta and Ruth, learned how to disengage from others' challenges and stand firm in their positionalities, even as they shifted.

Third, being perceived as White created both pain and privilege. There were several stories acknowledging privilege when others perceived them to be White. Elizabeth, for example, talked about how the Filipina/os in her life valued Whiteness. Linda acknowledged that her Whiteness brought her privilege. Diana talked about the greater degree of acknowledgement she received from White people when she dyed her hair blond and was perceived as White. Yet, being perceived as White also brought pain. Mindy, for example, was expected to perform Whiteness in certain ways by White people, and when she did not live up to the expectations, she felt ostracized. In addition, although her Filipina mom revered her Whiteness, because Mindy acknowledged the link to colonialism and White supremacy, the praise she got was disconcerting to her because she recognized it as a sign of internalized racism. Bobbi talked about the painful experience of hearing negative comments about her own race. Janet discussed the confusion she felt in forming her identity as a person singled out for her brown skin. Oftentimes passing as White is automatically associated with privilege, yet because of the continuing presence of White supremacy, for these mixed race women, "passing" as White also brought pain and struggle.

Fourth, as has been a theme throughout all the chapters thus far, the women's identities shifted in varying contexts; they exemplify the notion of translocational positionality and highlight operations of White power. The women learned to act in distinct ways based on the situations they encountered. Katherine, for example, explained that she learned to act differently among White and Black people. Diana also shared stories of how she was expected to act (speaking the "King's English") and look a certain way (straightening her hair) to succeed in the business world with White people who held power.

Fifth, passing was an issue in these women's lives, not only in terms of "passing" as White but also in relation to passing as people of color. Several of the women shared stories of anxiety about being fully accepted by their communities of color and/or being accepted as people of color in general. While passing as White was not important to these women, being accepted as people of color, as Latina, as Black, and Asian, for example, was important.

Sixth, although passing in terms of race related to all these women's lives in some way, there was another issue of passing that was raised – passing as straight. Although there were eight queer, bisexual, or lesbian women in the group, only two discussed passing in terms of sexuality. They fell on opposite ends of the spectrum in relation to their values about passing for straight. Ruth said that she resists passing overall, and Joanna said that it is important that both she and her partner be able to pass for straight. For Joanna, she feared homophobia much more than she feared racism.

Passing is a complex issue because it is tied to issues of power and privilege. Although race is a social construct (Omi & Winant, 1994), the effects of racism are real in their consequences. As much as we might like to believe that we are the creators of our fates, the possibilities to which we have access are constrained to some extent by the social categories to which we belong, race being one. Given the topic of this research, race is highlighted, but it is also important to remember that social positionalities intersect, as do the related complex workings of power, privilege, and oppression. Race and hierarchy "are indelibly wed" (Dalton, 2002), but hierarchy is also played out in relation to gender, sexuality, and social class. Thus, racial politics are always tied to politics of gender, sexuality, and class-status.

Unfortunately, Whites are often blinded by issues of race and unable or unwilling to see themselves in racial terms (Bonilla-Silva, 2006; Dalton, 2002). Nonetheless, this does not stop many White people from believing that their ways of being are the best, most effective ways of being. With this self-perception comes an expectation that, if given the chance, all other people would want to be perceived as White.

Throughout history there have been attempts by mixed people and people of color to be considered White in hopes of gaining access to White privilege. Other times a label of "White" has been imposed upon people. Since the start of the colonized United States, Blacks have been assigned a subordinate status to Whites. In addition, the racial designation "Black" was placed upon anyone with "one drop of Black blood." However, now that the social construction of race is more widely accepted, the one drop rule is losing ground. Racial categories have developed and changed over time as White scientists have coded certain physical differences as belonging to distinct *types* of individuals (Spickard, 1992).

Just as the categorization of Blacks has changed over time, so have the categorizations and rights of various Asian ethnic groups. For example, Chinese people were not eligible for citizenship until 1952 even though Chinese laborers had been contracted to come to the United States beginning in the early 1850s (Takaki, 1998). Similarly, the definitions and distinctions of "Hispanics" have fluctuated over time. Mexican Americans, for example, "were accorded the racial status of White people" however "socially, politically, and economically…they were treated as non-Whites" (Foley, 2002, p. 49). Thus, although "Hispanic" is officially, according to government designations, an ethnic category comprised of Mexicans, Colombians, Puerto Ricans, Cubans, Dominicans, and other Latino ethnic groups, Latino people have historically been treated as people of color (Foley, 2002).

Although White people may not acknowledge individual and institutional White privilege, Whiteness is nonetheless linked to institutional power and privilege (Johnson, 2006). As a result, various people of color throughout history have tried to gain access to White identities and White privilege. One might assume that people would choose to gain access to privilege whenever possible. However, the women in this study provided several examples of the ways in which they repeatedly rejected White racial identities. That said, it is important to acknowledge that the majority of these women *had the privilege* of rejecting White identities. As Applebaum (2010) asserts, "One cannot transcend the social system that frames how one makes meaning of oneself and the social world within which one is embedded" (p. 14). Even if we reject imposed White identities, there are still several ways in which we may benefit from White privilege regardless. Furthermore, risks taken to reject racial identities vary greatly based on other forms of privilege a person may have. These middle class women, including myself, have social class status to fall back upon when standing up against racism and implicit forms of White supremacy, such as conformity to White cultural ways of being. While middle class status may add privilege, gender identities among these women might add to a marginalized status. We see that sexism factors into experiences related to race, for example as shared in other chapters, in the form of sexual harassment. Experiences of being rendered invisible or overlooked may be impacted as much by gender dynamics as race-based politics. Although Joanna never made the explicit link between her desire to pass as straight and her racial identity, it is important to consider what the distinct implications may be for her to come out as a queer or bisexual woman (both terms she used to describe herself) given her social positionality as someone who does not always benefit from White privilege. Location, context, and intersectionality of social positionalities matter. When one is struggling to be accepted, for instance, in communities of color as a mixed race woman, how might coming out impact that struggle? The complex issue of Whiteness will be further addressed in the next chapter.

CHAPTER 7

SECRET AGENT INSIDERS TO WHITE PEOPLE

Disdaining, Denying, and Reconciling Whiteness

I feel like I'm the secret agent insider to White people because my family's White. But I don't feel like I'm a White person. – Bobbi

The excerpt below is a conversation from the Oakland group interview that begins to illuminate the complexity of Whiteness in relation to these women's lives.

Bobbi: Like I don't consider my mom a racist person. I consider her a White person who has xenophobia as part of her culture. Like how my mom doesn't get it [racism], when I really need her to understand that someone is being messed up to me at the straw market in the Bahamas. I don't think that's racism, I just think that she's a White person and she's not seeing it. You think that's racism?

Alana: Yes I do.

Bobbi: I just think that's their culture.

Alana: It's a racist culture. It's part of White supremacy.

Bobbi: Have you guys ever read Cheikh Anta Diop? He's an anthropologist. He has a theory called the "two cradle theory." It's all about how people evolved in a society with limited resources. European people evolved only caring about their family unit, and all their stuff.[31] To me I just don't think it's something to change, I think it's just natural. That's just how they are.

Linda: So when you grow up with scarcity that produces xenophobia?

Bobbi: Yeah.

Silvia: How you define xenophobia?

Bobbi: People that hate outsiders, people like – and not just people that are distrustful, but people who hate them. I was telling you how I can't even read books by White people any more. Like a book will be about something totally different like Virginia Woolf or Hemingway and they always got to be talking shit about somebody. Nobody else [but White people] would write like that. It's like an obsession with other people and putting them down.

Silvia: How do you reconcile that with the White people in your life that you love? How do you reconcile believing it's just the way they are, like your mom?

Bobbi: Well I love my mom. And I think my mom is like, you know, special. She's not like that. I don't know. I don't think about it.

Marta: How do we reconcile that that is us?

Silvia: Yeah, that's a deeper question.

Linda: That is me. And that is why I'm trying to reconcile that. And like, you know, that is me, for sure. Maybe not to that degree, but there are times when I catch myself, and I'm like, "Whoa!"

Alana: Yeah.

Linda: I feel like it's outside myself, you know? But it's not, it is me.

Many aspects of Whiteness – what it is, how it is enacted, who is considered White, disdain for Whiteness, denying Whiteness, recognizing Whiteness in actions, White racism, White supremacy – arose in several individual interviews and were a large part of the conversation in two group interviews. In the exchange above, a dialogue that occurred in the middle of the Oakland group interview, the women were grappling with the complexity of what it means to recognize the negativity of White cultural ways of being (as some of them see it) in both family members and in themselves. There is a desire to externalize Whiteness – to speak about it from an outsider perspective.

Situating these women's stories within critical whiteness[32] theory brings new questions to current frameworks of critical whiteness and raises particular analytic questions regarding how the women define and interpret their experiences with Whiteness. Applebaum (2010) explained:

> Critical whiteness studies has developed as a result of a shift in understanding racism as exclusively a matter of overt practices involving prejudice or antipathy to understanding racism as a system in which covert and subtle forms of institutional, cultural and individual practices produce and reproduce racial injustice. (p. 8)

It is important to note that these "subtle" forms of racist practices are often only subtle for White people who lack the critical consciousness to see the systemic injustice in their practices. Authors writing about critical whiteness theory (Applebaum, 2008, 2010; DiAngelo, 2006; Hytten & Warren, 2003; Moon, 1999; Thompson, 2003) focus on the ways that White people are complicit in the maintenance of systemic racial oppression, often unintentionally. Uncovering White complicity in racism has often centered on deconstructing individual and collective investments in a "good" White identity (Moon, 1999; Thompson, 2003); "racism is often perpetuated through *well-intended* white people" (Applebaum, 2010, p. 3). Given that many of the mixed race women were perceived, at least at times, to be White, some might assume that they would likely fall within White conceptions of Whiteness in this critical whiteness theory; however, their perspectives often disrupted key aspects of Whiteness as defined within critical whiteness theoretical frameworks. For example, rather than having an investment in being "good" Whites, they often exposed negative aspects of Whiteness. Yet connections to White people, particularly through family, made this exposure double-edged. Furthermore, critical whiteness theorists (Applebaum, 2008, 2010; Hytten & Warren, 2003; Thompson, 2003) have argued that operations of Whiteness are mostly invisible to the people who benefit from it; in contrast, these stories reveal that the majority of the women could identify various aspects of Whiteness as they relate to privilege and oppression. I return to this critical whiteness theoretical framework in the chapter's conclusion, after the stories take center stage.

In the dialogue above, Bobbi was struggling to reconcile her mom's ignorance around issues of racism, denying that her mom was racist. Instead she argued that xenophobia was a "natural" part of her mom's White culture. She later defined xenophobia as people who hate and put down outsiders. When I challenge her to explain how she reconciled that in relation to her mom, Bobbi replied that she didn't think her mom was like that. Her mom was "special." So in the end, her argument unraveled. However, reconciling the argument is not what matters most; what the dialogue reveals is that, as mixed race women, we face the challenge of trying to understand White family members' ignorance about – and complicity in – racism, and White supremacist ways of being. In addition, we struggle to understand how negative aspects of Whiteness relate to our own lives. There is significant resistance to owning Whiteness to any degree.

As I previously stated, none of the women, including myself, wanted to be called White. No one identified as White and several stated specifically that they didn't consider themselves to be White. However, all of us had a White parent so we had some connection to Whiteness. All but one of the participants were raised at least in part by their White parent, sometimes exclusively by single White moms and sometimes by both parents. In addition, most of us "passed" for White to some degree. Thus, the deep question, as asked by Marta above is, "How do we reconcile our Whiteness?" In the individual and group interviews, many of the women provided clear descriptions of the ugliness associated with cultural Whiteness. The participants named specific undesirable characteristics of cultural Whiteness, and some women expressed a desire to avoid White people whenever possible. Whiteness was associated with racism and White supremacy, ways of being to which none of us wanted to be related. Yet, some participants delved into the conflict of recognizing cultural Whiteness and/or white skin privilege within themselves.

CONNECTION TO WHITENESS

There were several discussions in which the negative aspects of cultural Whiteness were identified. The conflict in defining cultural Whiteness occurred when we struggled to position our White family members, White partners, White friends, and ourselves in relation to these individual and co-created definitions of Whiteness. As a participant observer, I often engaged in these discussions, sharing personal stories. As a facilitator, I often challenged the participants to further explain their thinking in terms of how they positioned themselves in relation to their concepts of Whiteness, and sometimes I was challenged by participants to further explain my positionality as well.

In the Oakland focus group, Linda introduced the topic of Whiteness early on in the conversation, and it remained a theme throughout the interview, as evidenced in the opening dialogue above. Exemplified in the opening quote by Bobbi, most participants spoke as if they understood and could define Whiteness – not from a personal perspective as White people, but as "secret agent insiders." Bobbi was raised primarily by her White mom, giving Bobbi insight into Whiteness, yet she also grew up with African Americans and Somali people and, as a mixed woman, she did not identify as White even though she had an intimate connection to Whiteness and White people. Alana, who would never pass for White said, "It's the cultural Whiteness that I really identify with." She was raised primarily by her White mom and grew up surrounded by White people, spending time occasionally with her African American dad. Having been hurt by many racist White people, Alana stated that she did not feel safe anymore in White spaces. Nonetheless she retained the capacity to move within them when necessary. Linda chimed in that she also had the same "cultural knowing" of how to be in White spaces.

At that point in the interview, I acknowledged the varying levels of consciousness in the group about race relations and race politics, and added that with that consciousness there appeared to be, among the women, "a critique and also lots of anger." The group responded with lots of "mm-hmms" and then bold laughter. Linda spoke up naming the sentiment behind the collective response stating, "Isn't it interesting that we all like started laughing because I think that there is this nervousness because we all know that one of our parents is White." She shared a story of going to Bobbi's house and seeing a picture of Bobbi's (White, blond, blue eyed) mom and asking, "Is that your mom?" with perhaps some sort of surprise in her voice. She remembers that Bobbi's response felt very protective as she replied something to the effect of, "Yeah, that's my mom and I love her very much; she's very important to me." Linda explained that the nervousness in the group about critiquing Whiteness came from having a real connection to White people and added, "That dichotomy of how we feel about our own Whiteness is really about ourselves."

This led to another exchange that revealed more about Whiteness in relation to their lives:

Bobbi: I feel guilty that I don't feel White. And I feel like, I don't know, I was telling you I feel fucked up because if I walk into a room and it's like all White people, I'm like, "Oh, god." But if I walk into a room of Filipino people, I feel more comfortable around them. Like if I walk into a job and they're all Korean people, I'm just like, "Wow, okay, that's cool." And it's weird. It's like, am I shady, or...?

Linda: (interrupting) It's that we live in a fucked up society where there is a reminder that we have to experience oppression and White supremacy, you know? And if you're not White then you're going to experience some sort of oppression. So of course you are going to be like, "Oh, you're Korean? Okay cool." Because you're like, "At some point in your life, you've had some experiences similar to mine." You know?

First Bobbi admitted that in addition to not feeling White, she didn't feel comfortable around a group of all White people. She was more likely to feel comfortable in a group of all people of color, even if they didn't share her background. She was confused by this and questioned her feelings. Linda took an educative role in that moment and explained to Bobbi that because she had experienced oppression (something we already knew from Bobbi's stories) it made sense that she was going to be leery of White people who might enact White supremacy. It's understandable that Bobbi would feel more comfortable with people of color who would be more likely to share experiences of oppression.

Bobbi listened to Linda's response and continued with her concerns, opening up a dialogue with other members of the group.

Bobbi: But I feel like I just don't like to talk to them [White people]. I just don't want to be in their company, you know? Like not to be – I just feel like, I just feel like there's something very aggressive and selfish with them.

Tina: But at the same time you feel guilty for being half White?

Bobbi: And I feel, I don't know, I just don't feel aggressive and selfish. (Lots of laughter by everybody.) So I'm like, "Why am I viewing a group of people in that way?" You know? Like Somali people, I've met aggressive and selfish Somali people, you know? But I just, I really just don't feel like I'm like that. So I just don't know what's wrong with all of them. But then I feel like, you know that's fucked up because I'm thinking of them as all one thing, and that's stupid, you know? I was racist.

Linda: No you're prejudiced. You don't have the power to be racist.

Alana: Actually I do feel aggressive and selfish, like I feel like I take up a lot of space in spaces of color. This is something that I'm working on, like for the first time here [living in the Bay Area]. I don't think I'm experiencing... it's just weird. I don't want to say anything like White guilt because I think it's very different, but I've experienced a lot of class guilt for the first time here I think. And it's really since I've been immersed in spaces with predominantly people of color for the first time in my entire life. And it's like all these ways that like, sort of like this other sense of entitlement that's in my culture... I was talking with Silvia earlier [about] the first house I lived in with all women of color, they were all first and second generation immigrant families from all over the world. And I grew up as an only child with my White mom, and I'm a spoiled brat; I'm used to getting my way all the time. It was really intense to be confronted day after day after day after day of the ways that my privilege, because I was acculturated in Whiteness, how that played out in like the way that I live, and the way that I interact in the world, and how I take up a lot of space, how I'm demanding, all these things. So this is like something that I attribute only to Whiteness. All those bad qualities that I have, they are specifically White to me.

Bobbi: Are we right to attribute that to Whiteness?

Alana: I mean like yeah, I think, because I don't notice those things come up for me when I'm around other White people. It's exactly, it's totally normalized to like, to take up space, to speak when not spoken to, to live life in a certain way.

In the dialogue above the group begins to describe what cultural Whiteness entails. Bobbi describes White people as "aggressive and selfish." Immediately Tina challenges Bobbi asking if she feels guilty for being half White. Throughout Tina's interviews, her stories about herself and her identity resonated White guilt; so her question can be interpreted to be as much about her own feelings about herself as it might be about Bobbi. Bobbi, in response, didn't claim guilt, but rather, once again distanced herself from Whiteness, claiming that she didn't possess those "White characteristics" of aggressiveness and selfishness. However, then she wondered out loud if it was racist of her to label those characteristics as "White."

Linda, once again taking an educative role, informed Bobbi that her comment was not racist. It was prejudiced. Linda's view came from a theory of diversity and social justice in which racism is defined as "racial prejudice plus power." Definitions from the book, *Teaching for Diversity and Social Justice* can help further elaborate on Linda's point. Prejudice is "a set of negative personal beliefs about a social group that leads individuals to prejudge people from that group or the group in general, regardless of individual differences among members of that group" (Goodman & Shapiro, 1997, p. 118). Thus, one can see how Bobbi's comment was a prejudiced one. Social power is defined as "[a]ccess to resources that enhance one's chances of getting what one needs or influencing others in order to lead a safe, productive, fulfilling life" (Griffin, 1997, p. 73). In the book there is an elaborate explanation of how oppression operates; social group membership (for example membership to the White race), because of historical inequalities, creates differing access to social power and privilege depending on whether or not your membership is that of a target group or an agent group. Putting racial prejudice and power together, racism is defined as "The systematic subordination of members of targeted racial groups who have relatively little social power in the United States (Blacks, Latino/as, Native Americans, and Asians), by members of the agent racial group who have relatively more social power (Whites)" (Wijeyesinghe, Griffin, & Love, 1997, p. 88). Within that theoretical framework, only White people can be racist. Negative comments made by people against White people and other people of color are considered prejudiced but not racist. Linda names that distinction, arguing that because Bobbi is not White she cannot be racist.

Steering the dialogue away from a more abstract discussion of racism and prejudice, Alana personalized Bobbi's claim in relation to her own life and admitted that she did feel "aggressive and selfish." In fact, through the use of the phrase "when I am around *other* White people [emphasis added]" she positioned herself in relation to White people, rather than in opposition to White people. Alana then added to the growing definition of cultural Whiteness, remarking that she "takes up a lot of space" and is "demanding." She specifically attributed those qualities to Whiteness; however, earlier she made a connection between the negative attributes and middle class social status. This raises the question, are these specifically White *middle/upper class* ways of being? Bobbi, still unsure, again asked if it was right to attribute such characteristics to Whiteness. Alana thought the characteristics were White; her proof was that those qualities are normalized with White people, but not among people of color. As the focus group interview progressed, there was a continually unfolding definition of cultural Whiteness and sustained discussions about how the women perceived their relationship to Whiteness.

In the group, Bobbi shared a story in which she described White people as people who "don't ever want to learn anything new." The topic changed but returned again to the topic of Whiteness during which Linda revealed that she and her friends "talk shit about White people" in front of Linda's White girlfriend. Linda admitted that such comments were difficult for her girlfriend (and consequently her, because she cared about her girlfriend's feelings), yet she felt that her girlfriend shouldn't take them personally because she and her friends were referring to racism as an institution. She said to her girlfriend, "This is institutional, and this is you, and unless you are doing that fucked up shit, I'm not talking about you." From there, the group interview conversation developed into the dialogue at the opening of this chapter in which Bobbi discussed her mom and xenophobia. During the discussion related to struggles with reconciling Whiteness, Marta chimed in and said, "I think that for me it's different. I'm pretty proud of both sides. I'm not embarrassed by my White Jewish side." Bobbi then admitted that's how she felt she should be – proud of her White side.

At that point in the conversation, I spoke up, reflecting on their statements and adding my opinion. First, I recognized that everyone in the group up to that point had talked about wanting to have distance from, or even having hatred or disdain for Whiteness. I admitted that there is a part of me that also wants to be distanced from Whiteness, which is related to my desire for acceptance by people of color, and part of relating to people of color entails disdaining Whiteness. There were many head nods and uh-hmms in response to my statement. Marta was the first to speak, stating, "But I think I feel dishonest if I am like that. I feel like I have to deny my Whiteness that way when I'm with people of color." Linda confirmed her thought stating, "You do." Marta continued, "I hate American culture as much as the next person, but I'm also not willing to write off every person who is White." She then shared that one of her best friends is White and "she's never said anything offensive." Bobbi added another perspective and said, "Except for my mom, every family member on my White side is racist." Alana then stated that she has a lot of anger because many White people have hurt her. She said, "I have had a very conflicted relationship with White people always." For instance she loved her mom, but her mom also hurt her. In addition she had White friends who hurt her deeply but also White friends who were very supportive in a time when she most needed support. Alana then elaborated that it isn't so easy for mixed people to just choose to embrace their White cultural side because there is "the issue of power and the issue of imperialism and colonialism, which is dominated by White folk." It's just not "so simple," Alana explained.

Alana made an important point. There is something distinct about being a person mixed both White and of color. We and our family members are often victims of racism, yet we are expected to embrace cultural Whiteness, which entails a history of colonialism and imperialism. It means embracing our torturers. Yet, as Marta explains above, it is implausible to write off White people, not only because we have White family and friends, but also because we are part White. Still, embracing White culture is difficult because, as Alana asked, "What is White culture?"

CULTURAL WHITENESS AND OUR LIVES: LIKE HAVING A RELATIVE WHO'S A CRACKHEAD THAT YOU LOVE ANYWAY

A piecemeal definition of cultural Whiteness unfolded in the Oakland interview as: selfishness, aggressive behavior, taking up a lot of space, being demanding, being racist, and supporting White supremacy. In the Boston group interview, cultural Whiteness was a topic raised throughout as well, only it was discussed in a more abstract, much less personal manner. Diana introduced the topic of White culture early on in the interview opening a dialogue about White privilege and White supremacy. She said, "I don't think that most White people get it, but the country is

Browning...They don't know that there is a way to be White. They just think it's the normal way and everybody else is different." Joanna then speculated as to why White people may not understand that the country is Browning, wondering if it is because "a lot of people live in all-White neighborhoods in small towns." Joanna felt that "White people in the city, they are fully aware of the constant changing of the culture, that America is Browning. But the majority of White people... are not in the metropolitan areas." Then Mindy raised the issue of how the media portrays the topic, posing a question at the end that Diana answered.

> Mindy: But is that even reflected in our culture? Because every time the subject comes up, like I know *Time*[33] did the thing about the Browning of America and they had a picture of a woman who looked really kind of White. And it was like, this is the face of the new America? And it's like, well she looks pretty mixed. It's not, it's a less threatening sort of way that they're spinning the whole Browning of America. And then you have to think, what is so threatening about someone who's darker and someone who's not White?

> Diana: White supremacy is at stake.

> Mindy: Exactly.

Similar to the discussion in the Oakland group, these Boston based women argued that White people are invested in White supremacy. During the Oakland group interview, in response to Bobbi's speculation as to why White people might fear people of color, Alana argued that White culture is a racist culture connected to White supremacy. The Boston group interview argument above led to the same conclusion: "White supremacy is at stake."

Later in the Boston interview, Joanna referenced more popular media bringing up the cable television show *Black.White.*, which she said was "poorly done" but "interesting." The show highlighted two families, a White family and a Black family, the members of which wore make-up in order to "switch" races. They then shared their experiences "living" as a different race. Joanna admitted that she only saw the highlights but Mindy had seen the show and gave her analysis. She said:

> And I think the problem with that is that they never address White privilege. They never talk about the history of racism. It's just like "Oh, it's just a matter of perspective. We'll just have people put on face paint." And you know everyone's prejudiced. And that's not the history of the country. It's like since the 1600s there was this whole idea of White is best, and everyone else is Other.

In the statement above, Mindy expressed frustration because prejudice was portrayed in the show without acknowledgment of the historical context of White supremacy. Joanna added further analysis to Mindy's statement, saying, "Everyone is prejudiced but one group has always had the power." These comments echoed the Oakland group exchange in which Linda named the distinction between prejudice and racism and argued for the importance of recognizing power differences between Whites and people of color.

Mindy continued her point, stating that it is frustrating that "American culture" looks at "individuals" rather than "culture as a collective." She said, "They never say 'Oh, let's look at how Whites, or White ethnics have continually advanced.'" In response, Diana asked, "History books don't say that, do they?" Ruth replied, "History books don't tell any truths at all." At that point I spoke up and said, "It is getting better. There are books like *A People's History of the United States*." In the book, the author, Howard Zinn (1980), recounted history from multiple perspectives, including history from the perspectives of American Indians, Black people, women, and poor people. During individual interviews at people's homes, I had noticed that several of my participants had the book on their bookshelves, including Ruth. Ruth argued, "Yeah, but that's not required reading in school."

As the women in both group interviews talked, a collective vision of Whiteness unfolded. The participants' words demonstrated anger towards White people as a group, highlighting how "they" (Whites) act in racist ways and protect White supremacy. However, there was also an acknowledgement that racism and White supremacy are situated in a cultural context in which the media and history books shade the truth about oppression against people of color. Thus the conversation about Whiteness flowed from a focus on the actions of individuals, to that of White people as a collective, to an acknowledgement of institutional media and cultural influence.

More telling comments regarding views on cultural Whiteness surfaced in the interviews. At the end of the Boston interview, Katherine, who was one of the quieter group participants, said:

> One of the things that I said in my individual interviews – and I wonder if other people feel this – is that for me in thinking about Whiteness, I guess actually, through the process of interviews and reflecting on it, I see that one way I think about it is having the freedom not to think about this at all.

Katherine then made reference to her liberal White ex-boyfriend. Both she and he spent time doing work in different parts of Asia. His positionality as a White man afforded him the privilege to "choose" whom he wanted to work for, and he was always praised and rewarded for his work. He was never challenged in ways that would cause him to examine his Whiteness. Katherine, however, faced challenges in Asia related to her positionality as someone mixed Black and White. In her individual interview, Katherine explained how, for example, she was turned down for a job to teach English in Taiwan because "it's not really about teaching. A lot of it is for show. They really care to have a white faced, blue eyed person teaching them English." She had to send a picture with her application. There were a "gazillion jobs" Katherine said, and no one would hire her even though she had experience teaching English as a second language. She was surprised by the blatant discrimination: "They didn't try to hide it." Katherine said that it is warm in Taiwan and consequently she was tan and darker than she was while in Japan. Given that foreigners often perceive U.S. Americans as White people, in Taiwan she got questioned a lot more often about her American identity and was not hired for jobs. Katherine said, "I say it's because my skin is darker, but I don't know if that's the reason." In addition, her identity and her alliances were at times called into question because of the choices she made to work with a cultural group that was not her own. Katherine's comment came on the heels of a comment by Mindy about the difficulty of reconciling her identity and her relationship to Whiteness. Katherine was not "White enough" to be hired in some cases and she was simultaneously challenged for not choosing to work with African Americans.

I responded to Katherine's comment about White people having the freedom to not think about their Whiteness by sharing how I struggled with accepting a prestigious assistantship working with a Carnegie initiative, an assistantship that I knew meant I would be working predominately with White people within academia when I longed to do more community based work with people of color, as I had done prior to returning to graduate school. After applying for the assistantship I went away for a week during which time I contemplated what would be lost and gained personally if given the position. Feeling increasingly disconnected from communities of color in graduate school, I had decided I did not want the job, but upon return found out that I had been chosen for the position by both fellow classmates and faculty who had to weigh in on the choice. I shared with the group:

> And that was really hard. I think any White person would've been like, "Of course I want this assistantship. It's prestigious, it pays," all the stuff. But for me it was making a choice to not work with my community. And I think of my community predominantly as other Latinos and Latinas but also people of color.

In response, another participant, Joanna, shared her sense of isolation within her predominately White graduate program of trying to combine her career as an engineer with her personal interests of teaching children of color about engineering and serving as a role model. The White people around her did not have those kinds of goals. Thus, other aspects to add to the list of cultural Whiteness are the freedom to not think about what it means to be White and the liberty to not feel torn between succeeding in predominately White spaces and supporting people of color.

In the very last few minutes of the Oakland interview, Bobbi summed up the complexity of having a disdain for cultural Whiteness while negotiating having White people in your family. She said, "It's like having a relative who's a crackhead that you love anyway." A chorus of mm-hmms from the group rang out in response. Then Bobbi added, "It's like, what are you going to do?" In her mind, there was no choice but to accept and love the family and parts of ourselves that are difficult to face and sometimes cause pain.

Although one could surmise from these stories plenty of reasons why we might not want to be considered to be White, as the facilitator in the Boston group interview, I asked pointedly, "What makes it really important to not be identified as White?" Joanna responded first saying, "Fear of being seen as a sell-out. That's part of it." Ruth added:

> I think fear of being categorized in a group of people that I have a lot of opinions about, you know as far as, as far as what Whiteness is, just Whiteness. But I don't ever get mistaken for White.

Ruth is naming explicitly that it is hard to acknowledge a connection to something about which you have negative opinions. Ruth who "looks Black" would never get mistaken for White, but her White mom worked in the predominately Black K-8 school she attended, so those around her knew she had White heritage.

Katherine shared that she once was asked by a Black woman, who didn't understand why someone would not pass as White, given the option, "What is there to be gained by clearing misconceptions about who you are?" Katherine admitted that she "had a hard time answering her question." Others in the group wondered if the woman who asked was older (she wasn't much older than Katherine, who was 27), and Joanna, who was 23, argued that even though racism continues today, passing never feels like a matter of survival, as it might have in the past. She said:

> I feel perfectly comfortable to go through this world as a person of color... I think that part of it too is because I know that I'm not White. Even if I could pass for White in my skin tone, my parents, my mother and her race and her family have had an effect that – that's now my life, and the attachment that I feel to Black culture, and the way that I feel when I see images of Black culture on TV, and that's a part of who I am and my identity, and what I care about in the world. Even if no one knew that I was attached to my culture because it's part of my heritage, it's still a part of who I am.

Joanna acknowledged that she had the privilege to claim an identity as a person of color without fear of harm. She argued that this privilege stemmed from the fact that racism is not as life threatening as it used to be. Although this may be true, there are many other factors – her class privilege, her lighter skin tone, her residence in diverse cities, etc. – that may contribute to her "comfort" in "going through the world as a person of color." However, it is important to acknowledge that for Joanna, to claim to be White felt like denying her mom's culture, which meant denying a part of her identity and a culture to which she feels attached.

Diana validated Joanna's sentiment, exclaiming, "That's exactly why I don't want to be White. Because I'm at home in my ethnic culture." Diana's experiences, as a 56 year old woman raised in a predominantly Black community were distinct from Joanna's as a 23 year old woman raised in a Black and White racially mixed community. However, both of them emphasized the importance of their attachments to Black culture.

THE PERVASIVENESS OF CULTURAL WHITENESS

Discussions about Whiteness were not limited to the group interviews. They permeated the individual interviews as well. Whiteness relates to every major theme discussed thus far: positionality, insider/outsider status, fluidity and ambiguity, and passing. Yet Whiteness was such a prominent topic of discussion in the interviews that it warrants its own space. The women often had sophisticated analyses of Whiteness as a broader cultural concept as well as more personalized stories about how Whiteness related to their lives.

Participants approached Whiteness in distinct ways. These approaches were impacted by such factors as degrees of passing, the races of people they dated, academic knowledge about race issues, and political ideologies. Alana, a master's student in Education during the time of the interviews, often provided sophisticated analyses of White supremacy, colonialism, and Whiteness as a cultural concept. During a dialogue about dating, Alana discussed issues that came up for her when she dated White people. To explain her reactions, she said:

That's just the historical reality that we live in; Whiteness can't be separated from White supremacy and how White people benefit from racism. It's different. They're completely different things. Dating White people is really different than dating a person of color regardless of what their racial background is, you know?

For Alana, understandings of interactions with White people always included an acknowledgement of power differentials between White people and people of color.

Because Alana used the term cultural Whiteness in both her individual interviews and the group interview, in her second individual interview I asked her specifically, "What is cultural Whiteness?" She provided a more expansive, yet overlapping, definition to those collectively created in the group interviews. She said:

What is cultural Whiteness? That's a big question, because what is culture? It's hard to talk about it because White people are invisible, the culture is invisible, the mainstream, sort of dominant culture. Definitely, I would say it varies from place to place, and from region to region. Where I grew up I definitely think that there is something about everything, from theaters to music aesthetics to literary access, to knowledge, cultural capital and language – White references. I don't want to say popular culture references, but activities of leisure time and what you do in your spare time. I know part of that is class, but class and race are so mixed. Also family, like being in more isolated communities I think is very White, not being around as much extended family. Language, Standard English, you know, having access to that. A lot of it is just naming unnamed things, like ways of being, mannerisms, behaviors, knowing how to react, knowing how to decode behavior and knowing what someone's trying to say or not trying to say. And being able to not feel intimidated by certain authority positions, whether it be teachers, police officers, counselors, you know? Does that sort of answer your question?

In this definition, Alana touched upon some of the main points made in the group interviews, for instance that White culture is dominant and invisible. Whereas several of the comments about cultural Whiteness in the group interviews focused on individual characteristics of White people enacting White culture, Alana discussed cultural Whiteness in terms of access to and an implicit understanding of mainstream culture that permeates all aspects of culture including music, knowledge, language, and leisure time activities; she described cultural capital. In her last sentence she implied that cultural Whiteness also carries a sense of certainty or self-assuredness with cultural authority figures.

I asked Alana to elaborate on her earlier comment about cultural Whiteness being related to space. She responded:

Yeah, I definitely think that that's embedded within the culture. Even if you think about it going back historically, how White people take land, and this idea of land tenure, which was introduced to indigenous folks who didn't have that. Needing all this space and this land, and these resources, they [White people] were like, "Well you're not using it so we are going to buy it; we are going to take it from you." I think that really is embedded within the history of that.[34] And the types of things that White folks like to do in their spare time, which is very much about leisure and leisure being very much attached to citizenship in this country, being able to purchase that leisure for things like outdoor activities like skiing and golfing. Golf – I hate golf. Golf courses are just so wasteful… So even just thinking about, taking up a lot of physical space just with all the different things that need land, whatever. But also there's no space for the voice of the other. There is dominating of the knowledge base, you know? Like this semester in one of my classes we talked about codified cultural schemas. We talked about the scientific method as being a culturally codified schema. I thought that was so cool. Just like thinking about the way that science is culturally codified. Just like this absolute truth and absolute knowledge that goes uncontested. It's completely culturally situated, all the different ways of acquiring scientific knowledge… So thinking about the Enlightenment and how Western modernity dominates everyone's ways of thinking and rationalizing, normalizing.[35] All that stuff takes up a lot of space. So I think that definitely impacts the way that White people feel entitled to that space. And they feel entitled without earning it in any sort of way, you know? It's this unearned sense of entitlement just by virtue of being White. And that is embedded within the culture, whatever cultural Whiteness looks like. So I think that that's part of it, the ways that I have been acculturated. I definitely know that I have participated in that and it comes out.

Here, Alana provided a sophisticated definition of cultural Whiteness focusing on how it is embedded in the historical and cultural ways that White people think and take up space. Cultural Whiteness entails a historical legacy of colonialism with an uncontested concept that land can be owned, bought, and taken. Cultural Whiteness is also made visible through examining dominant ways of thinking, which relate to the concept of "rational thinking" and "absolute truth." Finally, cultural Whiteness is marked by unearned entitlement – to land, to space, to knowledge, to people. Class is an integral but unnamed factor in these definitions of cultural Whiteness. Although White entitlement can cross all class status groups, cultural Whiteness often operates differently among people depending on their socioeconomic status with a greater sense of entitlement correlating with more material wealth (Bonilla-Silva, 2006). Gender performativity too, of course, has an impact on how cultural Whiteness gets enacted. For example, exalting rational thinking is not only related to Whiteness, but also patriarchal notions about what kinds of knowledge should be most valued (Jaggar, 1989; Johnson, 2005).

The majority of the participants had a politicized, social justice oriented, critical consciousness. As such, identity formation and negotiations often involve a critique of personal behaviors and the behaviors of others in relation to conceptions of cultural Whiteness. For example, Alana, at several points in her interviews, critically examined her actions in relation to Whiteness. She acknowledged that she possessed cultural Whiteness and at times acted in culturally White ways. Alana, as an adult, chose to immerse herself in communities of color. This is because as someone who has experienced a fair amount of racism, she felt "safer" in groups with people of color than White groups. At the same time, she also appreciated the ways in which people of color challenge her to examine her privilege.

EXAMINING WHITE PRIVILEGE

As discussed in previous chapters, several women named and examined White privilege in relation to their lives. Bobbi, Alana, Ruth and Joanna have had prominent voices in this chapter thus far. Tina and Mindy, as two women who almost always were identified by others as White, both acknowledged their White privilege. Tina, for example, talked about how she would not get in trouble for inadvertently breaking things at work while her co-workers of color would. Mindy and Elizabeth both explained how, in their Filipina/o culture, Whiteness is revered. Katherine stated specifically that one of the benefits of being mixed is "White skin privilege." Similar to Katherine, in a discussion about why she felt called to be an ally to people who have darker skin, Marta said, "I have White skin privilege." Diana explained that she was treated with more respect and friendliness by White people when she dyed her hair blond and people assumed she was White. Susan shared how her mom always "tried to make [her] look more White." In her individual interviews, she discussed the privilege of having her White mom put her in school; her mom became her representative.

Whiteness was not discussed as much in the Albuquerque group interview or among the Albuquerque based participants. Maria, for example, talked more about racism than Whiteness in relation to her life. She did say that her "biggest challenges" came from her family in that both her mom and dad at times questioned her Chicana identity claim. Maria also acknowledged that the only other "Brown" person in her graduate program, who was Native, was also light skinned. She and her light skinned Native classmate would have conversations about what it meant to "technically" be the Brown people. Maria felt that the school had certain expectations of how she would act, perhaps White like them; her response was to bring up racism consistently and never "let anyone off the hook." I too noticed while in graduate school many of the people of color in my program were light skinned and/or mixed. I recognize that a very complicated relationship between racism and White privilege played out in my ability to be in graduate school and the fact that many other people of color were not represented.

Brittney took a less critical approach to race issues, stating that "race never really came up" for her. She emphasized her ability to get along with anybody and her desire to be friends with anybody regardless of race. Ana similarly said, "I feel like I've always been able to hold my own in all the spaces I go to." Brittney speculated, "New Mexico is really like mixed up, I think, anyway so it's not as common here to hear racist things as much." Ana added that instead for her, "negotiations were more about being a girl, or being gay, or something like that." Yet, Ana did say that "one of the greatest challenges is being asked to be a token sometimes," especially in work situations. Similar to Maria's experience in graduate school, Ana had the privilege of fitting in enough to be hired but then dealt with the racism of being tokenized. Janet was the one participant in the study who did not participate in a group interview. In her individual interviews she elaborated on her complicated relationship to Whiteness as a brown skinned person raised in a White community. So discussions of Whiteness and White privilege were present among the Albuquerque participants but there were no explicit discussions about what constitutes cultural Whiteness and White supremacy as there were among the participants in the other two cities.

Linda stands out among all the participants because of the quantity of time she spent discussing Whiteness in relation to her life. Recall that Linda lived in Oakland, her mom was Filipina, and her biological dad was White but was minimally present in her life. She was raised by her mom and Black stepfather and attended racially diverse schools in the Bay Area. Linda and I had numerous conversations about Whiteness in both of her individual interviews. Linda was sometimes perceived to be White, but not always. She worked in the Bay Area for a non-profit organization that promotes the rights of people of color; the entire staff was comprised of people of color. The interview exchanges I had with Linda about Whiteness were often very dialogical; I shared several stories and thoughts of my own in response to Linda's narrative. Many of these discussions came about as Linda processed her positionality in relationship to her friends, who were mostly women of color, and her partner, Tracy, who was White. In light of the politics of Whiteness and racism, for her, negotiating relationships was a balancing act, especially when her friends of color and her White partner came together in the same space. For several years I had a White partner and experienced many of the same challenges Linda described when I tried to integrate my partner with my friends of color. Linda was a friend of one of my closest friends, and I felt an instant rapport with her. This led to deep discussions about painful and challenging issues related to Whiteness.

Discussions about Whiteness with Linda began early in the first individual interview. Linda often positioned herself as an outsider even in communities of color because she was usually "the lightest person" and didn't always feel like she fit in. She said, "It's interesting, actually, that whole Whiteness part has come up a lot in conversations with my partner." Her partner, Tracy, was "not very politically educated," and Tracy's dad was "inflammatory" and "antagonistic." Linda said that she loved Tracy's dad and that he reminded her of her (Black step) dad in many ways because her dad could be similarly antagonistic. Tracy's dad, however, said "racist shit" and simultaneously challenged her to embrace her White side. He once said to her, "You're half White. Why don't you embrace your Whiteness? Next time I see you I want you to know some Polish dances, and know some Polish food and know some Polish culture." Linda replied to him that she didn't have access to that (because she didn't have a relationship with her White Polish dad or his family). But she admitted that the dialogues with Tracy's dad were "really kind of intense."

Later in the interview she explained that her internal reaction to Tracy's dad's challenge was, "Well, White people are fucked up. That's why I'm not proud of being White." Linda added that being Japanese American with family in Hawaii, she was well aware of the racial oppression her family experienced; "They were interned, and there was a lot of racism after the war." White U.S. Americans created and imposed those laws. I asked Linda to expand upon what she meant when she said, "White people are fucked up." She said:

The history of America, I mean really it comes back to America and being American. I am, ironically, just getting over the lie of freedom for all and justice, and all that crap. Really, I did internalize that. I did want to believe that there is justice, and that America is great. And my perspective – and just to keep it real, I know that in other countries they don't get to experience the same kind of freedoms that we do. But we don't live in a just society. And I'm just coming to terms with how fucked up America is, not just to our own people, but to everyone in the whole fucking world, you know? That's kind of hard. It's been really hard, removing the blinders and being really depressed at the injustice everywhere and most of it was perpetrated by White men. Men are in power all over the world. And there is so much injustice, so I don't want to align myself with that. But I think that's why I've never really been [aligned]. It's been easy too, not having my dad be a part of my life. Having my dad be an asshole makes it easier to not be nice to White people, you know?

Linda, in her explanation above, described a cultural history of White and male supremacy.[36] Her knowledge about the institutional injustices perpetuated by White men, along with her personal negative experiences and lack of contact with her White father, made it easy for her to disdain Whiteness and wish to disassociate from that. However, I wondered then why she chose a White partner, so I said, "But your partner is White."

During the interviews Linda described Tracy as almost perfect. Linda shared:

Actually, when I first started dating her, what I would say to all my friends is, "She's perfect in every way except (1) she's White, and (2) she's not politically educated." And you know, I think that part of that fear was because I haven't felt like this before about someone, so the fear of falling in love. I'm falling so quickly, and so hard.

Linda acknowledged that she loved Tracy, but it was difficult for her to reconcile Tracy's minimal understanding of racial politics and racism. However, most of Linda's partners had been White; she confessed, "I think that's another issue around power." Linda admitted that having a White partner shielded her from the possibility of being less politically educated about issues of race. Furthermore, she would never have to deal with feeling like she was "oppressing somebody" as she might with a partner of color.

However, being partnered with a White person brought her a distinct set of challenges. A major challenge was dealing with Tracy's discomfort around Linda's friends. In those situations, Tracy felt uncomfortable because Linda's friends made negative comments about "White people." In addition, Linda had to negotiate straddling her desire to be with women of color friends in women of color spaces and her desire to be with her girlfriend. She shared her story of going to a gay pride event where there were "a lot of people of color" and her girlfriend later told her she felt "really out of place." Although Tracy never named race as the issue, Linda realized that her friends did not really include Tracy and added:

And she's the one White girl, with five people of color. It is really hard to negotiate, because that's probably where I should be translating, but I don't. That's where I should be like trying to include her, by being more of a bridge, but I'm not. Because I am, like, people of color aligned... These [friends] are people I've known for a long time, and that's how we are when we're together, you know? We talk smack about White people, and our conversations are racialized. And I want to be sensitive to my girlfriend's feeling of alienation. And it's really hard because, like you said, when she says something like, when she said, "I feel like you're generalizing about all White people," I'm like, "Well I am. I sure am. I'm generalizing about all White people, but that doesn't mean it's you." It's really hard, because I'm not sensitive in that way. I'm not sensitive to stand up for her when my friend was like "Oh, your people..." And Tracy was like, "I didn't do that." But like, I'm not good at being her champion really. That's what I feel like I need to be, and I haven't been. I feel bad about it, like I need to go make amends with my girlfriend. I mean it definitely highlights that it has to be really hard for her.

Linda felt torn between supporting her girlfriend and allowing her friends to have the space to speak freely as women of color who had experienced racism in a White supremacist society.

As a facilitator, I then tried to focus the discussion on Linda and said, "You talk about the difficulty for Tracy, but there are also difficulties for you, being in the middle." She responded candidly:

Well also, then to be White, because that's always the part that's not said. That's always the part that's not talked about. And it's funny because it came up more recently where I was really conscious about that, because these dialogues are happening with Tracy. Because, like I said, this is really the first time I'm being challenged with someone being like, "Well why aren't you praising your White side?"

Linda argued that we don't talk about our own Whiteness as mixed people. What Linda said resonates with the research data; as I analyzed the interviews, I found that there was relatively little discussion by most people about their Whiteness. Whiteness was more often discussed in relation to White family members or cultural Whiteness in general.

Linda then shared a story of how she was hurt by a comment someone made about Whiteness. She said:

So, a friend of mine in passing, I don't even remember who it was, said something like "Oh yeah, I found out recently that I have White in my family, and I'm just really upset about it." And they said this to me, you know?

Linda said that she was "floored" by the statement but didn't say anything in response to her friend. Yet Linda understood the friend's desire to not want to admit White heritage. She added:

But then also I've been villainized by my own White heritage too, like I'm down on the White man for sure. That's not me and that's not my family. Maybe that's not my dad, maybe it is. I'm working that out too.

Linda's biological White dad was a weekend dad when she was younger and then, beginning when Linda was in college, they were estranged for ten years up until her father passed away. Linda said this disconnection from her father made it easier to "put [her] Whiteness somewhere outside of" herself. Linda said, "How we notice our Whiteness I think is the biggest challenge."

All of the discussions above occurred during my first interview with Linda. Soon after, she shared some of our interview discussions with her partner. This sparked more dialogue between them and more conflict surfaced as a result. At the time of the interviews, Linda was on the verge of moving in with Tracy. Linda was admittedly "scared" and "freaking out" but felt "serious love" for Tracy. Nonetheless, the impending move made the conflict with her partner feel extremely threatening for both of them.

During their conversation, Tracy challenged Linda's negativity stating, "Whenever you talk about White people, it's really negatively." Linda conceded that she did "White bash" with her friends and needed to be more sensitive about how it would affect Tracy. She recalled that she said to Tracy:

But I tried really hard to be really clear with you, and really like break down the difference between this and you and your relationship to that [Whiteness and racism], and saying that you can only take responsibility for White people as a whole when you've done the oppressing, when you're the one who's being unconscious[ly racist], when you're the one acting like that. That's when you take ownership of it, but you don't need to own all of that shit.

Linda wanted Tracy to understand that there is a difference between oppression as a larger concept and her individual responsibility. However, in talking to Tracy, Linda also appeared to be trying to convince herself of the same point; as Linda shared that story she added, "I don't need to own all of that shit, you know? And yet, maybe I do because that's why I don't want to identify as White, you know?" Linda divulged that she had been asking herself:

Why is it that I really just want to identify as a person of color, a woman of color? Like, where is my White identity? And I've superficially said, "Oh yes, I acknowledge I have skin privilege," and not superficially, but that's what I say to myself. I know that I have skin privilege; I know that I'm White.

Linda said that the conversations where she asked herself those hard questions were "peripheral" conversations that came up with "other mixed people who are mixed with White." With one of her mixed friends she was able to have deep conversations about not feeling like she belonged in people of color space, the difficulties of being seen as White, and recognizing the experiential differences for people of color who don't have white skin privilege.

Linda and her partner resolved their conflict. Linda agreed to be more sensitive to Tracy's needs. In Linda's words, Tracy disclosed, "I realize that I'm having a hard time separating out institutional racism and my personal involvement on the individual level, and all that, breaking that apart." When Linda said, "What are we going to do?" Tracy replied, "I was thinking that I could get some books."[37] Linda shared with Tracy that she too had been challenged by her friends of color and promised to continue to help Tracy to further her understanding of racism just as friends had done for her.

At the end of the interview Linda said, "This Whiteness thing is huge. It's really huge." Linda then again brought up the story of her friend who found out she had White heritage, sparking a dialogue between us:

Linda: Yeah, yeah. It is really hard though. It is really hard. Why didn't I say something to my friend who was like, "I just found out that I have White in me and I'm just really upset." You know?

Me: I think it's too risky. I think, for me, the fear is that they are going to start seeing me as White.

Linda: Right. Mm-hmm, because you are.

Me: Right. No, don't say that. No I'm not. That's what I want to say, you know what I mean?

Linda: Totally. Totally. It's interesting because that's coming up with these conversations with Tracy because early on when she was like, "It's just really upsetting and blah, blah, blah." And she was like, "You wish that you weren't White." And I was like, "But I am White. And whenever I give you a hard time, you know you can say, 'Well you're White, too.'"

Me: Oh, I would never give anybody the opportunity to say that to me.

Linda: But it's *true*. But it *is* true.

Me: Right.

Linda: And that's part of what I really am trying to work on, what I need to work on that's coming up in these fucking interviews, that's coming up like her dad is saying "Claim your Whiteness, be proud of being White." You know? It's interesting too because I feel I can, this last year I have been able to say – we've made comments about my half Whiteness. We've made comments about the racial stuff. It's coming up. It's on the forefront of my mind. Yeah, and it is hard. Because you know what, we're dealing with all the same stuff that Tracy is trying to work out right now. Does that mean that I'm bad? Does that mean that I can't be a person of color anymore? Does that mean that my experience as a person of color is not authentic because I am White also? What is the experience of a person of color? It's how I define it because really… they see me as an exotic other, an Asian too, the model minority. Come on, seriously there's not a lot of discrimination. No one is calling me a freakin' banana or twinkie or whatever. Just putting myself in the framework of thinking that I'm White in this every day racialized context, within that framework.

Me: I haven't heard the term "twinkie" used before.

Linda: Well, a twinkie means that you are yellow on the outside and White on the inside. What that means for me is something totally different because I am a twinkie. [whispering] I am a White person. I'm more like the sunshine cookie, those lemon cookies, the White cookie with the lemon inside. So whatever is a person of color is what I define, it's what I have to define, that's my privilege, because I'm a person with fairly fair skin who could pass as White maybe. That's the funny thing about queerness too, because people who aren't queer aren't seeing you as queer. Or people who are White don't see you as a person of color. Asian people are totally like, "Oh, I see the Asian in you." But White people are just like, "Whatever." Straight people are like, "Whatever. I don't see it." It's not as obvious. So I get to choose. I get to choose if I want to identify as a person of color. That is my privilege.

In this exchange, Linda named our connections to Whiteness that as mixed people we often don't want to name: the privilege of choosing, the fear of being called White, the ways we have to own our connection to Whiteness and all the related questions that arise:

Does that mean that I'm bad? Does that mean that I can't be a person of color anymore? Does that mean that my experience as a person of color is not authentic because I am White also? What is the experience of a person of color?

It is the same fear and defensiveness that Tracy experienced, only it is exacerbated by a fear of being disconnected and/or rejected by people of our own cultural backgrounds, by people of color, groups to which we belong. It is no accident that

Linda's voice fell to a whisper when she said, "I am White." It feels like that which must not be named, it is our Voldemort[38]. Linda challenged me on this when I resisted her saying to me, "But you are White." I carry at least as much white skin privilege as Linda. I am part White, as is Linda. It feels much easier to admit "part" Whiteness or "half" Whiteness than just Whiteness. We want to say that it is because we don't want to deny our wholeness or our families of color. This may be true, but the resistance comes from a deeper place than that, evidenced by the fact that we don't wince or whisper when we claim to be people of color or Latina, Asian, Black, etc. without simultaneously naming our Whiteness. Perhaps Linda named it perfectly with the question, "Does that mean I'm bad?" As insiders to people of color spaces, many of us hear frequently all the negative terms associated with Whiteness. We know that to claim Whiteness carries with it a responsibility to examine our complicity in the negative aspects of cultural Whiteness.

CONCLUSION

These women's stories, both personal and analytical, expand critical whiteness theory. Definitions of cultural Whiteness unfolded as the women spoke about their views and their experiences. There was a simultaneous connection to and separation from cultural Whiteness as well as a complex relationship to White privilege.

Cultural Whiteness for Mixed Race Women as it Relates to the Culture of Power

The women collectively defined cultural Whiteness. In *Other People's Children,* Lisa Delpit (1995) defined what she called "the culture of power." Delpit, a teacher educator, wrote specifically about issues of power within the classroom; however, several of her points about what the "culture of power" entails relate to the participants' definitions of "cultural Whiteness." Delpit defined five aspects of power. We can examine the participants' words and experiences in relation to Delpit's framework.

First, Delpit (1995) argued that "Issues of power are enacted in classrooms," including that teachers hold power over students, and publishers hold power over curricula (p. 24). Even though all the participants were all asked to talk about their experiences in schools, they spoke little about their experiences with teachers. Virtually all the participants were successful "good" students. Thus, one could deduce that conflicts with teachers were minimal. In this chapter, however, the issue of what is taught in history was raised. Ruth argued that the truth about history isn't taught in school, referring to a lack of education about White privilege and issues of power. This leads to an incorrect mainstream view among White people that "their way is the normal way."

Second, Delpit argued that there is a "culture of power" which she defined as "codes or rules for participating in power" (p. 25). These codes include language forms, strategies of communication and ways of being, including "ways of talking, ways of writing, ways of dressing, and ways of interacting" (p. 25). The participants gave a similar definition for what they often called "White culture" or "cultural Whiteness" or simply "White people." Perhaps Alana summed it up best in her definition of "cultural Whiteness" when she shared that cultural Whiteness is about, among other things, having access to standard English (ways of talking), "ways of being, mannerisms, behaviors, knowing how to react, knowing how to decode behavior" (strategies of communicating), "dominating the knowledge base" (ways of writing), and knowing "what White people do in their spare time" (ways of interacting). The fact that virtually all the women excelled in school might point to some level of participation in and understanding of the cultural codes of power in the classroom.

Third, Delpit argued, "the rules of the culture of power are a reflection of the rules of the culture of those who have power" (p. 25). In her book she shared an example of how children from middle class homes tend to do better in school than those who are not from middle class homes. It is important to note that Delpit used an example that refers to socioeconomic status and not race. The dialogues in relation to a culture of power in the interviews focused almost exclusively on race (Whiteness), not class. Although, Alana did state, "I know part of that is class, but class and race are so mixed." In other words, Alana and Delpit both acknowledged that often, Whiteness is connected to middle to upper class cultures and people of color are connected to poor and working class cultures. It would be incorrect to conflate the two; there are poor white people and middle to upper class people of color (Bettie, 2003; Bonilla-Silva, 2006; hooks, 2000). However, it is important to note that class and race are intertwined and class-based cultural capital may contribute to race-related cultural capital, but not necessarily. There were several instances in which connections were made between White people and those in power, implying that White people are those at the top of the hierarchy. For example, Alana stated that White culture is invisible because it is the "mainstream" and "dominant" culture. She also stated that there is a historical legacy of White people taking land from people of color which has a current manifestation in White people feeling an unearned sense of entitlement to space.

Fourth, Delpit asserted, "If you are not already a participant in the culture of power, being told explicitly the rules of that culture makes acquiring power easier" (p. 25). Delpit argued that members of any culture implicitly transfer information to co-members. This works among members of a culture, but when there are attempts to implicitly transmit codes *across* cultures, there is frequently a breakdown in communication. People are left saying, "What's wrong with them, why don't they understand?" (p. 25). Clearly, although the participants tended to name Whiteness as something outside themselves, these women learned many of the codes of the culture of power from their White parents and perhaps other White family members. The majority of them had learned enough to be perceived as White by others. This requires more than a particular skin tone, it requires an understanding and demonstration, to some extent, of White cultural ways of being. It requires cultural capital (Bourdieu, 1986). Since all of the women except Linda had significant relationships with their White parents, it would stand to reason that they would understand and exhibit White cultural ways of being that they were most likely implicitly taught. However, there was a mixture of understanding and confusion among the women in relation to cultural Whiteness. There were definitely White cultural ways of being that surprised participants and left them asking, "What's wrong with them?" For example, this is evident in Bobbi's questioning of how White people can be "selfish and aggressive." Mindy also shared stories of being expected to know certain things about White ways of being that were foreign to her.

Finally, Delpit asserted, "Those with power are frequently least aware of – or least willing to acknowledge – its existence. Those with less power are often more aware of its existence" (p. 26). Delpit stated that it is "distinctly uncomfortable" for people with power to admit participation in the culture of power. "On the other hand," she states, "those who are less powerful in any situation are most likely to recognize the power variable most acutely" (p. 26). The participants were border crossers here, in that they were both uncomfortable admitting participation in the culture, yet also able to recognize power. The participants occupied a dual position of operating both within and outside of the culture of power in relation to race. It is important to note that most of the participants were raised middle class and most of them were living middle class lives at the time of the interviews. Delpit's definition of the culture of power is not limited to "cultural Whiteness," it is also about those who hold power, which relates to other social categories as well including class, gender, and sexuality. These women occupied multiple outsider and insider positionalities in relation to the culture of power more broadly defined. They also lived insider and outsider positionalities in relation to the more specific White culture of power. Furthermore, the reality is, as Alana aptly stated, that issues such as race and class cannot be easily separated.

Cultural Whiteness for Mixed Race Women as it Relates to Critical Whiteness Theory

We can also examine the participants' stories in relation to critical whiteness theory. Critical whiteness theory is dependent upon a distinction between White people and people of color. One major aim of critical whiteness studies has been to disrupt previous writings that centralized people of color in discussions of racism focusing on victimization rather than systematic oppressive practices. Thus, critical

177

whiteness to some extent flipped the script, examining and deconstructing White behaviors, discourses, habits, and dispositions that contributed to White supremacy. Within this theoretical framework, certain key aspects of Whiteness emerge including, but not limited to, the ideas that: (a) well-intended White people who perceive themselves to be good can still reproduce and maintain systemic racism (Moon, 1999; Thompson, 2003); (b) White privilege is typically invisible to White people (Applebaum, 2010; Hytten & Warren, 2003); and (c) all White people are complicit in racism by benefiting from White privilege, something they cannot renounce voluntarily (McIntosh, 2000; Tatum, 1997). Applebaum (2010) further deconstructed critical whiteness, revealing even greater intricacies. She argued, for example, that "White denials of complicity are an illustration of whitely ways of being" (p. 18). However, acknowledgement of complicity through "white confessionals or public self-disclosures can serve to reinscribe privilege" (Applebaum, 2010, p. 19). It's not that White people *do not mean* what they say, Applebaum explained, it's that such assertions do not *do* what they say. White people are thus caught in a paradox: damned if they do acknowledge White complicity in racism and damned if they don't. Applebaum, however, did not take a nihilistic approach; White people can, in fact, work on challenging racism. However, doing so, she argued, requires "a specific type of vigilance that recognizes the dangers of presuming that one can transcend racist systems when one attempts to work to challenge racist systems" (p. 20).

Examining the participants' stories in relation to critical whiteness theory reveals an in-between state; the participants occupy a liminal space in relation to binary positioning of White people and people of color. If, for example, White privilege is typically invisible to White people, then these women, who more often than not name privileges connected to their White heritage, do not fit that categorized White way of being. Yet most of us do have the "privilege," given "passing" skin-tones, at least in some contexts, to name ourselves; recall Linda's assertion in which she stated, "It's not as obvious. So I get to choose. I get to choose if I want to identify as a person of color. That is my privilege." However, being White is much more than white skin, it is, as Applebaum (2010) explains, "whitely ways of being" (p. 18). All of the women demonstrated success in negotiating White spaces and institutions; and Alana, who as a brown-skinned person could not pass as White, even stated outright that she benefitted from cultural Whiteness, from knowing how to navigate White habitus. Yet, we also see instances throughout the interviews where the opposite of easy navigation occurs. Mindy, for example, shared stories of feeling isolated in predominately White spaces due to lacking some expected whitely ways of being even though she was most often perceived by others to be White based on her looks. Throughout many of the interviews, the women demonstrated vigilance as they thought through their positioning – self-positioning and imposed positioning – as mixed race women in the context of a systemically racist society. Thus, these women's borderland experiences in relation to

Whiteness challenge current frameworks of critical whiteness theory which are built upon a clear-cut split between White people and people of color. The connections we have to Whiteness position us, to some extent, automatically in the White role, but our positioning is much more complicated than that. For mixed race women, acknowledging complicity in White privilege has the potential to both reinscribe privilege *and* reinscribe oppression simultaneously in our own lives. Naming our White privilege has the potential to provide fuel for people to dismiss our experiences related to being people of color, related to being mixed.

Breaking the Binaries of Theoretical Frameworks Related to the Politics of Race

Perhaps these stories reveal that although theoretical frameworks are necessary and help us to make meaning of situations, people's experiences do not always fit so neatly into the outlines provided. Frameworks such as the culture of power and critical whiteness theory are built upon positioning White people and people of color as binaries. However, as mixed race women, we can occupy multiple racial/ethnic positionalities simultaneously. The distinctions between prejudice and racism in social justice theoretical frameworks serve as another example of a dualistic conceptualization. This distinction is often appealing to those of us who teach about diversity and social justice, because we want people to begin to understand issues of power that have been historically erased and silenced. However, where do White/of color mixed race people fall in that framework, especially those who pass and/or have a fair amount of cultural capital? One of the arguments in the participants' dialogues is that because they identified as women of color they could not be racist: they could only be prejudiced against others because they did not hold the social power of Whites. But the question is, do we hold the social power of Whites? Sometimes we do, at least to some extent. I would argue, in line with the authors in *Teaching for Diversity and Social Justice*, that discrimination affects people of color as a whole in more detrimental ways than prejudice against White people because of institutionalized power imbalances (Adams, Bell, & Griffin, 1997). As such, I wouldn't call prejudiced remarks against White people racist, no matter who makes them. But when mixed race people are prejudiced against people of color, is that racism or internalized racism? If at times we don't "get it," if we are unable to see the operations of the culture of power, does that automatically make us White in that circumstance?

These questions relate to the questions Linda raised at the end of her second interview. If we examine our connection to Whiteness, specifically our White privilege and the ways in which we are complicit in the culture of power, does that mean that we cannot be people of color? We are caught in a trap. To talk with White people about these issues makes us vulnerable to racism/prejudice, but to talk to people of color makes us vulnerable to being disowned or potentially oppressing others. Linda said that she had the deepest discussions about where she stood in relation to Whiteness with other mixed people who were mixed with White. She also stated that dating White people freed her from any worry about "oppressing others." She would never be in the position of being an agent of racial oppression, only a target. Perhaps what is most striking is the sense of division, the segregation that exists even in our own lives between White people and people of color. We sometimes bring White people and people of color into our lives together, but to what level of integration?

In the next chapter, we will hear stories of participant roles as mediators, translators, and educators. We will discover how participants claimed agency through educating others and when and where participants felt obliged to build bridges and how that was attempted. Participants also shared the ways in which they refused to take on the burden of being an educator. It is another chapter in the story of insider/outsider positionality, border crossing, and mediating differences.

CHAPTER 8

BRIDGE BUILDERS, TRANSLATORS, AND ALLIES

The Responsibility, Burden, and Privilege of Educating Others

You need to be the translator. You have to speak their [White people's] language in order for them to hear. – Susan

I recognize that my feelings have changed and probably will keep changing, but I feel like it's both at the same time. The strongest part of me wants to say, "Yeah, it sucks that I have to be in this position where I can educate people, and they need educating sometimes." But nothing is going to get better without somebody doing it, so I want to do it. But then at the same time, sometimes I don't want that responsibility. I don't want that burden, and I'm tired of it. – Katherine

I just want to acknowledge how much power we hold, that we are the bridge between many communities and many people. – Marta

The participants' stories relating to their roles as educators focused primarily on ways they enlightened White people about racism, White supremacy, and more generally about the lives of people of color. Decades of debates have ensued regarding who should carry the burden of educating White people about racism. In response to a growing White feminist movement in the 1960s, 1970s and 1980s, women of color began to speak up and claim space in the public eye, demanding to be heard and acknowledged. Women of color have always been active in women's issues, but their experiences and work were often overlooked (Hurtado, 1996). In *This Bridge Called My Back: Writings by Radical Women of Color* (Moraga & Anzaldúa, 1983), a signifier of public space claiming, women of color told their personal stories and shared theoretical perspectives related to oppression; the editors emphasized the need for community with each other and demanded that White women listen to and *hear* their stories. Writers wrote simultaneously about the unfairness of being expected to teach White women about women of color and racism.

In *This Bridge Called My Back,* Yamada (1983) wrote, "If the majority culture knows so little about us, it must be *our* problem, they seem to be telling us; the burden of teaching is on us" (p. 72). She argued that White women need to teach themselves. In the same book, Moraga (1983) made a similar argument; however, as a mixed race Latina/White woman, she called for dialogue. She said:

I think: what is my responsibility to my roots – both White and brown, Spanish-speaking and English? I am a woman with a foot in both worlds; and I refuse the split. I feel the necessity for dialogue. Sometimes I feel it urgently. (p. 34)

The women's narratives in this project speak to the same struggles that were being discussed back in the early 1980s by mixed race women and women of color. These women struggled with the burden, responsibility, and privilege of building bridges between White people and people of color.

The participants shared many thoughts, feelings and stories related to educating people about racism and being mixed race. They discussed a variety of issues: the burden of having to educate in a way that White people can hear, beliefs in change and skepticism, a desire to reject educating others without compensation, a responsibility and a calling to be bridge builders and educators, the need to educate people they love, and the fear that they are not prepared to teach others. Collectively, they grappled with the desire to educate, the knowledge to do so (or lack thereof), the emotional drain of being a teacher, and the anger associated with being expected to teach others.

BURDEN OF EDUCATING IN A WAY THAT WHITE PEOPLE CAN HEAR

In the Boston group interview, Katherine shared a story of a time when one of her sisters was challenged around issues of race by a White man. Katherine said, "I don't remember what she told me that she ended up saying, but I was trying to think with her, what could you say, to call somebody out on that kind of the comment?" A discussion followed among several members of the group concerning the difficulty of educating White people. Joanna commented first.

Joanna: Part of the difficulty of this situation is finding a way to respond in which the person will actually hear what you have to say. Especially because if you get defensive, it's very clear to me in watching my own interactions, and watching interactions with other Black women, as soon as your neck starts moving, people stop listening.

Ruth: This is true.

Joanna: And that's genuine. That's what happens when I get angry. It just starts going. And people do stop listening. And so you have to find a way to educate them in a way that they will actually hear it.

Mindy: But yeah again, the idea of White supremacy, even in language and how you interact with people, it has to be this very narrow way. You can't get emotional because they don't understand that. They don't even see that their idea of objectivity is messed up, you know? Or they don't even have the baseline of the understanding that identity is made up of all these different things and not just based on appearance. They don't even understand color then, or economic discrimination or class, and homophobia, you know? And it's a lot of burden to place on individuals like us.

Joanna: [interrupting] To educate the masses.

Mindy: It's like, "Okay we're going to educate you," just based on our personal [experience]; it's a huge thing.

Joanna: Yet it's very hard to detach the emotion from their response. But then they write you off as an angry Black woman, or just an emotional woman, you know? It's obviously a touchy subject. And clearly they've hit on something and it's hard to respond and try to keep yourself in check when it's something you feel so passionate about.

Diana: They want us to respond as a White person.

Joanna: Right.

Ruth: I get "the angry Black woman" all the time.

Susan: You need to be the translator. You have to speak their language in order for them to hear.

Diana: You have a professional façade, your public façade, and your real self. And you have to know which hat to put on in different situations if you're going to survive, like in the business world. There is a certain culture where you work, how you're supposed to behave. You need to pick up those clues and get with it if you want to work here. If you can't, you know, get with that, then move on. Because no matter what validity you have in your response in your way of delivering information for your research, whatever it is, if it isn't the White way, it isn't right. You are, you're, you're incompetent.

After Susan's comment, Diana remarked on the impact of information delivery; she argued that White people believe that "if it isn't the White way, it isn't right" and when someone does not communicate in "White [dominant, middle class] ways" they are seen as "incompetent."

In the exchange above, Joanna and Ruth started the discussion by talking about the cultural expectations of body language by White people, and the need to self-monitor behaviors perceived as Black to be heard. Mindy then steered the conversation away from the personal to interject her theoretical analysis of what occurs in that type of situation. She argued that when White people expect other people to talk and interact in a very "narrow" White way, a way that is non-emotional, that their expectation is a form of White supremacy. She said, "They don't even understand that their idea of objectivity is messed up." Mindy was referring to a White, patriarchal history in which reason is expected to be detached from emotion. This analysis coincides with Alana's analysis quoted in the previous chapter where she defined cultural Whiteness as being situated in scientific knowledge emerging from Western modernity in a way that "dominates everyone's ways of thinking and rationalizing, normalizing." This belief in rationalization is culturally codified in Whiteness. The connection between cultural Whiteness and White supremacist thinking blinds people from "understanding that identity is made up of all these different things and not just based on appearance." As a result, White people are not going to understand racism, classism, or even homophobia. Ultimately, that places a "burden" on us as mixed race people and people of color to educate White people.

Joanna continued the conversation, bringing the focus back to the personal, claiming that it is "hard to respond and try to keep yourself in check when it's something you feel so passionate about." It takes work to "respond like a White person," as Diana described, and it is unfair. The group agreed that in order to get White people to listen, one has to speak and act like White people. Susan referred to this as being the "translator." Diana took it a step further and called it a survival skill.

After Diana's final comment above, Joanna shared a story of a play she saw titled, *Slanguage*, in which the neighborhood slang of Latino and Black youth is not accepted in school.

> It was clear in this play and in the things that they were reading that there was so much validity in these terms, in these phrases that they were using. But it was [not seen as valid] because they were not "proper;" you would never use them in an office.

Here, Joanna expanded on what it means to teach in a way that is both accessible and acceptable to people of the dominant culture. The expected and accepted explanations require not only White cultural body language but also dominant White Standard English. Diana responded, "Their loss. They don't listen and learn."

Although Diana said, "It's their loss," there were several stories she shared throughout her interviews of having to act culturally White in the sense of speaking "the King's English," straightening her hair, and minimizing her emotion. Diana attended Harvard Business School and worked as a top executive in corporate companies. In that role she had to create a "professional façade" in order to be viewed as competent. Also, as one of the older participants, at 58, Diana had lived through times in which blatant discrimination happened more regularly and went unchecked. She had to know "which hat to put on in different situations" to "survive."

Diana shared an example of a way she learned early on to influence White people so that they would listen to her and respect her. She explained that she was "always sort of a goody two shoes and a straight A student." She told a story about when she was in the eighth grade she had a long-term substitute math teacher. She explained:

> So, the first time we were going into the class the kids said to me, "Diana, talk like a White person and you can be the only White person in the class and let's see how – if the teacher adopts you." So, we all played this game on the teacher. I did not speak any Ebonics and the teacher did actually take to me and not to the other kids. It was a very interesting social experiment.

It was clear to Diana and her classmates that she received special treatment because she "talked White." Her stories of needing to "code switch" from one context to another are not unique to the mixed race experience (Greene & Walker, 2004). People of color have been doing so throughout U.S. history in order to survive (Du Bois, 1996). What is notable is that, as the mixed race kid, she had the capacity to do so from a young age. Her peers picked her to do what in all likelihood they could not do as well.

A fine line exists between educating others and enacting cultural Whiteness in order to achieve success in White dominant institutions. In other words, sometimes the necessity to act culturally White is more about finding a way to achieve success in White dominant culture than it is about educating others so that they gain a greater consciousness of race issues and racism. Diana, for example, was not using her ability to act culturally White in the example above in order to educate; she and her classmates never revealed their secret to the teacher. In order for that experiment to have been potentially educative, they would have had to confront the teacher's bias. However, she learned in that instance what privileges she could receive by "acting White." Throughout her interviews, Diana shared stories about times she felt the need to act culturally White to succeed in the business world. Other participants, however, talked specifically about striving to communicate with White people in "White ways" with the intentional purpose of helping them gain greater understandings of racism dynamics. In those instances the women used their cultural Whiteness to help educate. When these efforts succeeded, often the White people's increased understanding, in turn, helped them.

Moments arose in which the role of educating others was more of a choice than a matter of survival. This may be more likely for the younger generation, as well as for those who may more easily enact White cultural ways of being. Joanna, who is 23, said in her individual interview:

> I can manipulate what I say so that I do not compromise what I believe, but not step on people's toes. Sometimes if I think they can handle it and they need to be educated, I'm very blunt about a lot of things. I especially take people off guard. Because I'm a woman and the things I say – I have a really dirty mouth sometimes. I'm very, very comfortable about my sexuality and I don't have a problem talking about it. I know sometimes it's not appropriate, and I don't bring it up. People are often shocked, especially older people.

> Older women are appalled by the things I have to say. They think it's great and wish they could be as upfront about it. But they're always shocked. Even my mother who agrees with what I have to say, and wishes she could say the things I say, is still taken aback by it sometimes. So sometimes I use that to my advantage, and I stretch people's comfort zone. But it's to a degree and with compassion. Because it's not to make them so uncomfortable they don't want to hear anything you have to say. I don't want to make anyone that uncomfortable. I just want to push their limits a little bit.

In this quote, Joanna described the liberty to speak her mind and "manipulate" in a way that did not feel like a "compromise" to her integrity. She explicitly acknowledged that her ways of being shocked "older people," alluding to a freedom she may have possessed as someone younger, living in an era that was less tolerant of discrimination. Key points in her description are that (a) she stretched people to come out of their comfort zones, but only to a degree; and (b) that she taught with compassion.

Griffin (1997), in *Teaching for Diversity and Social Justice*, shared an activity that described how being on the "learning edge" requires us to stretch our "comfort zones," but only to the extent that we don't withdraw or completely resist (p. 68–69). Several people who have written about teaching to promote social justice have emphasized the need to have compassion for learners (Bettez, 2008; Boler, 2003; hooks, 1994; Shapiro, 2005). Hence, Joanna, an engineering graduate student, employed techniques that diversity and social justice educators advocate to teach effectively about oppression.

It is notable as well that in this instance she referred to educating around issues of sexuality rather than race. Although she stated in the quote that she had no problem talking about her sexuality, that comment was situated in a larger context; in an earlier quote she remarked that she would not date someone who could not pass for straight out of fear of homophobia. This is a reminder that decisions about whether or not to educate others are always made in a complex web of intersecting power dynamics of privilege and oppression. Nonetheless, here is a clear example of taking on an educator role. Similarly, in another quote above, Mindy referred to teaching about racism, sexism, and homophobia. Many of these women indicated that it was important to educate others about all forms of discrimination, not merely racism, which acknowledges that all forms of oppression overlap.

In an individual interview, Janet shared that she found it difficult to educate others when individuals were putting down her people, Latina/os; it was easier for her to defend attacks against groups of people to which she did not belong. She said:

> I definitely experience the same thing [difficulty], and it's definitely when they're comments about Brown people. I feel like it's a personal attack on me and my people, and you know I get that knot in my throat, and in my heart,

and I feel my body tense up, and yeah, it's a different reaction but with any kind of comment that's coming from this anger and fear, you know, when people make comments about gays and lesbians in an offensive way. I mean all of that, I get angry, and it's hard. And I think it's harder to defend when it's about Brown people. Because I feel like, as a straight person, if someone says something about, like if someone called someone a fag or something like, I can really – it's easier for me to say something, as a straight person, in defending that community. Because for some people it's easier to hear things when it's coming from someone that's like them, so if I'm talking to like a straight man or a straight woman, it's easier for me to say, and I think for them to hear. But it's always hard.

Janet raised an important point about the distinctions between supporting others as an ally and defending one's own group of people. More is at stake when we have to speak up for a group to which we belong. Some sociologists have argued that we have an imperative to stand up as an ally and use our privilege to assist in dismantling oppression (Johnson, 2006; Schwalbe, 2007). It is understood that it is not fair to expect oppressed people to put themselves further in jeopardy of discrimination by speaking up against their own oppression. This distinction gets blurred for mixed race people. Are we expected to use our potential access to White privilege (for those that have it) to stand up for our own oppressed identities of color? Are we allies or targets of oppression, or both?

BELIEF IN CHANGE AND SKEPTICISM

The women displayed varying degrees of faith and skepticism about the power of education to dismantle racism. Tina believed in people's capacity to unlearn oppression. In the group interview she said:

I always make allowances for people, and I always recognize that people can unlearn these things. They can unlearn racism; they can unlearn classism. So I try not to come at them in a hateful way but more like, "I suggest this book to you." I don't know.

This comment came at the end of a story she told about how she learned to think about race in new ways because of the exposure she had. Because she "passes as White all the time everywhere, every day" (even when she is with her Mexican family), she believed that if she never went to college she "wouldn't be thinking about being mixed race at all." Marta revealed that she too gained a deeper understanding of oppression in college when she "got the vocabulary to make things make sense."

Other people followed suit, acknowledging the learning process. Alana said, "I've definitely been called out a lot" after which Tina admitted that she also had been called out by people of color. In a separate interview, Linda talked about how she had been educated about race issues by people of color. She said that her best friend of 15 years, a Latina, pushed her and talked to her about race to help her consciousness grow.

> I have these few key people in my life that have been really key to my growth as well, and she and I became feminists together, women of color feminists together. And our race and political consciousness were growing at the same time. I was like, "I like this book. Check out Ana Castillo. What do you think of that?" and "Let's talk about this."

Thus some of the women admitted their own growth processes around issues of race. They were taught by peers of color to better understand racism and learned through readings in college authored by people of color to better understand issues of race and oppression. Acknowledging their own growth process allowed some of the women to have greater compassion and belief that White people can unlearn racism.

Joanna similarly argued that some people have just not had the exposure needed to understand issues of oppression.

> Like last weekend we went to see a movie, it's a documentary about the persecution in Tibet, and all the mess of what's going on over there. I was telling [a fellow graduate student] about it before I went to go see it. I said, "I don't really know too much about it. It's about the Buddhist struggle in Tibet." She was like, "Buddhists are being persecuted in Tibet?" It's like, "Do you read the newspaper?" And you know, I understand why; she's so sheltered. It makes sense; it's just difficult for me. I kinda take on this personal charge to educate her, which feels really arrogant. But at the same time, it's not that she doesn't care. Because when she finds out about these things she's really interested in them, but she just hasn't been exposed.

Joanna, acknowledging that her classmate's misunderstanding came from lack of exposure, was not only willing, but felt obligated to educate her friend. However, perhaps key in that story is that her classmate was always "really interested." She was willing and wanted to learn. Later in the interview, Joanna stated that she liked it when people showed interest in learning about her background. She preferred it when people showed interest as long as they did so respectfully. She said:

> They want to ask but don't know how and don't know what's appropriate, which I think is cute and endearing. As long as they're being respectful, which is most of the time, and it's a true curiosity, I think that's cute. I enjoy watching people be awkward and struggle with it, not know how to ask, because I'm happy to tell them my experiences. I'm happy to educate them. I'm happy to share my view. But sometimes I just wait for them to ask. And I know they want to.

It may sound cruel to watch people squirm when they are curious, but it seems that Joanna's main point is that when others demonstrate a genuine interest in learning, that creates in her a desire and willingness to educate.

Ruth, in one of her individual interviews, shared a similar sentiment. She said:

> I actually prefer that people just show me their curiosity because to me if they can do that, they're going to learn something and that's one step closer to people getting along better, I think. It's just some things that I don't like. I think people have to have conversations more often about things that are different or scary or new or unusual or uncommon to them because then they ultimately realize, "Okay. You're really not as different from me as I thought." And it's good.

Ruth recognized that change can happen through human interaction when people are willing to take the risk to ask questions and others are willing to respond. Ruth was willing to educate when others were eager to learn. Coming from Chicago, where, according to Ruth, people generally say what they think, she carried that way of being with her. She found, however, that in Boston, where she was living, people did not always want to know the answer.

Ruth shared a story of telling a woman outright that she didn't want to hang out with her because the woman was elitist. She explained:

> She [the woman] asked, "Why don't you want to hang out with me?" I said, "Well, I don't think we'd be good friends." I said, "If you want me to explain that further, I can." She goes, "That's okay. That's okay." She said, "Well, good luck in Boston." I said, "Okay. Thanks." Then she wrote me back and said, "Actually, I do want to know." So I told her. And so many people were like, "Oh, my God. Why would you ever say that to somebody? Why would you ever say that you thought that she was elitist?" I thought, "Because she wanted to know the truth." She asked. I didn't put it out there to crow. I'm not – I don't believe in being unnecessarily cruel to people, but if you want my honest answer, I'll tell you.

For Ruth, it was "bizarre" that people would "sugar-coat" how they felt about a situation; she felt it was important to tell her truth.

Diana and Bobbi, however, were much more skeptical that people are teachable. Diana asked about White people, "What's their motivation to change?" Diana reported that Boston is now a minority-majority city, yet that is not reflected in people who hold government offices, and people of color are "still getting less resources and less attention and less respect than White people." She added, "So you have to ask yourself, 'How Brown does America have to get before White people get it?'" Later she talked about how even though there are more "minorities" in the country, they are "still clustered in the bottom level of the economic ladder and the educational system and the job market." She said:

> So, why are these White people going to change? Nobody gives up power. You have to take it, and I think the only way you can take it is either by force (and there's not enough minorities to do it by force), or by getting inside and changing things.

Diana was focusing on White people's *motivation* to change. However, her final sentence implied that she believed in *capacity* for change, by "getting inside and changing things." In other words, she believed that her presence and the presence of other people of color inside White institutions could ultimately change the power structure.

Diana shared a story of walking out of a staff meeting when a co-worker said something about the drawback of having to work with a "nigger." As she was exiting, her boss begged her not to leave, and the woman who made the remark apologized soon after. Diana remarked:

> So, that may be an example of why White people – how White people had to change. But had I not been in that job, and if I had not stood my ground, there would never have been any recognition of their wrongfulness.

Often Diana's stories focused on issues of social class. She believed that in order to make it ahead in life people had to gain access to money and White ways of being. If she had not gone to Harvard, she probably would not have had the kind of job where she would have been in a meeting like that, and thus would not have been able to affect that kind of change. Although skeptical about the capacity to educate White people, Diana believed it was possible, in large part, through access to money and subsequently, social status.

Bobbi, if you recall, was the person who believed that White culture is a xenophobic culture. She believed that it is in White people's "nature" to put down people of color and be "hateful" and "distrustful" of outsiders. She said, "With White people it always comes back to race. Like they'll always say some shit that's so stupid." She didn't believe in White people's willingness and capacity to unlearn racism.

From these stories it is apparent that there was a continuum of belief in the capacity of people with power to unlearn and understand oppression. Most of the participants believed in other people's capacity to change. The only participant who stated that she truly didn't believe change was possible was Bobbi; yet, she wavered on this stance in relation to her mom.

THAT'S THEIR PROBLEM OR I SHOULD GET PAID FOR IT

In the Oakland group interview there was a discussion about whether or not people felt a responsibility to educate. Bobbi responded, "Are you talking about educating White people? No. No way. That's their problem. That's what I think. It's just like too draining, you know?" Linda also admitted, "I didn't want to be an educator ever. I was always like, 'Fuck you. Go away. I don't want to deal with your shit because it's too hard.' Then I started dating White people." Thus Linda didn't want the role of educator, but later changed her attitude based on her intimate involvement with White women. Ana also discussed not wanting to take on the burden of educating. She said:

> My work world is very White, staff wise. Yet, I work with a lot of Brown young people. That's kind of interesting being a minority in lots of different ways with my staff, feeling like I have an outsider perspective, and feeling like I'm the only one who has that. Not wanting to have the burden to be the one to always speak up about certain things, or educate about how oppression works.

Although Ana didn't want the burden, she often took on the role of educator or bridge builder, as will be discussed later in the chapter. Alana didn't outwardly refuse to educate but felt she should be compensated for her work. She said:

> I don't feel I can talk openly with most White people without having to explain to them things and constantly breaking everything down. And then it becomes about me serving them and educating them, which I do all day long in school, and with my students. And then it becomes, it's like I want to get paid to do that. I don't want to have to do that constantly in my life all the time.

As a graduate student who also taught, Alana felt she often acted as an educator regarding issues of oppression with her White students. Thus, she did indeed get paid for some of her educating. Alana felt she needed to put energy into herself and "other people of color in the ways that we've been hurt" when outside of her professional role. She didn't refuse to educate, but she put boundaries around how much, with whom, and when she expended energy to teach people about oppression.

Ruth had a similar approach to educating others, which surfaced when I asked how her parents felt about her being queer. She said that they were not okay with it at all, but she felt like it was up to them to deal with their feelings. She said, "I'm going to be who I am and then everybody else can figure it out on their own. It's not my responsibility to make them get it." I asked her how she kept that perspective. She responded:

I don't know. I think maybe it's knowing that it's just way too much – it would involve way too much work and way too much energy to get people to come around. I can't educate the world on this stuff. I've got shit to do. I can educate – I can try to educate people to a point, and then I'm done. I don't want to take that on. It's too much. It gets old educating people on how to treat people. It's tiring. I can say it once, but I'm not going to do it too many times after that. I can only hope that they figure it out. I think it's also realizing that you can't change – you can't necessarily change people, but you can change the way you respond to them and my response is to just go about my business and stay true to myself and make sure I'm happy.

Ruth, like Alana, was willing to educate people, but she limited the amount of time she invested in others. She recognized that it was up to her to stay true to herself, and she could only control her own actions. Ultimately people need to take responsibility for their own learning.

A RESPONSIBILITY AND A CALLING TO BE ALLIES, EDUCATORS, AND BRIDGE BUILDERS

In the Oakland group interview, Tina said that because she could pass, she felt it was her responsibility to be an "ally" to people of color "as much as possible." Marta felt similarly and said:

I feel like because I have white skin privilege, I feel like it's my calling to do that... to be an ally to people that have darker skin and get much more racism than I do. So I do speak up a lot, especially when it's about somebody else. I have a much harder time speaking up about myself.

Alana chimed in:

I definitely feel like I do [have a calling to educate], as hard and frustrating as it is to educate White folks all the time every day. It's my life. And I feel I should be getting paid to do so. It's something that I feel a responsibility to do because I understand Whiteness.

Alana repeated her conviction that she should get paid for her time and effort spent educating White people; nonetheless, she felt a calling to educate "White folks" because she understood Whiteness. Alana then added:

I also feel like, more so I'm thinking in terms of education around sort of identifying my community, whatever that is. Thinking about doing education around sexuality and gender stuff within communities of color is also something that I'm thinking a lot about in terms of like, I want to say providing resources in sort of a paternalistic way, for poorer working class folks specifically. Because I've had access to theory, and the academic theory specifically, I feel like that is a resource. And I definitely want to feel like I can provide that for folks who don't have that resource. So that's actually something I've been thinking about, how to start doing that work. And it's also doing work around privilege, for people of color with class privilege. That's something else I've been thinking about. Because I don't feel like I have a lot of conversations with a lot of other people of color with class privilege as people of color specifically. That's also something that I would like to start thinking more about and having conversations with folks about.

For Alana, the call to educate moved beyond the scope of educating White people about racism and included educating people on issues of sexuality and gender. Specifically, she named a desire to work with other people of color, to work with her community to share her academic knowledge as a resource. Yet she also realized that she needed to seek out her own education in order to better understand her class privilege.

As mentioned earlier, there was a high level of consciousness among the women about the intersectionality of oppressions. Linda summed this up:

As much as I've always been like, I don't want to be an educator, I don't want to have to teach people, blah, blah, blah. It is real though, and that is kind of our role, often. I'm not saying as people of color, but as human beings, like to change the world and to make it more of a better place. We need to speak to one another as humans and recognize that we're not always in the same place, where everyone has the same background, or political education, or experience even, to not be homophobic, and not be sexist, not be racist, not be ageist, or fat phobic; there are almost 50 million ways we can discriminate against each other. And all it takes is a few minutes of being like, "Well, what about this," or having that kind of dialogue. So that was a big learning experience; that was a big step for me.

Several of the women in the Oakland group felt a calling or responsibility to educate. This sentiment arose among participants in other cities as well.

In the Boston group interview, Susan said that she used to "feel a responsibility" to teach but she no longer concentrated on the intention of teaching. In that way, "the burden of translation is taken off" of her shoulders. She still responded when people asked her questions. However, instead of focusing on responding to educate, she responded however she wanted to, and recognized that the listener could "hear whatever they want from it." By not "catering" what she said to someone else, she found that it freed up her "emotional energy." Thus she was still educating but not claiming "responsibility" to do so.

Shortly after that statement, Katherine responded with her thoughts on the topic; she took a position of feeling both a responsibility to educate and a desire to shuck the burden of being an educator. She said:

I recognize that my feelings have changed and probably will keep changing, but I feel like it's both at the same time. The strongest part of me wants to say, "Yeah, it sucks that I have to be in this position where I can educate people, and they need educating sometimes." But nothing is going to get better without somebody doing it, so I want to do it. But then at the same time sometimes I don't want that responsibility. I don't want that burden, and I'm tired of it. I think people even when they ask harmless questions, you know, they are asking you, and for them it's the first time that they've thought about it or asked somebody. But for you it's like the umpteenth time this week that somebody's asked me that, and they don't understand that.

Thus, Katherine teetered between owning responsibility and wanting to release the burden of educating. Katherine, as you may recall, was described by her sister as the most "exotic" sibling, and she was the participant who was most often asked the "What are you?" question. It makes sense that she would want to evade the responsibility to educate because, with her highly ethnically ambiguous look, people confronted and questioned her about identity and race issues constantly.

Ruth also acknowledged that her identity as a mixed race woman made her "a lot more sensitive to race relations." In addition, watching her mom deal with issues of race helped her "to have conversations with White friends without it being scary for them." She said:

I think I'm able to give them [White people] a safe space to talk about that stuff without making them feel like they should feel ashamed, because I think it can be hard to be a person of color, but I think it's also hard to be White, too. That is hard. On one hand, you get privilege to be White, but on the other hand, it alleviates some privilege because a lot of people direct their anger toward you in maybe a blanket way that's not fair.

Ruth's empathy for her mom's experience as a White woman dealing with issues of race and her understanding of race issues as a mixed race woman helped her talk to White people in non-threatening ways.

In the Albuquerque group interview, Maria and I both discussed the feeling of responsibility we each held to confront others on their racism as light skinned people of color in graduate school. I said, "People who often have a hard time interacting with people of color sometimes feel more comfortable around me. Then I wonder, 'What does that mean, what are their expectations, and how can I challenge those?'" Maria recalled her time in graduate school and how she and the other person of color in her program were both light skinned and felt that others expected them to be complacent. She said, "Because of that I know that I went in even stronger. I mean, even in theory classes I was bringing up racism. I was just not going to let anyone off the hook." We felt the added responsibility of educating

White peers about issues of race, knowing that issues of racism contributed to the fact that many of the people of color in graduate school were light skinned.

Participants also discussed the concept of bridge building in relation to their thoughts on educating responsibilities. Ana said:

> I think I spent a fair amount of time thinking of myself as a bridge builder. Which in a natural way became thinking of myself as an outsider. I think at some point, I was thinking "Where are the people that match me? Where are they? Where are they?" I felt like an outsider in that way and an outsider as a vaguely Brown person in a mainly White peer group I hung out with in college or just feeling like an outsider in different ways, but also utilizing [the fact] that I have these neat perspectives, because I live between different worlds. To me the bridge building is being comfortable with things that are simultaneously true, and sometimes may be in conflict with each other, and you still have to deal with it and move your way forward.

Ana, feeling like an outsider as a "vaguely Brown person" in mainly White communities, took her positionality as someone living "between different worlds" as an opportunity to build bridges. She added:

> I think I've accepted some level of responsibility in terms of being a bridge builder. I'm just trying to figure out where my natural talents and my life experiences come together in a way that I feel like I've got a contribution to make to the community. Bridge building is definitely one of the things. But I acknowledge that when stuff happens, yeah, I'm not a super girl. And people need to have responsibility for things that happen. They need to be accountable, either they will be or they won't.

Ana began to accept a level of "responsibility" as a bridge builder. However, she simultaneously learned that there were limits to her bridge building capacity, which were dependent upon other people's willingness to be accountable for their actions.

Linda similarly articulated her positionality as a bridge builder:

> But yeah, the bridge, and the power that we hold, an opportunity we have, I think it's really exciting, and like I feel that we are on the forefront of transnationalism on like a whole new generation. My little cousins, they can say it's all around us, it's all around us.

Not only did she have the power to build bridges, but she highlighted the increasing power to do so that will come with the new generation of mixed race people. Linda informed me that all of her Japanese aunts married White people, so all of her cousins are mixed race. In her world, there was a clearly growing population of mixed race people who would also have the power to build bridges.

TEACHING PEOPLE WE LOVE

It is clear that many participants felt a calling and/or responsibility to be educators and bridge builders about issues of oppression. Several of them stated that this responsibility came from either living in two worlds, understanding Whiteness, and/or having the privilege to pass. However, there was another reason why these women found a need to be educators around issues of race – because they had White people in their lives that they loved. Some of the women found it easier to educate people they were close to, others found it more difficult.

In the Oakland group interview Bobbi said, "I'm not trying to call my mom on her shit. She's an adult." Linda validated her, stating that it is hard to go there with people "who you love and care about. That's hard. Because the risk is that they're going to be hurt terribly." Throughout her interviews, Linda talked about the difficulty of trying to educate her White girlfriend about racism, knowing that she often felt hurt in the process. Her girlfriend at the time had little education around race issues and, as a result, would at times make comments that were "kind of off." Linda explained:

> She said something that rubbed me the wrong way, and I freaked out. I was like, "Oh shit, I can't tell you to fuck off because I love you." And I came to the realization that this is my role. I feel like we have a responsibility to talk to each other, even if it's hard, even if it means that I'm the one being like, "Okay you're pissing me off, but I will be really calm and talk to you about it and help open your eye about it." And it's weird because I'll do it with random ass strangers before I'll do [it] with people I love.

Linda, who had the tendency not to want to educate, found herself in a position where she had to in order to maintain a relationship with someone she loved. Later in the interview Bobbi said, "I call people out." I challenged her, saying, "Except for your mom." She responded, "I have to deal with my mom for the rest of my life, you know? I don't want to make waves now."

Alana then said:

> I have the opposite experience with my mom. I'm trying to educate her every chance I can with this consciousness around the Whiteness and privilege about the ways that she hurt me, and the ways that her family hurt me. And it's been hard. It's really almost destroyed our relationship at times.

Alana explained that her mom "knows some of the language around antiracist White stuff" and knows what "White privilege is" because of being privy to Alana's struggles and experiences with racism. Still she found herself wanting and needing to educate her mom and other White people in her life. She recognized that she needed to "set some boundaries" but felt a responsibility to talk to people she loved. She stated:

I have to say something that, honestly, I don't think that most White people really change or understand racism without interpersonal work, really learning from people that they love and care about. Like, they can read every book in the world about imperialism and colonialism and not understand how they actually act in the ways that they do, not recognize how they treat people and understand what it means to be a White person, without people of color that actually love them and are willing to get in that conversation with them. And it's hard, it's hard. But I feel like for me, those White folks I have in my life that really have changed, have done so from people of color continually schooling them and calling them out on their shit. So it's kind of a slippery [slope], you know, like how much? Well we get to choose, we still get to choose, and it makes sense for us to do what we can. For me, when it makes sense for me, I do it, and when it doesn't make sense I can set boundaries and say "No, I'm not going to do that for you."

As much as Alana didn't want to take on the burden of educating others, she really believed that interpersonal communication between White people and people of color about issues of race is the most effective way for White people to begin to understand racism. As such, she felt an obligation to "school" White people, but she also realized that she needed to set limits for herself, to take care of herself.

Janet, like Alana, found it easier to talk to people she was close to. Janet struggled in general with speaking out, but admitted:

The closer I am to someone, it's easier for me to speak out. You know, like with my father for example, but if it's like my friend's friend or something and we're all sitting in like a bar or something, it's like that's not lecture time, and I don't want to be your teacher, and always feeling like I have to teach people too. And I don't always want to do that. Like I just want to relax and not have you say these comments to me. So that's hard.

Janet found it easier to challenge people with whom she was close.

Racist comments and actions can be exponentially more painful when the perpetrators are loved ones. Although teaching others about oppression runs the risk of causing strife and hurt, not teaching others entails the risk of being continually hurt by ignorance. Participants varied in their feelings about whether or not it was easier and/or more important to educate White people they loved about oppression. Perhaps most striking is Alana's argument that White people won't change unless they learn about the impact of oppression "from people that they love and care about." This means that if we are invested in creating a more socially just world, then it is imperative that we act as educators.

NOT NECESSARILY PREPARED TO EDUCATE

Janet struggled with feeling inadequately prepared to educate others. Reflecting back on her life, she realized that she rarely stood up against racism, for herself or her friends. She harbored feelings of guilt for her failure to act. To compensate, she began actively arming herself with the knowledge to confront people through her media literacy work, and she continually strived to "show stereotyping in the media."

Tina still was unsure of her abilities to challenge people regarding issues of oppression. She said:

> I don't know if I can be an educator because I don't feel completely educated myself. I don't know, I know how to confront people around racism, but I don't know how to, I guess, guide them from doing that. I still have to deal with that myself.

Tina admitted her lack of skills in confronting others. She also was actively working toward gaining new knowledge, for example, taking courses in graduate school to further her understandings. Throughout the interviews, she shared several stories of calling people out on oppressive remarks. So, despite her feeling of not having enough knowledge to educate others, she still spoke up against injustice and prejudiced remarks.

Brittney told stories in which she could be identified as a victim of racism, yet she, self-reportedly, didn't really see racism. However, as a result of the group interview and the project, she began to interpret her experiences through a new critical lens. With this new lens, she felt she would educate and challenge others more often, stating, "I won't just blow it off. I would tell them why it was offensive and hopefully me telling them will make them not do it again."

Ana shared a story of an experience in which she was "caught between two perspectives" when a White person and a person of color entered an argument related to race issues. She explained:

> I felt very loyal to both of them. I think both of them were right and both of them were wrong. One was more wrong than the other. It all happened so quickly, and then it was over, and I was just there. I felt I wasn't equipped to deal with it.

Although Ana came across as articulate in her thoughts on race, racism, and other forms of oppression, she still felt she had more to learn in order to be an effective bridge builder.

Overall, the women struggled with various complications of educating others, including: the fear of hurting people they loved; not feeling adequately equipped to confront people; and struggling with taking on the responsibility to educate while simultaneously setting boundaries necessary for self-care.

CONCLUSION

As mixed race women straddling the borderlands of several social categories, these women often found themselves in the position of educating others. The women had complex and sometimes conflicting feelings regarding educating others about racism, being mixed race, and oppression more generally. Their ability to educate others, both in terms of experience and opportunity, was perceived as a responsibility, a calling and a burden. There were times when these women wished and wanted to say, "No, I won't do it." Overall, however, they appeared to take on the challenge of teachable moments.

Three main motivating factors emerged for accepting the responsibility of teaching about oppression. First, for some, in order to be perceived as "competent" in predominately White institutions, they had to educate in order to pave the way for their own success. Second, these women collectively had a strong sense of commitment to social justice. Several of them stated, through the telling of their stories, that they desired a world without racism, sexism, and homophobia. Thus, as women fighting for social justice, they felt the need to do their part to eradicate oppression, to use their borderland positionalities, and (for some) their privilege to pass as White to build bridges between White people and people of color. Third, they all had White people in their lives whom they loved. In negotiating those relationships, at times the White people they loved made comments or took actions that felt oppressive and hurtful, or failed to take actions against oppression. As such, they were caught in a trap of either educating the people they loved so they would be hurt less often, not educating and continuing to be hurt, or not having the people they loved in their lives any longer (which sometimes, as in the case of White moms, was not an option). These women had strong motivations, in both public and private spheres, to educate others about issues of oppression, especially related to race.

In light of some of their motivations, it is useful to look at the more complex factors that played into the relationship dynamics as the women tried to educate. Their stories speak to two important theoretical concepts related to race issues and racism: double consciousness and code-switching.

W.E.B. Du Bois coined the term "double-consciousness." He wrote about double consciousness in his autobiographical book *The Souls of Black Folk*. Du Bois (1996) said:

> ...the Negro is a sort of seventh son, born with a veil, and gifted with second-sight in this American world, – a world which yields him no true self-consciousness, but only lets him see himself through the revelation of the other world. It is a peculiar sensation, this double-consciousness, this sense of always looking at one's self through the eyes of others, of measuring one's soul by the tape of a world that looks on in amused contempt and pity. One ever feels his twoness, – an American, a Negro, two souls, two thoughts,

two unreconciled strivings; two warring ideals in one dark body, whose dogged strength alone keeps it from being torn asunder. (p. 5)

Du Bois wrote about Black people's ability to understand the viewpoint of White people – "the American." People of color, in order to navigate White culturally codified institutions, have always needed to understand White consciousness. Thus, the double consciousness that these women occupy, in understanding culturally codified habits and practices of both White people and people of color (at least the ways of their respective racial/ethnic groups), is not something unique to mixed race people.

This double consciousness also connects to Lisa Delpit's (1995) articulation of the culture of power. Double consciousness entails understanding the operations of the culture of power. In terms of race, this refers to understanding the culture of White people. Of course, White people have the greatest access to the White culture of power and because White culture is the culture of power; White people have the freedom to never have to understand other people's cultures. Most institutions – work, school, healthcare, etc. – are dominated by White leadership and structured around White culture. White people are thus advantaged to succeed. People of color, however, have been forced to adapt to White ways of being to successfully navigate White institutions. They have had to "code-switch."

Scotton and Ury (1977) defined code switching as "the use of two or more linguistic varieties in the same conversation or interaction" (p. 7). The term has since been expanded upon. Greene and Walker (2004), for example, stated that code-switching, "can involve the alternation between two different languages, two tonal registers, or a dialectical shift within the same language, such as Standard English and Black English (Flowers, 2000)" (p. 435). They argued, "it is a linguistic tool and a sign of the participants' awareness of alternative communicative conventions" (p. 435). Although theories of code-switching focus on linguistic patterns in verbal communication, the women's stories indicate that non-verbal cues need to be switched as well in distinct contexts. Greene and Walker (2004) argued that code-switching "is a strategy at negotiating power for the speaker. Code-switching reflects culture and identity and promotes solidarity. A rhetorical tool, the mastery of code-switching enables the speaker to maneuver through a variety of publics" (p. 436). Diana's story of talking White as a student with a substitute teacher and consequently garnering special attention is a strong example of how code-switching can be used to negotiate power. However, altering speech patterns alone may not be enough. As exemplified in Joanna's echoed statement, "It's very clear to me in watching my own interactions, and watching interactions with other Black women, as soon as your neck starts moving, people stop listening." The women's stories convey that in order to be heard, to claim power, they not only need to *talk* White, they need to *act* White, to display non-verbal cues that are considered "appropriate" in mainstream White culture.

Again, code-switching is not unique to mixed race women; people of color in the United States have been code-switching since colonization. Diana's story of "acting White" in her eighth grade classroom, however, reveals a capacity to code-switch from a very young age, something to which she had been granted access by having White culture modeled in her home. All but one of these women (Linda, who was raised by her Japanese mom and Black step dad) had been heavily immersed in White culture in their homes, so it was not so much a switch as a need to emphasize one way of being over another. Linda was granted access to White culture as a person who could pass in a society in which Whiteness is dominant. Regardless of how and to what extent these women had access to White culture, the stories these women told support writings by people of color who emphasize that White culture is dominant and that sometimes acting White in terms of spoken language and mannerisms is necessary in order to be heard and respected by White people.

There was a general sense among the women of a responsibility to educate, coupled with anger that the education must be conducted in a manner that suppresses any of their cultural ways of being that are not in line with dominant White culture. However, several of the women stated that they felt they must take the opportunities they had, especially those who had light skin privilege, to help others unlearn oppression. At the same time, however, some emphasized the need to set boundaries to take care of themselves and to hold others accountable. Ana, for example, said that she wanted to use her "perspectives of living between different worlds" to build bridges but recognized that "would only work insofar as people were willing to be accountable for their actions." Throughout the participants' stories there is a sense that overall, these women believed in the capacity of White people (and other people who hold social power) to unlearn and understand oppression but that capacity is only as great as people's willingness to learn.

Linda felt that she learned the most about racism and oppression from dialogues with people of color. I asked Linda specifically, "So how do we dialogue with one another?" She said:

Well, one, we have to actually speak to one another. I think it has to happen in schools. I think it has to happen at a way young age. I think people need to be learning about other cultures, and learning race tolerance and cultural understanding at a very young age. And with fucking homophobia too. We need to get it [anti-oppression education] to elementary school and be like, "Look, gay kids are cool, Brown people are cool, be tolerant of each other. You have a lot to learn, look at all of this diversity around you, and look at all the cultural riches that you have to learn from. That's a gift. That's a blessing, and not something to be afraid of, or stereotype, or ostracize, or otherize, or whatever." We should be talking about it, definitely.

It creates a sense of hope that these women were willing to take on the responsibility of bridge building. People of color have been stepping up to educate White people for centuries, and many White people have stepped up to be allies of people of color (Thompson, 2001). However, I agree with Linda; we need to approach the issue of eliminating oppression on an institutional level. It needs to happen in schools on a systematic level starting at a young age.

Some of the most important messages in these stories are being sent to people who hold social power, most specifically White people who hold racial power. The participants said, "Listen to us, other people of color, and mixed race people and learn about who we are and what we have to offer. It is not fair that we are expected to always speak to you in ways that are most comfortable to you. Step out of your comfort zone and meet us. Don't force us to talk and act 'White' to be heard. Listen to us and treat us with respect and dignity."

These women emphasized that it makes a difference when others demonstrate genuine interest in learning. Thus, the reciprocal exchange can be that White people make the effort to listen with demonstrated interest while mixed race women share their time and effort to educate with compassion. In order to continue the exchange, White people need to be accountable for their actions and statements. This means that when White people are being "schooled" about racism they need to be willing to actively listen to what they are being told, take responsibility for oppressive actions, and strive to avoid racist actions and statements in the future. In addition, White people can make efforts to *educate themselves* through courses and books about racism, privilege, and other forms of oppression.

Although these women's stories focus on educating about issues of race, it is important to remember that racism is intricately intertwined with sexism, homophobia, classism, and other forms of oppression (Collins, 2000; Johnson, 2006). As mixed race women we can be bridge builders, but education about issues of oppression needs to happen on a much grander, institutional level. Change toward justice will only work insofar as people with power are willing to be accountable and actively pursue ways to dispel stereotypes and unlearn racism and other forms of oppression.

EXPOSING ANALYSIS

Further Decoding Meaning

> Being mixed is very difficult in a society/culture that does not have a complex notion of race; you are gray in a context where only Black and White are seen to exist. But that is also the gift of being mixed, to be able to see the subtleties in all sorts of contexts, not just when thinking about race, where others cannot. – Susan

Having the power to decide what to emphasize in the conclusion places me in a precarious position. What and who will I expose yet again? What will be highlighted? What will be left out? What is at stake in such revelations and omissions? What collectivity will the daughter of a dark skinned mother and a White father attend to? My goals are multiple, and I hope to attend to various individuals and groups of people. For me it's helpful to return to why I embarked upon this work at the onset: I hoped to discover what mixed race women might know that could aid all interested individuals in taking actions to facilitate cross cultural communication and minimize oppression. I still believe, perhaps even more than when I began this work, that the more interconnected people feel, the less segregation and oppression will occur. This requires taking time and exerting the effort to connect with others across cultural differences and, ultimately, taking action to create structural change. While ideally, these links would occur through face-to-face interactions, connections can also be made by learning about people's life stories, at least as an initial step or perhaps to augment understandings of personal interactions. Thus, I hope that readers have taken the time to read the chapters that precede this conclusion. The complex stories the women tell are what bring this analysis and interpretation to life.

As I write these words, I imagine the varied readers: the mixed race woman searching for a sense of belonging, a White mother hoping to better understand her mixed race daughter, a sociology of education student wondering what this has to do with anything, a person of color skeptical of the ways a mixed race person might add to the dismantling of affirmative action – the possibilities are endless. For grounding I return to the participants – whom did they care most about and worry most about when exposing themselves through storytelling? The answers seem to vary: some worried about how people of color in general might perceive them, others were concerned about how White people might misuse the information they shared. For a few there were particular individuals that seemed to matter most, such as parents or partners. I also think about my own life. Who matters most to me? If I am honest, it is a mixture of other mixed race people, White people, and people of color, queer and straight, academic and non-academic; basically there is too much diversity among those I care about to narrow it down, and isn't the whole point to make connections across lines of difference? Thus for structure, I focus on a particular, perhaps peculiar, question. Let me explain.

In my original conception of this work, I had an entire chapter on "Dating, Mating, and Kids" that centralized information about whom the participants chose to date, what they wanted in a partner, and what thoughts went into who their kids might be/are, particularly related to race and ethnicity. Many of the ideas and quotes are infused throughout this book, but it was suggested that I concentrate that information as a final data chapter. I was prompted to tell my readers the answer to this question: "What vote do these mixed race women make with their bodies?" That question has been echoing in my head ever since. I find it problematic on several levels. The question places an emphasis on dating and partnering choices above all else, however, this is but one small facet of the complexity of their mixed race lives. The question implies that whom the women chose to sleep with (implied with the word "bodies") is some kind of "vote." What would that "vote" be regarding? Does the asker of the question (or you) think it reveals leanings in racial politics? Would the race of a chosen partner imply choosing that race above others? Regardless of what one might think such a "vote" implies, the assumption that it is a "vote" is troubling. However, answering the question, in multiple ways, has the potential to get at the heart of much of what has been shared throughout this text.

EMBODIED HYBRIDITY: "WHAT VOTE DO THESE MIXED RACE WOMEN MAKE WITH THEIR *BODIES*?"

First, the question, "What vote do these mixed race women make with their *bodies*?" highlights embodiment. The stories told do not emanate out of faceless, bodiless individuals, they are descriptions of embodied experiences. This relates to one of my main critiques regarding contemporary discourses of hybridity. As I argued in Chapter 2, I have been disturbed by the ways in which "hybridity" has been reconceptualized. Historically, "hybrid" persons signaled the potential demise of the "great White race" in racist politics (Young, 1995). In the new postcolonial conception, removed from biological origins, Bhabha (1996) named hybridity as a "Third Space" in which colonized individuals can claim agency through discourse (p. 58). However, this "Third Space" theory, I argue, has been co-opted by voices of dominant culture (see Grossberg, 1993; McLaren, 1997) to simply mean "cross-cultural exchange" (Ashcroft, Griffiths, & Tiffin, 2003, p. 119). This subtle shift, from hybrid person to hybrid space, risks disregarding power relations. The postcolonial concept of hybridity often overlooks the experience of actual hybrid persons, and focuses instead on the theoretical construct of border crossing (for a more detailed explanation, see Chapter 2). The hybrid positionalities of third space, liminality and border crossing are thus opened to everyone and, once again, the mestiza herself is rendered invisible while her theoretical consciousness is co-opted. In this text, I have been committed to recentering the voice of the hybrid person, which in turn brings a focus back to issues of power.

I recognize that this argument rests on a slippery slope of potential essentialization of race; what does it mean, after all, to be a "true" hybrid? I return, once again, to the concept of translocational positionality (Anthias, 2002). These women do not occupy fixed identities; race and gender remain social constructs (Butler 1990; Lorber, 2001, Omi & Winant, 1994). However, by virtue of historical race constructions, coupled with who gave birth to us, we hold particular raced positionalities that mark our experiences of "hybridity." Being mixed both White and of color is a distinct positionality. We, and our family members, are often victims of racism, yet we are expected to embrace cultural Whiteness, which entails a history of colonialism and imperialism. This requires us to embrace our torturers, our oppressors. Yet, it is also improbable for us to dismiss White people entirely, because we not only have White family, friends, and sometimes partners, but we ourselves are part White. Thus we can see the distinct, complicated power dynamics of the embodied hybrid experience that becomes lost in co-opted reconceptualizations of hybridity. The hybrid space that Bhabha (1996) described in which the colonizer and colonized meet is not as charmed as it might seem in theory. Although as mixed race women, we are in a unique position to ask questions that imply "acts of love" that "address [the] oppressed as well as the oppressor" (Noddings, 1989, p. 167), the politics of racial divisions continue. These participants' stories recenter hybrid, subaltern voices and experiences and demonstrate that embodiment matters. Linda exemplified the embodied conflicts in grappling with sustaining the contradictions of a "mestiza" consciousness as she admitted:

I'm really struggling with this. I just feel really negative. It's just the downward spiral of feeling bad about stuff. I don't feel like I can sustain contradictions or turn inner hurts into something else. I can't even hold those. I don't. And I am always choosing one. I'm always going to be identifying as a person of color. I'm never like, "I'm White." That's what I'm struggling with right now, is learning to acknowledge, to be in the contradiction and embrace it, and all that. Sustaining the contradictions, to turn the ambivalence into something else. I don't feel like that's even a comfortable place for me to be, to be in both. I love thinking that, yes it makes me pluralistic, it makes me, you know, think differently, and it does. But, every day I'm making choices about how I'm presenting my gender, how I'm presenting my sexuality, and how I'm being White or not, and I'm never being White. I'm never choosing White. I don't think that I've ever chosen White in my life because, because that's how the world views me in a lot of ways. I'm sure it's different a lot of times, but a lot of times I pass too. And I'm in the space of then of not even choosing it. I'm not saying I'm going to pass as White, and this is what feels good for me, you know? I don't know if I'm holding the contradictions.

Her narrative demonstrates how her embodiment of hybridity is more complicated than a theoretical "Third Space" or "mestiza consciousness." Because of her hybrid positionality there were certain external constraints that she negotiated as she endeavored to name and position herself; as she said, she didn't always get to choose, often certain identities were imposed upon her.

MULTIPLE POSITIONALITIES: "WHAT VOTE DO THESE *MIXED RACE WOMEN* MAKE WITH THEIR BODIES?"

Second, the question, "What vote do these *mixed race women* make with their bodies?" highlights the interplay of gender and race; this question would have a completely different connotation if the participants were men, and perhaps might not have even been asked. Highlighting gender and race simultaneously reminds us of the ways intersecting identities create multiple positionalities that impact experiences and related narratives, which is another main point emphasized throughout the text. Reality is constructed and performed through narrative; how stories are situated and their constructed meanings provide information about the hierarchies of social positions. The stories shared in the book reveal multiple layers of hierarchies related to race that are impacted by other socially constructed factors, including gender, socioeconomic status, and sexuality.

Self-positioning

With the question, "What vote do these mixed race women make with their bodies?" one might start with examining how the participants define their bodies, how they define themselves. In Chapter 3, we learned – through echoed statements such as "I do strongly identify as *not* White" (Joanna) and "I don't want people to think I'm White" (Bobbi) – that, in terms of race, the participants did not identify as White. Although gender might be assumed to be a given – these are women – a variety of stories serve as reminders that gender is created through performativity. For example, tomboy and butch identifications among some of the women impacted gender positioning, which also impacted experiences and positionalities related to race. Marta, for instance, used the word "Latin" to describe herself, purposefully rejecting both the feminine and masculine implications of the words "Latina" and "Latino." Maria's stories of the disconcerting change from elementary to middle school, when all those around her seemed to have grown from girls to young women overnight also highlights the impact of gender performativity on positionality. We see that identity is not fixed; many of the women shifted how they identified in terms of race and/or ethnicity and altered gender performances depending on the situation, as well as over time. Positionalities, we find, are impacted by myriad structural and cultural influences, such as upbringing, peer groups, geographic location, appearance, life changes, institutional pressures, other social identities, and personal challenges. The participants describe their identities as mixed race women as simultaneously painful and powerful.

Race and Gender Hierarchies

Throughout the text, stories abound that reveal operations of dominant White culture and racial hierarchies. The details of the stories reveal the nuanced operations of privilege and oppression. The narratives, for example, demonstrate that White people were most likely to assume participants were White and most likely to suggest that participants suppress their mixed race identities. This points to entitlement. White people were entitled to not have to examine cues that reveal race or ethnicity; they had the "luxury of obliviousness" (Johnson, 2006, p. 22). They also felt entitled to tell others how to be and act. This stands in direct contrast, for example, to Katherine's story of being asked by a Black woman about her background; the Black woman explained that she learned she had to act in different ways around White people than people of color for survival. White entitlement and power is also revealed in the many stories the women shared of recognizing that in order to be heard and respected by White people, they were expected to talk and act "White." This information may not be new, as it supports much of the research related to racism and White supremacy (Bonilla-Silva, 2006; Delpit, 1995). However, there is something particularly powerful and revealing about the moments in the stories where the women chose to shift a behavior, action, or aspect of appearance because these shifts revealed a resultant increase or decrease in acceptance by dominant culture individuals. Consequently the women gained or lost privilege. Several of Diana's stories stand out related to this. We learned of her quick entry to being the substitute teacher's favored student when she, with peer support, conspired to conscientiously act and talk "White." She informed us that she was treated differently on a daily basis after dying her hair blond and subsequently was perceived as White. She exclaimed that she learned that she had to speak "the King's English" to make it in the business world. We see, in the moment that she revealed her race as "Black" to a White gas station attendant, that she was reduced to being treated as less than human when asked to parade her body for him and his co-worker. The power of code-switching highlighted in these stories exposes racism, and indicates the nuances of power politics. For example, in order to gain the greatest privilege, the switching must be not only verbal, but also non-verbal to include "White" ways of acting – no neck moving allowed, we learn. Careful examinations of the narratives also reveal interplays of racism and sexism; it is because Diana is a *woman* that she was asked by a man to parade her body. We see too, that non-verbal communications are coded in multiple ways; neck moving is not only raced, but also gendered.

Thus, the stories expose interplays of race and gender hierarchies. Of course other social identity categories, such as class and sexuality, also affect power dynamics. Diana's middle-class positioning, for instance, influenced her opportunity to enter the business world and learn how to speak "the King's English." In the next section we will see further how sexuality in particular impacts power politics.

INTERPLAY OF AGENCY AND STRUCTURE: "WHAT *VOTE* DO THESE MIXED RACE WOMEN MAKE WITH THEIR BODIES?"

Third, "What *vote* do these mixed race women make with their bodies?" implies agency, something I have aimed to emphasize throughout the text, although always situated within the dialectical relationship agency occupies with structural constraints (Giddens, 1979). In fact, the question itself demonstrates the complex relationship between agentic options and structural limitations; even though the women have a "vote," norms based on patriarchal, racialized, institutional structures would dictate that one could deduce something about a mixed race woman's racial positionality based on whom she chooses to sleep with, to partner with, to conceive children with. The women recognized this assumption and some stated reactions to it.

After providing a detailed history of whom she dated – which included both men and women who were both Brown and White – Maria shared this:

> I have a [Brown] friend who told me one time that if she ever liked a White guy she wouldn't go there. She was just like, "now I just want a Brown guy," or whatever. And I hear that. I think I could consciously make those choices too, but I also know that in my world I have been and am attracted to a variety of people. I don't think that makes me less Brown or more White or less White or more Brown. If I let my partner define that for me then I'm fucked, you know? I think I'm at a place where it's just like "No, I can't." …
> For me, what I get interested in is that, if I'm with a White person how I think I'm seen as being in a mixed relationship, and if I'm with a Brown person then I'm not seen as being in a mixed relationship. And what does that really mean then? Because either way I'm operating in that mixed space.

So Maria has agency to choose whom she wishes to date, and she realizes that her choice may be perceived as a marker of her identity "more White or less White," but she rejects the idea that her partner defines her racial identification.

Katherine similarly points out her awareness that whom she dates is often read by others to have implications about how she identifies racially. She explained:

A lot of times, in terms of dating or what groups I hang out with, I definitely notice I have felt that people see those choices that I make as the choice of my identity. If I date a White person then it's my preference to be White. I don't think I've consciously thought [about it] that much, but that's been a concern that I have.

Thus, I could provide a list of information about the racial backgrounds of whom the women were dating or married to and votes could be tallied, but I won't, because the supposed "votes" mean nothing. This concept of voting implies what are likely, given the examples above, to be false assumptions about what matters to these women and their chosen positionalities. The stories reveal the nuances that matter in these mixed race women's complex lives.

Ana, for example, talked in detail about her hopes and fears for her four-year-old son. Ana is Filipina and British, and her partner, Stephanie, is a light skinned Black woman. Their son, Roberto, is Stephanie's biological child and the donor is a White Jewish friend of theirs. Ana wanted Roberto to have a Filipino/Spanish-sounding name (many Filipino names are Spanish because of colonization), and Roberto was chosen because it relates to a family name on Ana's side. Although he is Stephanie's biological child, Roberto actually has "ambiguously beige" skin much like Ana's. They have not yet decided how they will talk with Roberto about who he is in terms of his background given the multiple factors involved. Ana is considering carrying their second child and said:

I would love for our child to be half Black and half my mix because that represents our family. Reality is I don't think we'll have a male Black donor that's the right person. So do we do unknown? Because the cultural part of our child looking like who we are, would that become important? Or do we approach our son's godfather and ask him if he'll be a donor again. If that's the case, will I birth a child who's lighter than me? And what would that be like? Being a Brown woman, I just don't know.

Although Roberto has Ana's skin color, she realizes that he might have "experiences that are very different" from hers. Ana is concerned that Roberto will likely be assumed to be White unless he states otherwise, "and he'll have to decide for himself how he identifies." However, she conscientiously chooses to spend two weeks every summer in a city where she is around other light skinned Brown people and now takes Roberto. "And hopefully," Ana said, "something will rub off along the way and he'll realize he's Black. Who knows how he'll identify." Later in the conversation, she named her deepest fear:

I think one of my greatest fears is our child runs around unconsciously with privilege he never bothers to question. And he will because he's male. But hopefully we'll be good, not super militant, moms about that.

Much is revealed in Ana's narratives related to her family. Foremost, we see the impact of multiple positionalities – gender, race, skin color, socioeconomic status (ability to travel, choice of donors, and other factors mentioned in the full version of Ana's story) and sexuality. Race is/was only one factor of many in decisions about partnering and having children. Her stories also demonstrate a deep examination of privilege.

In an individual interview, Joanna shared a story that echoed some of what both Maria and Ana discussed.

> It's also how you define interracial. If one of those people in that relationship is not clearly one race or another, then everything is interracial… Even if I feel like dating other people who are [mixed] Black and White, that would feel interracial to me. Partially because, you know, nature vs. nurture. Where I grew up had so much to do with my racial identity and my race politics and the kind of family I grew up in. Even if you have the same ethnic background as me, it doesn't mean anything about your race politics or how you view it…My mom asked me if I viewed myself as being in an interracial relationship. Because my mom comes from the old school of the one drop rule. This is speculation, but I'm pretty sure that's why she was asking, 'cause she didn't view it as interracial, and she was kind of curious as to how I viewed it. The one drop rule is part of how I see it, but I definitely don't buy into it, at least not in that context. And I was saying, "Yes, I absolutely think it's an interracial relationship." . . . And I mentioned this to my girlfriend at the time, I was trying to make some other point, but she got hung up on that. I'm like "Yeah, my mom asked me if we were in an interracial relationship," and she's like "What did you say?" I'm like "Yes." And she's like "Really?" Like, hello! It was so obvious to me. It's funny because I was telling [my girlfriend] about it and she doesn't, she didn't feel our relationship was interracial. Whereas she felt like her relationship with her ex, who is White, was interracial. But my relationship with my girlfriend, who was Black, was not. Which was like "Whoa!" to me.

Joanna, like Maria, argued that all relationships for mixed people are interracial. Race, as Ana emphasized, is only one factor in how individuals might relate. Joanna pointed out that racial identity and politics factored into the equation. We see in her story that there can be multiple viewpoints regarding one situation.

Ruth explained that she tended to date women of color. Her experience with dating White people had been "kind of weird" because of the ways they were constantly "noticing differences." Ruth shared:

> Them noticing differences and pointing out my skin and "Oh, this and that," and blah, blah, blah. Just irritating. Irritating. Focusing on my hair, on my skin, or chalking up everything that's different about me versus other people

before me to my Blackness or mixed raceness. Mixed raceness, I don't know if that is a word, but – which is irritating, and really it's a gross simplification. It offends me, and I really didn't feel like having a side-by-side comparison so often. That and also just arguments about them perceiving me as being over-sensitive to things that I perceived to be as coming from racism.

Ruth stated that she would be open to dating White women but acknowledged that she usually ends up being interested in Black women. I admitted that I was surprised to hear that given all her difficult experiences in high school; Ruth, you might recall, was harassed throughout her schooling in her predominately Black school by Black students. She responded simply, "But those problems were external." Ruth was looking for someone who would understand her and not make her exotic. She elaborated that she previously had a "half German, half Filipino girlfriend." Ruth said:

She passed for White, and she had no sense whatsoever of what might be difficult about being of mixed heritage. She just didn't get that, and I felt like she didn't really identify much with being Filipino at all, and that was really weird to me. I just didn't understand why. I didn't understand why. To me it was obvious that she did not have two White parents, but that's not obvious to a lot of people and that might be why her experience – she moves through the world like a White person, in my opinion. Maybe she would tell you something different, but that was really bizarre to be with somebody who – I thought we would have more overlap in terms of experience and we didn't. I learned something about that. You can't assume that just because somebody's of mixed race that they're going to have – that there's going to be a lot of overlap, because I dated a woman who had a Jewish mom and a Black father also, and she was angry. I don't know why, but she was angry that we had different experiences.

So, although not averse to dating people of different races, as someone who could not pass for White, Ruth's experience had been that she was better understood by Black women. She stated, "So my girlfriend now is African American also. Well, I shouldn't say *also*, but she's African American, both parents."

Again, the nuances reveal power dynamics and differences. Ruth's stories reveal how racism operated in her relationships through her White girlfriends' positioning of Ruth as "different" and "exotic." When she confronted them, instead of recognizing that their actions might be racist, they accused Ruth of being too "sensitive." One might assume there would be overlaps among all mixed race people, and indeed in this study overall, we see several points of connection among the women as a group. However, in Ruth's story of dating mixed race women she highlighted the fact that she had little in common with them regarding how they experienced being mixed. She emphasized the connection she felt with Black women, but yet, in describing her current girlfriend, she was careful to name the distinction between herself as a mixed woman and her girlfriend who had two African American parents.

Brittney summed up her viewpoint regarding dating succinctly. She said, "I don't really look at race when I date. I mean if you are nice to me, and you treat me good, then I don't care what color you are." What stands out here is Brittney's desire, above all else, to be treated well. Given her history of having been the victim of both sexual harassment and rape, this is not surprising. Here we see that her choice of partner would not, for her, indicate any kind of vote in racial politics. Regarding having children she stated, "You know, if I can have kids, I wanna have my own kids, rather than adopt, just because I wanna see a reflection of me, you know?... And I don't care what race it is, just as long as it's got me in it." Brittney has described her mixed race experience as often feeling like "the only," so it is not surprising that she longs for a "reflection" of herself.

Each woman has her own unique story, but perhaps what is telling in these stories is that each was ultimately looking to be treated well, to find points of connection, and to acknowledge places of difference. Most of the women in the study, when describing whom they date/partner with and why, examined how privilege and power played out in the relationships. This is particularly evident in the multiple stories shared throughout the book by Linda regarding struggles in her relationship with Tracy, a White woman. We see this theme – striving to recognize how power is playing out in interactions – in most discussions of relationships (with parents, teachers, friends, co-workers, etc.) throughout the text.

Thus, through answering the question, "What vote do these mixed race women make with their bodies?" we gain insights into several of the themes highlighted in the women's stories throughout the book: embodied hybridity, self-positioning, positioning by others, the impact of multiple positionalities, operations of racism, White entitlement, the power of code-switching (when coupled with dominant norms of non-verbal communication), the interplay between agency and structure, conscientious examination of privilege, and the desire to be heard and understood. Yet, there is still more to discuss.

COMMON EXPERIENCES OF THESE MIXED RACE WOMEN

One research question I had approaching this project was: Are there shared experiences that U.S. mixed women identify with that cross racial and ethnic lines? Here, I reflect upon shared experiences among the women in the study that cross racial/ethnic borderlands.

Each chapter illuminates shared experiences. Perhaps one of the most surprising commonalities among the women relating to positionality was the shared strong desire to not identify as White. None told stories of consciously choosing to identify as White while several shared stories of consciously rejecting

White identities. Another less surprising commonality was the experience of fluid identities. The women relayed experiences of identifying and being labeled by others in various ways, both over time and situationally. The participants articulated a shared desire to name their racial and ethnic identities for themselves and did not want to be told how they should identify by others. Perhaps the largest common denominator is that being mixed was related to both pain and privilege. This is evidenced for example in examining their lives in relationship to school in which they had the tools and privilege to be academically successful, but the majority of them also suffered from feelings of alienation and exclusion based on race. Among many of the women there was an overarching sense of belonging nowhere and belonging everywhere simultaneously.

A desire for community with other mixed race people also arose as a common theme. In an often alienating and challenging atmosphere, several mixed race participants created a space that felt like home through friendships with other mixed women. Sometimes having these safe spaces allowed them to have more confidence in facing the pressures and constraints of being mixed in a milieu of overly simplified notions of racial politics, "in a context where only Black and White are seen to exist" (Susan).

EXPOSING RIFTS IN THEORETICAL MODELS OF OPPRESSION

Theories help guide us in our actions. Those of us striving to enact social justice work recognize the importance of praxis, the combination of theory and practice (Freire, 2000). The women told several stories that support well-known social justice theories. Much of what participants described relating to "Whiteness" coincides with discussions of how oppression operates in *Teaching for Diversity and Social Justice* (Adams, Bell, & Griffin, 1997). For example, in a detailed dialogue (see Chapter 7) the women explained the difference between prejudice and racism in ways that align with what is written in the text.

It is evident from these women's stories that racism is enacted in various ways – culturally, socially, and institutionally. What is not always clear is where these mixed race women fit in relationship to Whiteness, racism, and White privilege. In the *Teaching for Diversity* book, White privilege is defined as:

> The concrete benefits of access to resources and social rewards and the power to shape the norms and values of society, which Whites receive, unconsciously or consciously, by virtue of their skin color in a racist society. Examples include the ability to be unaware of race, the ability to live and work among people of the same racial group as their own, the security of not being pulled over by the police for being a suspicious person, the expectation that they speak for themselves and not for their entire race, the ability to have a job hire or promotion attributed to their skills and background and not

affirmative action (McIntosh, 1992). (Wijeyesinghe, Griffin, & Love, 1997, pp. 97–98)

If I included only the first half of the definition above without the examples, one might argue that almost all the participants had White privilege because 13 of the 16 participants were at times taken to be White, especially by White people. However the women demonstrated that racial identification goes beyond skin color. Many participants, including those who didn't "pass" as White, would admit that they sometimes benefitted from White privilege in certain situations because they had access to cultural Whiteness. At the same time, many of the women, including those who "passed" as White, could provide examples of being denied access to several privileges, such as those in the examples provided in the quote above, afforded to White people.

One of the main arguments made by Adams, Bell, and Griffin (1997) in their theory of oppression is that people of color cannot be racist because they lack institutional power. When people of color are prejudiced against other people of color, they are considered to be operating from internalized racism, not racism. So what happens, then, when mixed race people are brought into this theoretical framework? When White/of color mixed race people are prejudiced against people of color, is that considered racism or internalized racism? Who has the power and who has the right to answer that question? What would the response reveal? Mixed race experiences raise important unanswered questions.

Delpit's (1995) theory of "the culture of power" is another powerful tool that can be used to deconstruct how codes of power operate, especially regarding race and class dynamics. Delpit has five main assertions related to "the culture of power." Using her framework to analyze participants' stories (see Chapter 7 conclusion), we can deduce that the women, for example, had access to the codes and rules of the culture of power, evidenced by their overall high degree of success in institutions of education. Although the participants tended to distance themselves from Whiteness, they had learned and could enact White codes related to power. We find that the participants were border crossers, however, based on Delpit's (1995) final assertion that "Those with power are frequently least aware of – or least willing to acknowledge – its existence. Those with less power are often more aware of its existence" (p. 26). Although uncomfortable admitting participation in the culture of power, the participants collectively shared several stories demonstrating that often, they were able to recognize and willing to acknowledge its existence.

Similarly, related to critical whiteness theory, the stories the women told trouble the framework of critical whiteness that relies on a dichotomy between White people and people of color. Thus, we see that the experiences of the mixed race women may not fit neatly into the provided structure of existing theoretical models of race-based oppression that are configured upon racial dichotomies. This indicates the need for more nuanced theories and points to unexplored complexities about how privilege and oppression operate.

EXPOSING THE PRIVILEGE AND POLITICS OF CULTURAL WHITENESS

Scholarship on critical whiteness theory is increasing (Applebaum, 2010; Hytten & Warren, 2003; Thompson, 2003). To deepen our understandings of racial politics, which can assist us in listening across difference, we are tasked with understanding the interconnections between White supremacy and racism. This requires an understanding of how cultural Whiteness and "the culture of power" (Delpit, 1995) operate. The perspectives and words of these mixed race women, who embodied a combination of racial privilege and oppression, offer a unique lens with which to view the operations of cultural Whiteness. Discussions of Whiteness permeated the interviews. Thoughts about cultural Whiteness revealed in this text may not be surprising to people of color and other mixed race people. What I heard in these stories I have heard before in spaces inhabited predominately or exclusively by people of color. Rarely have I heard such forthright descriptions told in White/of color mixed company.

In the individual and group interviews, many of the women explicitly named undesirable aspects of cultural Whiteness. White people enacting cultural Whiteness were described as aggressive, selfish, demanding, taking up lots of space, critical of others, closed-minded, entitled, and individualistic. Cultural Whiteness was associated with racism and White supremacy; Alana stated outright, "It's a racist culture; it's part of White supremacy," and Bobbi asserted, "Xenophobia is a part of their culture." Nuances of White privilege were revealed in statements such as "They don't know that there is a way to be White. They just think it's the normal way and everybody else is different" (Diana) and "A lot of it is just unnamed things, like ways of being, mannerisms, behaviors, knowing how to react, knowing how to decode behavior, and know[ing] what someone's trying to say or not trying to say. And being able to not feel intimidated by certain authority positions," (Alana) and "I think about it [Whiteness] as having the freedom to not think about this [race] at all" (Katherine).

The participants highlighted the ways in which White people enact racism, consciously and unconsciously, that protect White supremacy and White privilege. However, they also acknowledged that such actions are situated in a cultural context of systemic racism in which White people are blinded to how people of color are harmed by oppression because of skewed media and history books that promote White dominant culture as the norm and typically as "good." Thus, conversations about Whiteness flowed from a focus on the individual actions to White cultural group behaviors to an acknowledgement of institutional systems of oppression. One participant acknowledged that the descriptions of cultural Whiteness related to socioeconomic status as well. Alana stated, "I know part of this is class, but class and race are so mixed." These descriptions of cultural

Whiteness intersect with Delpit's (1995) definitions of "the culture of power," yet again the framework is complicated by the hybrid space we occupy of being simultaneously people of color and White.

RECONCILING WHITENESS IN OUR OWN LIVES

As much as we desired to externalize Whiteness completely, it was impossible. Although none of the women, including myself, wanted to be called White, most of us were at times (to varying degrees) perceived to be White, and all of us had a White parent so we had some connection to Whiteness. Thus, the deep question, as asked by Marta (see Chapter 7) is, "How do we reconcile our Whiteness?" While several women named and examined White privilege and cultural Whiteness in relation to their lives, Linda stands out among the participants because of the quantity of time she spent discussing the topic. Many of these discussions came about as Linda processed her positionality in relationship to her friends, who were mostly women of color, and her partner, Tracy, who was White and not politically educated. In light of the politics of Whiteness and racism, for Linda, negotiating relationships was a balancing act, especially when her friends of color and her White partner came together in the same space. Linda alternated between feeling guilty and feeling justified for not being her girlfriend's "champion" in such spaces. She wondered if she should "translate" and be "more of a bridge" between her friends and her girlfriend, or if she was warranted in being "people of color aligned," which included "racialized" conversations in which she and her friends of color would sometimes "talk smack about White people." At the time of the interviews, Linda's compromise was to have side conversations with Tracy about systemic racism, stating to her, "You can only take responsibility for White people as a whole when you've done the oppressing, when you're the one who's being unconscious[ly racist], when you're the one acting like that. That's when you take ownership of it."

However, as the conversation deepened, Linda turned the lens onto herself. She admitted:

> This last year I have been able to say – we've [Linda and her partner] made comments about my half Whiteness. We've made comments about the racial stuff. It's coming up. It's on the forefront of my mind. Yeah, and it is hard. Because, you know what? We're dealing with all the same stuff that [my White girlfriend] is trying to work out right now. Does that mean that I'm bad? Does that mean that I can't be a person of color anymore? Does that mean that my experience as a person of color is not authentic because I am White also? What is the experience of a person of color?

In this exchange and other dialogues, Linda exposed our connections to Whiteness that as mixed people we often don't want to name: internalized self-hatred, fear of being shunned by people of color, self-doubt about our ethnic/racial positionality and "authenticity," our privileges due to connections to Whiteness, and all the related questions that arise. Although similar to Tracy's fear, with our disclosures we run the risk of being rejected by people of our own cultural backgrounds, by people of color, a group to which we belong. We feel trapped. Revealing these thoughts to people of color makes us vulnerable to being disowned and sharing them with White people opens us to racism and being pathologized.

Returning to the question, "What vote do these mixed race women make with their bodies?" deeper more meaningful questions arise: Why do the women make the choices they make about whom they choose to share with most intimately? and What do such choices reveal?

Linda, for example, shared that most of her partners have been White, and she recognizes that her choices have been connected to issues of power. With a White partner, Linda did not have to worry about being insufficiently politically educated about race; she would not be challenged on her racial positionality. Also, she admitted, with a partner of color she might have to deal with feeling like she was "oppressing" somebody. With a White partner, she would never be in the position of being an agent of racial oppression, only a target. The same politics led to Alana making a conscious choice to not partner with White women; she wanted to be challenged on her privilege related to cultural Whiteness by people of color and over time had grown to "not feel safe" with White people. Ruth similarly typically chose not to partner with White women. After several experiences of girlfriends making racist remarks and making her exotic, Ruth did not want to be a target of oppression in her intimate relationships. Thus we see power dynamics related to issues of privilege centralized in the choices these women made. Typically in relationship dynamics between White women and women of color, social justice issues are described in the ways Alana and Ruth revealed; White women are perceived to have greater power due to their White privilege and capacity to enact racial oppression. It's notable that both Alana and Ruth could not pass for White and thus were more vulnerable to racial oppression.

Linda's Asian mixed race, light skinned positionality complicated the racial dynamics and politics of privilege. Her words indicated that she felt a greater sense of power in relationships with White women than she would in relationships with women of color. Yet she also feared that she might have had more power in relationships with women of color, particularly power to unconsciously "oppress." (Given who she is, she would not consciously choose to oppress). However, as Linda's stories reveal, having a White partner still brings a set of challenges; given that her friends were people of color, she was constantly placed in situations where she was being forced to choose. As has been described in detail, such choices are perceived as more significant than just favoring particular individuals. The choices are assumed to indicate larger politics and allegiances. This returns us full circle to the concept of how the choices we make about who we choose to be with, intimately or otherwise, are perceived by some as how we "vote" in racial politics. However, on the personal one-to-one (micro) level, race is but one (sometimes small) factor in the depth of interactions that can occur between two people; to place a primary emphasis on this minimizes all that goes into developing and maintaining healthy relationships

SEGREGATION AND COMMUNITY

Not surprisingly, Linda stated that her deepest discussions regarding her own Whiteness occurred with other mixed people who were mixed with White. Throughout the stories we gained an impression that the women were longing for a sense of community, a home. Many of the women shared stories of feeling that they had found the greatest sense of community with other mixed race people. However, several found and created community through other points of connection, including groups of open-minded people, progressively politicized people, eclectic people, and people who had experiences of straddling borderlands, such as immigrants, first generation people of color, and light skinned people of color.

Yet, inserted among the stories of desiring community, there were striking stories of division and segregation. The narratives reveal that we often are complicit in segregation, separating out the White people and people of color in our lives in an effort to delicately navigate complicated racial politics. When we do bring White people and people of color into our lives together, what level of integration occurs?

Yet, we see in the stories of schooling experiences that segregation was detrimental to the well-being of several participants. Many of the women shared descriptions of being isolated and alienated in monoracial peer groups. The participants who had the most positive school experiences were in ethnically and racially diverse schools, which points to the importance of increasing diversity and promoting cross cultural integration.

RELATIONSHIP TO SOCIOLOGY AT LARGE AND SOCIOLOGY OF EDUCATION

Although sociologists recognize that race is socially constructed (Omi & Winant, 1994), it is also understood among those in the field that human beings are placed in hierarchies and treated in particular ways based on racial categories; thus social positionalities related to race matter. Race based research is prominent in the field of sociology, but little research exists regarding qualitative work on mixed race people that is interpreted through a sociological lens (Telles & Sue, 2009). This work adds to the field of sociology through a focus on sociologically analyzed mixed race narratives that resist theoretical disembodiment. As exemplified in the sections above, this work exposes nuances in privilege and oppression politics as revealed through the lived experiences of mixed race women.

Sociologists of education claim a prominent role in uncovering ways that oppression is created and reproduced. This work centralizes operations of power related to oppression and privilege. The participants' stories provide some insights into the "stratification of knowledge and social stratification" (Weis, McCarthy, & Dimitriadis, 2006, p. 4). The women shared stories that reveal interplays between cultural capital, social capital and academic success. For example, we learned that two of the Latinas were placed in low tracks for reading due to assumptions about their lack of English language skills. However, with their social and cultural capital, each was able to gain access to higher academic tracks. Through Diana's story we learned how her ability to use dominant culture speech patterns helped her garner special treatment among her all-Black peers. All of the women in the study possessed the general speech patterns of the dominant culture and ultimately each achieved academic success in school; there is likely a correlation. There is little research and information within sociology of education that explores the stories of mixed race individuals. The combined macro and micro analysis employed here reveals complex dynamics of academic success that is often achieved at the expense of a large emotional cost. If we ask the sociological question, "What is the purpose of schools?" and the answer is deeper and broader than academic achievement, then there is much work to be done to make schools meaningful and safe spaces for mixed race students. The narratives are overwhelmingly filled with schooling stories of alienation. In debates about how to better serve the needs of students of color, one response has been to suggest that we stop trying to minimize segregation and instead concentrate on at least making segregated schools equitable (Ladson-Billings, 2007). Although understandable in the desperation to assist groups of failed students, such a move would likely be emotionally detrimental for mixed race students, increasing alienation and isolation.

We learned that the level of connections the women felt to their ethnic cultures – languages, personal histories, and cultural ways of being – influenced their sense of agency. This supports research regarding the importance of encouraging students to maintain their ethnic ways of being and the work teachers should do to incorporate students' home cultures (Delpit, 1995; Gay, 2000; Moll, 1992; Nieto, 2004). However, perhaps most importantly, the stories exposed nuances of power dynamics that can assist all educators and administrators in making informed decisions about both personal interactions with students, particularly mixed race students, and policy making.

COMMUNICATING ACROSS LINES OF RACIAL DIFFERENCE

In autobiographical writings, mixed race people often allude to having enhanced skills for moving in and out of various ethnic and racial communities (Camper, 1994; O'Hearn, 1998; Walker, 2001). I wanted to examine these women's stories for what they might tell us about cross-cultural communication and comprehension, particularly related to race and ethnicity.

There is a complex relationship between cross-cultural communication ability, desire, and need. These women had no choice but to communicate cross-culturally as they moved from one side of the family to another and talked with one parent or the other. Although they embodied the races of both their parents, the mixture created a third positionality – being *mixed*. How the women identified racially/ethnically would impact their perceptions about communicating cross-culturally. For example, if Joanna's primary racial identity was mixed, she was communicating cross-culturally when she interacts with both her Black mom and her White dad. If Katherine's primary racial identity was Black, then interacting with her White family would entail communicating across racial differences. Regardless of the identifications, each participant had to learn how to best interact with people of distinct races as they interacted with various family members. Consequently, these mixed race women did not have the option of avoiding cross-cultural communication on an intimate level.

In *Teaching for Diversity and Social Justice*, Adams, Bell, & Griffin (1997) argued that one of the best strategies for challenging oppression systematically is through building diverse coalitions. They also argued for promoting "a sense of social responsibility toward and with others" (p. 3). For those of us who wish to promote social justice, there is value in learning how these women built relationships across lines of difference.

These women's stories reveal a few key insights into cross-cultural understanding. As explained in Chapter 6, four main factors emerged related to how these women were able to communicate cross-culturally. The first three were learned. First, they learned from a young age that there are multiple ways of being, and each must be respected. Second they found that active, thoughtful observation was key to effectively learning about cultural differences. This conscious effort to recognize cultural differences, coupled with a demonstrated respect of each group's customary ways of being helped them to gain acceptance in various cultural groups. Third, they found that it was important not to co-opt habits and rituals of cultures to which they did not belong. Physical racial ambiguity was another influencing factor that contributed to their cross-cultural acceptance and understanding; this was not learned, but a given.

The women shared stories of being frustrated with White people who did not care or make an effort to learn about people of color and mixed race people. They also had stories of being confronted by people of color on prejudices and biases about race. Collectively, these narratives showed mixed race people to be both agents and targets of racism. Just as they wanted to send a message to White people to listen and learn from other people of color and mixed race individuals, they also challenged themselves to be better listeners and recognize the ways they may oppress people of color through acting in dismissive, culturally White ways. From these stories, we can learn techniques to better communicate across lines of difference.

THE POTENTIAL TRANSFORMATIONAL POWER OF A BOTH/AND
CONCEPTUALIZATION

Not surprisingly, the narratives reveal several both/and situations and positionalities. These women occupied positions of both privilege and oppression. They claimed agency and were confined by structure. They held contradictions, embraced ambiguity, and were plagued by uncertainty. They externalized Whiteness, yet examined how Whiteness played out in their lives. They loved White people and disdained cultural Whiteness. They craved multiracial spaces but often avoided integrating the people in their lives. They feared being both targets and agents of oppression.

The women in this study took the risk to expose the contradictions, hurts, and triumphs in their lives. The stories they shared add to the growing but still scant amount of qualitative research with mixed race people that moves beyond a psychological identity theory lens (DaCosta, 2007; Ifekwunigwe, 1999; Korgen, 1998; Mahtani, 2001; Renn, 2004). Like Ifekwunigwe (2004), I also argue for an understanding of multiple subjectivities that interrogates "taken-for-granted constructs of 'race,' nation, culture and family and their confluent relationships to gendered identities" (p. 193). By centralizing the concept of translocational positionalities (Anthias, 2002) I strived to simultaneously highlight fluid and negotiated subject positions while examining chosen positionalities and related experiences for what they might reveal about racial politics. For those who may still doubt the socially constructed nature of race, this project, along with other related research, "reveals the fluidity and subjectivity of race" (Korgen, 1998, p. 118). The nuances of the participants' stories expose subtleties of power dynamics related to privilege and oppression (as described throughout this chapter and the book as a whole) that are connected to and expand upon current mixed race and sociological research. What stands out in this work are those telling moments where participants delved into highly conflicted emotional places of describing and trying to hold contradictions related to the ways constructions of Whiteness impact their lives and those of people they love; they employed a both/and conceptualization that exposes hidden complexities that would otherwise be rendered invisible, in the form of dichotomous thinking and binary-based theoretical frameworks. This reconceptualization has the potential to transform our ways of being to create more equitable cross-cultural interactions and improve our work towards systemic change for the promotion of social justice.

This work of promoting equity and social justice, however, requires constant vigilance and continual self-reflection. The women as a whole demonstrated this in their critically self-reflective narratives throughout the book. I conclude with a story from Tina that she wrote in her response to reading a draft of the book. She acknowledged that my interpretations and portrayals of her at the time of her interviews were accurate but that "a lot has changed since then." Tina, upon reading the book, shared stories of the ways in which she had changed: she became comfortable calling herself mixed race, became confident just being herself, and had done much work related to "White guilt." She had become an educational leader with "a goal to build communities (students, staff and families alike) through empowerment." Tina's quote reminds us that positionalities are fluid and the developing story is never over:

> I feel so lucky to have been randomly born into my family. They were loving and supportive. I want try to bring that feeling of support into my leadership role. And that is what my family has gifted me - not a racial identity, but a loving, compassionate identity that has room for all the different developments that are sure to be on my horizon. I know my self-conception/identity will continue to shift, but I know that I will continue to claim a mixed race identity.

APPENDIX A

Appendix A: Participants Overview

Name	Age	Mom	Dad	Childhood Location	Current Location	Pass	Sexuality	Education	Childhood Class	Current Class
Maria	34	White	Mexican	Phoenix	Albuquerque	Yes	Queer	MA	Lower middle	Middle
Ana	32	British	Filipino	Los Angeles	Albuquerque	Yes	Queer	BA	Middle	Upper
Brittney	26	White	Black	Albuquerque	Albuquerque	No	Straight	HS Diploma	Middle	Working
Janet	25	White	Mexican	Kansas City	Albuquerque	Yes	Straight	BA	Middle	Lower middle
Linda	30	Japanese	White Polish	San Francisco	Oakland	Yes	Queer	BA	Working	Working/low middle
Marta	46	White Jewish	Peruvian	suburb of San Francisco	Oakland	Yes	Queer	BA	Working	Middle
Alana	32	White	Black	LA	Oakland	No	Queer	Getting MA	Middle	Middle
Bobbi	26	White	Somali	Phoenix	San Francisco	Yes	Straight	MA	Middle	Middle
Tina	24	White	Mexican	suburb of San Francisco	Oakland	Yes	Straight	Getting MA	Working/ middle	Middle
Diana	58	White	African American	Buffalo	Boston	Yes	Straight	MA	Working	Upper middle
Ruth	34	Russian Jewish	African American	Chicago	Boston	No	Queer	MA	Lower middle	Middle
Joanna	23	Black	White	suburb of Philadelphia	Boston	Yes	Queer	Getting MA	Lower middle	Middle
Katherine	27	Black	White	suburb of Philadelphia	Boston	Yes	Straight	Getting MA	Middle	Middle
Elizabeth	31	Filipina	White	upstate NY	Boston	Yes	Straight	MA	Middle	Middle
Mindy	33	Filipina	White	SE Massachusetts	Boston	Yes	Straight	BA, some grad	Working	Lower middle
Susan	36	Norwe-gian	Mexican	Minnesota	Boston	Yes	Bisexual	BA	Upper middle	Middle

223

NOTES

[1] In a pilot project I conducted, the majority of women that I interviewed told me that they would feel more comfortable speaking in a single sex focus group as opposed to a co-ed group.

[2] The flier used to attract potential study participants stated,

> I am a doctoral student of mixed heritage collecting stories from other women who identify as mixed for a dissertation research project. You have a unique story to tell, and I want to hear your story. The goal of this project is to learn about the life histories of mixed race women who have one White parent and one parent who is a person of color (Latino/a, African-American, Native-American, Asian/Asian-American, etc.). I live in Durham, NC, but will be doing interviews June-Sept 2006 in and around the following cities: Albuquerque, NM; San Francisco/Oakland, CA; and Boston, MA. If you live in or near the cities listed above, and think you might be interested, call Silvia or e-mail. I can tell you more about the project and you can decide whether or not you want to participate.

[3] Two participants I had scheduled to interview in Albuquerque had to leave town unexpectedly, thus making the total number in that city lower. The Boston interview number was highest, perhaps in part because the coordinator of a mixed race organization received my flier in time to advertise my project in the organization newsletter, which was distributed to over 100 people. All of my Boston participants were members of that organization. When I returned to North Carolina, after my research in the other three cities, I reviewed my field notes and realized that little had emerged in my earlier local pilot project that had not emerged in my interviews in the other cities. The interviews from the three cities I had visited already provided me with the stories and rich data I needed for this project. In addition, having 16 participants was already stretching the bounds of a feasible number for the readers of the project to hold. Having reached a saturation point (Bowen, 2008), I decided to forgo the local interviews for this project and never conducted further Southeast interviews beyond those in my pilot project.

[4] These were the original interview questions: 1) Tell me about who you are; 2) Who do other people think you are? 3) Talk to me about your family; 4) Tell me about who you hang out with. Describe your friends, partner, who you date...; 5) How have your friends changed over time? 6) Are there groups of people that you feel more or less comfortable with? Tell me about that; 7) What was school like for you? 8) Tell me about what it means for you to be mixed race; 9) How do you think that others view you? (parents, friends, general public, teachers); 10) What is it like being mixed in this area and other places you have lived? 11) (At the end of the interview) Is there anything that you haven't said that you think would be helpful for me to know?

[5] These are the five group interview questions: 1) Tell me what it's like to be a person of mixed heritage; 2) What are the ways that you identify yourself racially/ethnically? Does that change in different situations and/or has it changed over time? How so? 3) Talk to me about the benefits of being mixed; 4) Tell me about the challenges of being mixed; 5) Talk to me about how you navigate being with people of different cultures.

[6] At the end of the interviews I told each participant that she was welcome to write to me or call me with any information or new experiences she might want to add. Four people did this, sharing stories of, for example, a recent discussion with a parent about being mixed. After completing the transcription and coding I found that with a few participants I had particular questions, so I emailed them asking for clarification. All of the participants responded. Later, as I was finalizing my writing, I created a set of short specific questions I wanted to ask everyone. I sent individualized emails to each participant with the same set of questions; all but three responded.

NOTES

[7]   It was my intent to personally transcribe all the interviews, but I did not have the time required to both write about the data and transcribe the interviews, so I employed the help of others to aid me.

[8]   Due to confidentiality, I had only minimal records of how to reach participants, which is why I was unable to contact six of the participants.

[9]   This is what I stated in the emails eliciting feedback:

> In 2006, I interviewed you for a mixed race research project. I just received a book contract for that work, and I am contacting you to see if you would like to read a draft of the book before it goes to print. Mostly I want to be sure that what I wrote resonates with what you feel you shared with me at that time. I realize that your perspectives may have changed some given that four years have elapsed, but I want it to ring true to what you shared then. Of course, there is no obligation to read a draft, I just wanted to make the opportunity available to you. Anyway, let me know if you are interested. If you want to wait to read it until the book is published, that's fine too. I will let you know when it comes out.

[10] *The Daily Show with John Stewart*, episode 15082, June 23, 2010.

[11] The search was conducted in 2010 using the following words: mixed race, multiracial, biracial, and interracial.

[12] According to U.S. Office of Management and Budget Directive 15 (1997).

[13] Linda explained what the term hapa meant to her. She identifies with the term hapa "in a political context" that acknowledges mixed race Asian people. This is distinct, she explained, from hapa in a Hawaiian context (Linda's mom's family is from Hawaii), because "hapa is a little derogatory because it means you're hapa-haule, half White, and that's not really looked upon as something desirable in Hawaii."

[14] Linda mentions later that she doesn't know how to say the word in English. She is referring here to Freire's (2000) notion of conscientizacao. Freire explained, "the term conscientizacao refers to learning to perceive social, political, and economic contradictions, and to take action against the oppressive elements of reality" (p. 35).

[15] Cultural capital is a sociological concept coined by Pierre Bourdieu. Bourdieu (1986) defined cultural capital as knowledge and skills that advantage people in dominant cultural institutions, such as schools, that are acquired through socialization usually by parents. Alana, a master's student in education, had a sophisticated articulation of her identity in relation to theory. In this excerpt she located her experience in relation to Bourdieu's theory of cultural capital, in which she asserted that being raised by her White mom provided her with White cultural ways of being that advantaged her.

[16] Marta always used the term "Latin" to refer to herself. Because the more common term is Latina, I asked her why. She responded that she liked it because it was "nongendered." Marta did not feel that either gendered term "Latina" or "Latino" fit her because she considered herself "as much male as female." In Spanish, words that end in "a" or "o" are often gendered female and male respectively.

[17] In the Spanish language, nouns related to identity have an "a" or an "o" placed at the end to mark gender. For example, I would be considered a "Colombiana," while my uncles would be considered "Colombianos." Also, within Spanish grammar rules, when there is a mixed-gender group of people, the masculine plural is always used (so if I was with my uncles we, as a group, would be referred to as "Colombianos"), with the assumption being that the masculine plural form of the noun can encapsulate both the men and women. Some progressive writers are now using alternative representations such as "Colombian@s" or "Colombiana/os" to emphasize equity in gender through naming.

[18] Gloria Anzaldúa (1987) wrote a groundbreaking book about what it means to live in racial, sexual, language, culture, and gender borderlands titled, *Borderlands/La Frontera*.

[19] According to the online "urban dictionary," Suavecita posted the definition of chola that got the most votes. She said, "a Chola is a Latina that wears a lot of makeup: thick eyeliner, liquid eyeliner

on top going out of your eye dark brown or red lipstick and eyebrows drawn on or really thin. We mostly have permed hair with hella gel or straight and arched on top. We kick it with people in our own barrio and not really claiming a color mainly your raza (Brown Pride) or (Barrio) and wear baggy or tight clothes with nike cortez shoes." In other words chola is slang for a certain look displayed by some Latinas.

[20] Mija is an affectionate term for daughter, a shorted version of *mi hijita*, which literally translates to "my little daughter."

[21] Susan, upon reading a draft of the book, had this to say about this interpretation:

> I don't insist that it be changed or removed or anything, but I don't think my words are understood in the meaning they had to me (not rare given my problems with language), i just sound really naive. What I meant is that it is always offensive and it is always racist, I hate the question with a venom you can probably guess, but I am not surprised that people do not have the consciousness of their White privilege to such a degree that they say things that when explained to them, some people feel it doesn't represent their intentions even if the meaning seems to me clearly racist. I think having grown up with white people that did not go to college, that were struggling financially many times, rarely saw non-whites much less had meaningful relationships with any, had no sophisticated understanding of race issues or even race vocabulary. I guess I am not surprised they do not understand their role in racism and their white privilege, so I cut them some slack which translates to me just being annoyed instead of <u>ANGRY</u>.

[22] MEChA stands for Movimiento Estudiantil Chicano de Aztlán. It is a Chicano/MEChA student movement organization that has chapters in a large number of high schools, colleges, and universities.

[23] grandmother

[24] aunt

[25] Wise, T. (2005). *White like me: Reflections on race from a privileged son.* Brooklyn, NY: Soft Skull Press.

[26] Femme is a term often used in the Lesbian, Gay, Bisexual, Transgender, Queer (LGBTQ) community that means queer femininity (Rose & Camilleri, 2002). In their "femme" anthology, Harris & Crocker (1997) argued that:

> In reading femininity through femme, our project takes as its subject a femininity that is transgressive, disruptive, and chosen. For example, some women, who might otherwise reject dominant cultural standards of feminine beauty, graft a chosen and empowering femininity onto their bodies as femmes. Many femmes would not appear properly or conventionally feminine. Thus, femme identification provides for wide variations of femininities across differences of class, race, age, body image, and communities (p. 3).

[27] The Southern Poverty Law Center (SPLC), a nonprofit organization that fights for civil rights, tracks hate groups. They are a good resource for learning about active hate groups. See the SPLC hate map: http://www.splcenter.org/get-informed/hate-map.

[28] Elizabeth is one of the participants who took the time to read a draft of the book and responded via email. Although she stated, "I'm glad I was a part of your study," she also had a strong objection to what is written here. As the author, I debated what to do about her response. Although I was tempted to delete my analytical statement that prompted her objection, instead, I have chosen to include her full response here. I believe her explanation exemplifies the multilayered complexity of mixed race experiences. This is what Elizabeth stated:

> I object strongly to this characterization: "However, Elizabeth does not have the same critical analysis around the racist implications of favoring Whiteness and consequently views her

experiences of being favored positively." I disagree that I was unaware or not critical of the racist implications of my white privilege. At the time of the interviews, I had been acutely cognizant of American and Filipino racism for many years (and I think the mere act of acknowledging white privilege implies awareness of racism). I had been immersed in racial analysis and Asian American history when I was in graduate school in 2000-01 and, in my professional life, involved with organizations focused on issues of racial diversity and on Asian Americans specifically, and I know I thought and talked about race and racism a lot.

I think there's a distinction to be made between having a personally positive experience (which I have had, thanks to my whiteness) and having a positive (or at least not critical or antagonistic) view of a racist system or society. My own personal racial experience has been very much untroubled, but I acknowledge this is founded on Filipino and American racism. I don't think my lack of personal angst suggests naïveté, an intellectual blind spot, or endorsement of a racist system. Maybe what I'm trying to get at is that I don't think that, at the time of the interviews, I had a positive view of "being favored" because of my whiteness, although I would certainly say that my subjective experience as a person racialized as white was positive.

I feel as though that statement suggests that a mixed-race, part-white woman *should* be troubled by her whiteness/white privilege if she experiences it, and I don't agree with that. As a point of contrast, I think if a man could give a good account of the gender privilege he experienced, including a comparison with the obstacles his female relatives had experienced due to sexism, we would not necessarily expect him to express vexed feelings or guilt about being a man.

There is, I think, also a political element in my tendency to extol vigorously the virtues of being a mixed-race person. (Hapa power?) My pronounced comfort with my racial identity probably also has to do with growing up in a remote small town that's sort of anomalous in terms of race and class, as well as having a really wonderful, low-key, accepting, kind, and highly evolved (white) dad. And if I seem blithe about or comfortable with privilege in general, I think it has more to do with my being a very spoiled only child than having a less-than-rigorous critical analysis of racism.

[29] Participants had the opportunity to read through a draft of the book before it was published. In that process Marta corrected this information from her quote, "I was in a neighborhood where there were seven kids who were mixed Latin and White and a mixed race [they were actually Guamanian, not mixed] family moved in a couple of houses down...."

[30] This text has been changed from my original version based upon feedback from Maria upon reading a draft of the text. Originally I wrote:

She has a Spanish last name and, no matter what context she is in, she pronounces her first name as a Spanish-speaker would, with a slightly rolled *r*. Given this, as soon as she introduces herself to anyone, they will most likely assume that she is Latina.

Maria stated this in response:

The sentence about pronouncing my first name as a Spanish speaker isn't accurate because my entire name is in Spanish. If I pronounced it differently, I would be mispronouncing it. My suggestion is something along the lines of: "She has a Spanish name and given this, as soon as she introduces herself to anyone, they will most likely assume that she is Latina."

I agree with Maria, although, I believe that others might read the name and think, "that is not a Spanish name." Thus, I have included this information for that reason and also to highlight Maria's excellent point.

[31] Here is a brief explanation of Diop's hypothesis, from his 1978 book, *Cultural Unity of Black Africa*:

> In fact, if it were proved contrary to the generally accepted theory—that insisted of a universal transition from matriarchy to patriarchy, humanity has from the beginning been divided into two geographical distinct "cradles," one which was favorable to the flourishing of matriarchy and the other to that of patriarchy, and these two systems encountered one another and even disputed with each other in different human societies, that in certain places they were superimposed on each other, or even existed side by side. (p. 25)

[32] Whiteness has been intentionally capitalized throughout the book to denote connections to racial positioning; however, it will not be capitalized within the phrase "critical whiteness theory" in order to remain consistent with current critical whiteness literature.

[33] In 1993, *Time Magazine* ran a special issue. The cover portrayed a picture of a fair skinned, light eyed woman who was digitally created. Next to her face was the caption, "Take a good look at this woman. She was created by a computer from a mix of several races. What you see is a remarkable preview of..." Below the caption is the title "The New Face of America: How Immigrants are Shaping the World's First Multicultural Society." The picture of the cover can be viewed at http://www.time.com/time/covers/0,16641,19931118,00.html

[34] For a good synopsis of white supremacy and colonialism as it relates to education and the law, see Brown, E. (2009). Education and the law: Toward conquest or social justice. In W. Ayers, T. Quinn, & D. Stovall (Eds.), *Handbook for social justice in education* (pp. 59–87). New York, NY: Routledge.

[35] See Hemphill, D. (1999). The blues and the scientific method: Codified cultural schemas and understanding adult cognition from a multicultural perspective. Proceedings of the Adult Education Research Conference, Northern Illinois University.

[36] For those interested in learning more about this, refer to Allan Johnson *The gender knot* (2005) and *Privilege, power, and difference* (2006), and bell hooks *Cultural criticism & transformation* (videorecording, 2002).

[37] Linda suggested the book *Uprooting Racism: How White People Can Work for Racial Justice* by Paul Kivel and the article "White Privilege: Unpacking the Invisible Knapsack" by Peggy McIntosh.

[38] Voldemort is a fictional character in the Harry Potter book series written by J.K. Rowling. He is an evil wizard who is so feared that most characters refuse to say his name and refer to him as "He-Who-Must-Not-Be-Named."

REFERENCES

Adams, M., Bell, L. A., & Griffin, P. (Eds.). (1997). *Teaching for diversity and social justice: A sourcebook*. New York: Routledge.

Anthias, F. (2002). Where do I belong?: Narrating collective identity and translocational positionality. *Ethnicities*, *2*, 491–514.

Anzaldúa, G. (1987). *Borderlands/la frontera: The new mestiza* (1st ed.). San Francisco: Spinsters/Aunt Lute.

Anzaldúa, G. (1999). *Borderlands/la frontera: The new mestiza* (2nd ed.). San Francisco: Spinsters/Aunt Lute.

Anzaldúa, G., & Keating, A. (Eds.). (2002). *This bridge we call home: Radical visions for transformation*. New York: Routledge.

Applebaum, B. (2008). 'Doesn't my experience count?' White students, the authority of experience, and social justice pedagogy. *Race Ethnicity and Education*, *11*, 405–414.

Applebaum, B. (2010). *Being white, being good: White complicity, white moral responsibility, and social justice pedagogy*. Lanham, MD: Lexington Books.

Ashcroft, B., Griffiths, G., & Tiffin, H. (2003). *Key concepts in post-colonial studies*. London & New York: Routledge.

Bennett, C. (2006). *Comprehensive multicultural education: Theory and practice* (6th ed.). Boston: Allyn & Bacon, Inc.

Bennett deMarrais, K., & LeCompte, M. (Eds.). (1999). *The way schools work: A sociological analysis of education*. New York: Longman.

Bettez, S. C. (2008). Social justice activist teaching in the university classroom. In J. Diem & R. Helfenbein (Eds.), *Unsettling beliefs: Teaching social theory to teachers* (pp. 273–296). Greenwich, CT: Information Age.

Bettie, J. (2003). *Women without class: Girls, race, and identity*. Berkeley, CA: University of California Press.

Bhabha, H. (1994). *The location of culture*. New York: Routledge.

Bhabha, H. (1996). Cultures in between. In S. Hall & P. du Guy (Eds.), *Questions of cultural identity* (pp. 53–60). Thousand Oaks, CA: Sage Publications, Inc.

Boler, M. (2003). Teaching for hope: The ethics of shattering worldviews. In D. Liston & J. Garrison (Eds.), *Teaching, learning, and loving: Reclaiming passion in educational practice* (pp. 117–131). New York: Routledge.

Bonilla-Silva, E. (2006). *Racism without racists: Color-blind racism and the persistence of racial inequality in the United States* (2nd ed.). Lanham, MD: Rowman & Littlefield Publishers, Inc.

Bourdieu, P. (1977). *Outline of a theory of practice*. Cambridge: Cambridge University Press.

Bourdieu, P. (1986). The forms of capital. In J. Richardson (Ed.), *Handbook of theory and research for the sociology of education* (pp. 241–258). Westport, CT: Greenwood Press.

Bourdieu, P. (1987–1988). What makes a social class? On the theoretical and practical resistance of groups. *Berkeley Journal of Sociology*, *32–33*, 1–17.

Bowen, G. A. (2008). Naturalistic inquiry and the saturation concept: A research note. *Qualitative Research*, *8*, 137–152.

Bowles, S., & Gintis, H. (1976). *Schooling in capitalist America*. New York: Basic Books.

Brown, E. (2009). Education and the law: Toward conquest or social justice. In W. Ayers, T. Quinn, & D. Stovall (Eds.), *Handbook for social justice in education* (pp. 59–87). New York: Routledge.

Brown, N. G., & Douglas, R. E. (1996). Making the invisible visible: The growth of community network organizations. In M. P. P. Root (Ed.), *The multiracial experience: Racial borders as the new frontier* (pp. 323–340). Thousand Oaks, CA: Sage Publications, Inc.

REFERENCES

Brunsma, D. (Ed.). (2006). *Mixed messages: Multiracial identities in the "color-blind" era.* Boulder, CO: Lynne Rienner Publishers.

Butler, J. (1990). *Gender trouble: Feminism and the subversion of identity.* New York: Routledge.

Butler, J. (1993). *Bodies that matter: On the discursive limits of sex.* New York: Routledge.

Camper, C. (1994). *Miscegenation blues: Voices of mixed race women.* Toronto: Sister Vision.

Chavez, C. (2008). Conceptualizing from the inside: Advantages, complications, and demands on insider positionality. *The Qualitative Report, 13,* 474–494.

Childress, H. (2006). A subtractive education. *Phi Delta Kappan, 88*(2), 104–109.

Clifford, J. (1983). On ethnographic authority. *Representations, 1*(2), 118–146.

Coffey, A., & Atkinson, P. (1996). *Making sense of qualitative data.* Thousand Oaks, CA: Sage Publications, Inc.

Collins, P. H. (2000). *Black feminist thought: Knowledge, consciousness, and the politics of empowerment.* New York: Routledge.

Conquergood, D. (2003). Rethinking ethnography: Towards a critical cultural politics. In Y. S. Lincoln & N. K. Denzin (Eds.), *Turning points in qualitative research: Tying knots in a handkerchief* (pp. 351–374). Walnut Creek, CA: AltaMira Press.

Creef, E. T. (1990). Notes from a fragmented daughter. In G. Anzaldúa (Ed.), *Making face, making soul: Haciendo caras: Creative and critical perspectives by women of color* (pp. 82–84). San Francisco: Aunt Lute Books.

Creswell, J. (1998). *Qualitative inquiry and research design.* Thousand Oaks, CA: Sage Publications, Inc.

DaCosta, K. M. (2004). All in the family: The familial roots of racial division. In H. Dalmage (Ed.), *The politics of multiracialism: Challenging racial thinking* (pp. 19–42). Albany, NY: SUNY Press.

DaCosta, K. M. (2007). *Making multiracials: State, family, and market in the redrawing of the color line.* Stanford, CA: Stanford University Press.

Dalmage, H. (Ed.). (2004). *The politics of multiracialism: Challenging racial thinking.* Albany, NY: SUNY Press.

Dalton, H. (2002). Failing to see. In P. Rothenberg (Ed.), *White privilege: Essential readings on the other side of racism* (pp. 15–18). New York: Worth Publishers.

Delpit, L. (1995). *Other people's children: Cultural conflict in the classroom.* New York: The New Press.

Denzin, N. (2007). The politics and ethics of performance pedagogy. In P. McLaren & J. L. Kincheloe (Eds.), *Critical pedagogy: Where are we now?* (pp. 127–142). New York: Peter Lang.

Deyhle, D. (2009). *Reflections in place: Connected lives of Navajo women.* Tucson, AZ: The University of Arizona Press.

DiAngelo, R. (2006). The production of whiteness in education: Asian international students in a college classroom. *Teacher College Record, 108,* 1983–2000.

Diop, C. (1978). *Cultural unity of Black Africa.* Chicago: Third World Press.

Downing, K., Nichols, D., & Webster, K. (Eds.). (2005). *Multiracial America: A resource guide on the history and literature of interracial issues.* Lanham, MD: The Scarecrow Press, Inc.

D'Souza, D. (1995). *The end of racism.* New York: Free Press.

Du Bois, W. E. B. (1996). *The souls of black folk.* New York: Penguin Books.

Ferber, A. (2004). Defending the creation of Whiteness: White supremacy and the threat of interracial sexuality. In H. Dalmage (Ed.), *The politics of multiracialism: Challenging racial thinking* (pp. 43–58). Albany, NY: SUNY Press.

Foley, N. (2002). Becoming Hispanic: Mexican Americans and Whiteness. In P. Rothenberg (Ed.), *White privilege: Essential readings on the other side of racism* (pp. 55–65). New York: Worth Publishers.

Freire, P. (1995). *Pedagogy of hope: Reliving pedagogy of the oppressed.* New York: Continuum.

Freire, P. (2000). *Pedogagy of the oppressed* (30th anniversary ed.). New York: Continuum.

Freire, P. (2001). *Pedagody of freedom: Ethics, democracy, and civic courage.* Lanham, MD: Rowman & Littlefield Publishers, Inc.

Funderburg, L. (1994). *Black, white, other: Biracial Americans talk about race and identity.* New York: W. Morrow and Co.

Furedi, F. (2001). How sociology imagined mixed race. In D. Parker & M. Song (Eds.), *Rethinking 'mixed race'* (pp. 223–241). Sterling, VA: Pluto Press.

Gallagher, C. (2004). Racial redistricting: Expanding the boundaries of whiteness. In H. Dalmage (Ed.), *The politics of multiracialism: Challenging racial thinking* (pp. 59–76). Albany, NY: SUNY Press.

Gaskins, P. F. (1999). *What are you?: Voices of mixed-race young people.* New York: Henry Holt and Company.

Gay, G. (2000). *Culturally responsive teaching: Theory research, and practice.* New York: Teachers College Press.

Geertz, C. (2003). Thick description: Toward an interpretive theory of culture. In Y. S. Lincoln & N. K. Denzin (Eds.), *Turning points in qualitative research: Tying knots in a handkerchief* (pp. 143–168). Walnut Creek, CA: AltaMira Press.

Giddens, A. (1977). *Studies in social and political theory.* New York: Basic Books.

Giddens, A. (1979). *Central problems in social theory: Action, structure, and contradiction in social analysis.* Berkeley, CA: University of California Press.

Giddens, A. (1984). *The constitution of society: Introduction of the theory of structuration.* Berkeley, CA: University of California Press.

Gillem, A., Cohn, L. R., & Throne, C. (2001). Black identity in biracial black/white people: A comparison of Jacqueline who refuses to be exclusively black and Adolphus who wishes he were. *Cultural Diversity and Ethnic Minority Psychology, 7*(2), 182–196.

Giroux, H. (2009). Critical theory and educational practice. In A. Darder (Ed.), *The critical pedagogy reader* (2nd ed., pp. 27–51). New York: Routledge.

Glesne, C. (2006). *Becoming qualitative researchers: An introduction* (3rd ed.). Boston: Pearson Education Inc.

Glesne, C. (2011). *Becoming qualitative researchers: An introduction* (4th ed.). Boston: Pearson Education Inc.

Goodall, H. L., Jr. (2000). *Writing the new ethnography.* Walnut Creek, CA: AltaMira Press.

Goodman, D., & Shapiro, S. (1997). Sexism curriculum design. In M. Adams, L. A. Bell, & P. Griffin (Eds.), *Teaching for diversity and social justice: A sourcebook* (pp. 110–140). New York: Routledge.

Greene, D., & Walker, F. (2004). Recommendations to public speaking instructors for the negotiation of code-switching practices among Black English-speaking African American students. *The Journal of Negro Education, 73*, 435–442.

Griffin, P. (1997). Introductory module for the single course issues. In M. Adams, L. A. Bell, & P. Griffin (Eds.), *Teaching for diversity and social justice* (pp. 62–81). New York & London: Routledge.

Grossberg, L. (1993). Cultural studies and/in new worlds. In C. McCarthy & W. Crichlow (Eds.), *Race, identity and representation in education* (pp. 89–105). New York: Routledge.

Grossberg, L. (1996). The circulation of cultural studies. In J. Storey (Ed.), *What is cultural studies? A reader* (pp. 178–186). London: Arnold.

Hallinan, M. T. (1988). Equality of educational opportunity. *Annual Review of Sociology, 14*, 249–268.

Harris, L., & Crocker, E. (Eds.). (1997). *Femme: Feminist lesbians & bad girls.* New York: Routledge.

Harrison, R. (2010). Social Homelessness. In S. Steinberg, M. Kehler, & L. Cornish (Eds.), *Boy culture: An encyclopedia* (Vol. 1, pp. 199–203). Santa Barbara, CA: Greenwood.

REFERENCES

Hatch, J. A. (2002). *Doing qualitative research in education settings*. New York: State University of New York Press.

Hemphill, D. (1999). The blues and the scientific method: Codified cultural schemas and understanding adult cognition from a multicultural perspective. Proceedings of the Adult Education Research Conference, Northern Illinois University. Retrieved from http://www.adulterc.org/Proceedings/1999/99hemphill.htm

Herman, M. R. (2009). The black-white-other achievement gap: Testing theories of academic performance among multiracial and monoracial adolescents. *Sociology of Education, 82*, 20–46.

Hey, V. (2006). The politics of performative resignification: Translating Judith Butler's theoretical discourse and its potential for a sociology of education. *British Journal of Sociology of Education, 27*, 439–457.

Hoetink, H. (1985). 'Race' and color in the Caribbean. In S. W. Mintz & S. Price (Eds.), *Carribbean contours* (pp. 55–84). Baltimore: Johns Hopkins University Press.

hooks, b. (1994). *Teaching to transgress: Education as the practice of freedom*. New York: Routledge.

hooks, b. (2000). *Where we stand: Class matters*. New York: Routledge.

hooks, b., & Jhally, S. (Producer & Director). (2002). *Cultural criticism & transformation* [Motion picture]. Northampton, MA: Media Education Foundation.

Hurtado, A. (1996). *The color of privilege: Three blasphemies on race and feminism*. Ann Arbor, MI: The University of Michigan Press.

Hytten, K., & Warren, J. (2003). Engaging whiteness: How racial power gets reified in education. *International Journal of Qualitative Studies in Education, 16*, 65–89.

Ifekwunigwe, J. O. (Ed.). (1999). *Scattered belongings: Cultural paradoxes of race, culture and nation*. London: Routledge.

Ifekwunigwe, J. O. (2001). Re-Membering "race": On gender, "mixed race" and family in the English-African diaspora. In D. Parker & M. Song (Eds.), *Rethinking 'mixed race'* (pp. 42–63). Sterling, VA: Pluto Press.

Ifekwunigwe, J. O. (Ed.). (2004). *'Mixed race' studies: A reader*. London: Routledge.

Jaggar, A. (1989). Love and knowledge: Emotion in feminist epistemology. In A. Jaggar & S. Bordo (Eds.), *Gender/body/knowledge: Feminist reconstructions of being and knowing* (pp. 145–171). New Brunswick, NJ: Rutgers University Press.

Jencks, C., & Phillips, M. (1998). The Black-White test score gap: An Introduction". In C. Jencks & M. Phillips (Eds.), *The Black-White test score gap* (pp. 1–47). Washington, DC: Brookings Institution Press.

Jo, J., & Rong, X. L. (2003). Historical struggles for equity: Politics and language policies and its implications for Asian Americans. In R. Hunter & F. Brown (Eds.), *Challenges of urban education and efficacy of school reform* (pp. 25–48). Boston: JAI.

Johnson, A. (2005). *The gender knot: Unraveling our patriarchal legacy* (Rev. ed.). Philadelphia: Temple University Press.

Johnson, A. (2006). *Privilege, power and difference* (2nd ed.). New York: McGraw-Hill.

Johnson, B., & Christensen, L. (2004). *Educational research: Quantitative, qualitative, and mixed approaches* (2nd ed.). Boston: Pearson Education Inc.

Karabel, J. & Halsey, A. (Eds.). (1977). *Power and ideology in education*. New York: Oxford University Press.

Karis, T. A. (2004). "I prefer to speak of culture": White mothers of multiracial children. In H. Dalmage (Ed.), *The politics of multiracialism: Challenging racial thinking* (pp. 161–174). Albany, NY: SUNY Press.

Kich, G. K. (1992). The developmental process of asserting a biracial, bicultural identity. In M. P. P. Root (Ed.), *Racially mixed people in America* (pp. 304–317). Newbury Park, CA: Sage Publications, Inc.

Kivel, P. (2002). *Uprooting racism: How white people can work for racial justice* (Rev. ed.). British Columbia: New Society Publishers.

Korgen, K. O. (1998). *From black to biracial: Transforming racial identity among Americans.* Westport, CT: Praeger.

Kozol, J. (2005). *The shame of the nation: The restoration of apartheid schooling in America.* New York: Crown Publishers.

Knox, R. (1850). *The races of men: A fragment.* Philadelphia: Lea & Blanchard.

Kroeger, B. (2003). *Passing: When people can't be who they are.* New York: Public Affairs.

Ladson-Billlings, G. (2004). Landing on the wrong note: The price we paid for Brown. *Educational Researcher, 33*(7), 3–13.

Ladson-Billings, G. (2007). Can we at least have *Plessy*? The struggle for quality education. *North Carolina Law Review, 85,* 1279–1292.

Larsen, N. (2003). *Passing.* New York: Penguin Books.

Lather, P. (2003). Issues of validity in openly ideological research: Between a rock and a soft place. In Y. S. Lincoln & N. K. Denzin (Eds.), *Turning points in qualitative research: Tying knots in a handkerchief* (pp. 185–215). Walnut Creek, CA: AltaMira Press.

Lauder, H., Brown, P., & Halsey, A. H. (2009). Sociology of education: A critical history and prospects for the future. *Oxford Review of Education, 35*(5), 569–585.

Lincoln, Y. S. & Denzin, N. K. (Eds.). (2003). *Turning points in qualitative research: Tying knots in a handkerchief.* Walnut Creek, CA: AltaMira Press.

Lincoln, Y. S., & Guba, E. G. (1985). *Naturalistic inquiry.* Beverly Hills, CA: Sage Publications, Inc.

Lincoln, Y. S., & Guba, E. G. (2000). Paradigmatic controversies, contradictions, and emerging confluences. In N. K. Denzin & Y. S. Lincoln (Eds.), *Handbook of qualitative research* (pp. 163–188). Thousand Oaks, CA: Sage Publications, Inc.

Lorber, J. (2001). "Night to his day": The social construction of gender. In L. Richardson, V. Taylor, & N. Whittier (Eds.), *Feminist frontiers* (Vol. 5, pp. 40–56). Boston: McGraw Hill.

Lugones, M. (1990). Playfulness, 'World'-Travelling, and loving perception. In G. Anzaldúa (Ed.), *Making face, making soul: Haciendo caras: Creative and critical perspectives by women of color* (pp. 390–402). San Francisco: Aunt Lute Books.

Mahtani, M. (2001). 'I'm a blonde-haired, blue-eyed black girl': Mapping mobile paradoxical spaces among multiethnic women in Toronto, Canada. In D. Parker & M. Song (Eds.), *Rethinking 'mixed race'* (pp. 173–190). London: Pluto Press.

Mahtani, M., & Moreno, A. (2001). Same difference: Towards a more unified discourse in mixed race theory. In D. Parker & M. Song (Eds.), *Rethinking 'mixed race'* (pp. 65–75). Sterling, VA: Pluto Press.

McDonough, P. M., & Nuñez, A. M. (2007). Bourdieu's sociology of education: Identifying persistent inequality, unmasking domination, and fighting social reproduction. In C. A. Torres & A. Teodoro (Eds.), *Critique and utopia: New developments in the sociology of education in the 21st century* (pp. 139–154). Lanham, MD: Rowan & Littlefield Publishers.

McIntosh, P. (2000). White privilege and male privilege: A personal account of coming to see correspondences through work in women's studies. In A. Minas (Ed.), *Gender basics: Feminist perspectives on women and men* (2nd ed., pp. 30–38). Belmont, CA: Wadsworth.

McLaren, P. (1997). The ethnographer as postmodern flaneur: Critical reflexivity and posthybridity as narrative engagement. In W. G. Tierney & Y. S. Lincoln (Eds.), *Representation and the text: Re-framing the narrative voice* (pp. 143–177). Albany, NY: State University of New York Press.

McLaren, P. (2000). Developing a pedagogy of whiteness in the context of a postcolonial hybridity: White identities in global context. In N. M. Rodriguez & L. E. Villaverde (Eds.), *Dismantling white privilege: Pedagogy, politics, and whiteness* (pp. 150–157). New York: Peter Lang.

REFERENCES

Mengel, L. M. (2001). Triples - The social evolution of a multiracial panethnicity: An Asian American perspective. In D. Parker & M. Song (Eds.), *Rethinking 'mixed race'* (pp. 99–116). Sterling, VA: Pluto Press.

Moll, L. C. (1992). Bilingual classroom studies and community analysis. *Educational Researcher, 21*(2), 20–24.

Moon, D. (1999). White enculturation and bourgeois identity: The discursive production of "good (white) girls". In T. K. Nakayama & J. N. Martin (Eds.), *Whiteness: The communication of social identity* (pp. 177–197). Thousand Oaks, CA: Sage Publications, Inc.

Moraga, C. (1983). La Guera. In C. Moraga & G. Anzaldúa (Eds.), *This bridge called my back: Writings by radical women of color* (2nd ed., pp. 27–34). New York: Kitchen Table Women of Color Press.

Moraga, C., & Anzaldúa, G. (Eds.). (1983). *This bridge called my back: Writings by radical women of color* (2nd ed.). New York: Kitchen Table Women of Color Press.

Nakashima, C. L. (1992). An invisible monster: The creation and denial of mixed-race people in America. In M. P. P. Root (Ed.), *Racially mixed people in America* (pp. 162–180). Newbury Park, CA: Sage Publications, Inc.

Nash, P. T. (1992). Multicultural identity and the death of stereotypes. In M. P. P. Root (Ed.), *Racially mixed people in America* (pp. 330–332). Newbury Park, CA: Sage Publications, Inc.

Nieto, S. (2004). *Affirming diversity: The sociopolitical context of multicultural education* (4th ed.). New York: Longman.

Noblit, G. W., Flores, S. Y., & Murillo, E. G., Jr. (Eds.). (2004). *Postcritical ethnography: Reinscribing critique*. Hampton, NJ: Hampton Press.

Noddings, N. (1989). *Women and evil*. Berkeley, CA: University of California Press.

Noguera, P. A. (2004). Social capital and the education of immigrant students: Categories and generalizations. *Sociology of Education, 77*, 180–183.

Noguera, P. A., & Wing, J. Y. (2006). *Unfinished business: Closing the racial achievement gap in our schools*. San Francisco: Jossey-Bass.

Nott, J., & Gliddon, G. (1854). *Types of mankind*. Philadelphia: J. P. Lippincott.

O'Hearn, C. C. (Ed.). (1998). *Half + half*. New York: Pantheon Books.

Olumide, J. (2002). *Raiding the gene pool: The social construction of mixed race*. London: Pluto Press.

Omi, M., & Winant, H. (1994). *Racial formation in the USA: From the 1960s to the 1990s*. New York: Routledge.

Parker, D. & Song, M. (Eds.). (2001). *Rethinking 'mixed race'*. Sterling, VA: Pluto Press.

Patterson, O. (2000). Race over. *New Republic: A Journal of Politics and Arts, 222*(2), 6.

Pfeiffer, K. (2003). *Race passing and American individualism*. Amherst, MA: University of Massachusetts Press.

Power, S., & Rees, G. (2006). *Making sense of changing times and changing places: The challenges of the new political arithmetic of education*. Paper given to the BERA Symposium on the Future of Sociology of Education, Warwick, UK.

Reinharz, S. (1997). Who am I? The need for a variety of selves in the field. In S. Reinharz (Ed.), *Reflexivity and voice* (pp. 3–20). Thousand Oaks, CA: Sage Publications, Inc.

Renn, K. A. (2004). *Mixed race students in college: The ecology of race, identity, and community on campus*. New York: State University of New York Press.

Rich, P. (1990). *Race and empire in British politics*. Cambridge: Cambridge University Press.

Richardson, L., Taylor, V. A., & Whittier, N. (Eds.). (2001). *Feminist frontiers: Rethinking sex, gender, and society* (5th ed.). New York: McGraw-Hill.

Root, M. P. P. (Ed.). (1992). *Racially mixed people in America*. Newbury Park, CA: Sage Publications, Inc.

Root, M. P. P. (1996). *The multiracial experience: Racial borders as the new frontier.* Thousand Oaks, CA: Sage Publications, Inc.

Rose, C. B., & Camilleri, A. (Eds.). (2002). *Brazen femme: Queering femininity.* Vancouver: Arsenal Pulp Press.

Rothstein, R., & Jacobsen, R. (2006). The goals of education. *Phi Delta Kappan, 88*(4), 264–272.

Sadovnik, A. R. (2001). Theories of sociology of education. In J. H. Ballantine & J. Z. Spade (Eds.), *Schools and society: A sociological approach to education* (pp. 15–34). Belmont, CA: Wadsworth.

Sandweiss, M. (2009). *Passing strange: A gilded age tale of love and deception across the color line.* New York: Penguin Group.

Schwalbe, M. (2007). *The sociologically examined life: Pieces of the conversation* (4th ed.). Boston: McGraw-Hill.

Scotton, C. M., & Ury, W. (1977). Bilingual strategies: The social functions of code-switching. *International Journal of the Sociology of Language, 13,* 5–20.

Sexton, J. (2008). *Amalgamation schemes: Antiblackness and the critique of multiracialism.* Minneapolis, MN: University of Minnesota Press.

Shapiro, S. (2005). Lessons of September 11. In S. Shapiro & D. E. Purpel (Eds.), *Critical social issues in American education: Democracy and meaning in a globalizing world.* Mahwah, NJ: Lawrence Erlbaum Associates.

Siddle Walker, E. V. (1996). Caswell county training school, 1933–1969: Relationships between community and school. *Harvard Educational Review, 63,* 161–182.

Spickard, P. (1992). The illogic of American racial categories. In M. P. P. Root (Ed.), *Racially mixed people in America* (pp. 12–23). Newbury Park, CA: Sage Publications, Inc.

Stam, R. (1998). Hybridity and the aesthetics of garbage: The case of Brazilian cinema. *Estudios Interdisciplinarios de America Latina y el Caribe, 9*(1). Retrieved from http://www.tau.ac.il/eial/IX_1/stam.html

Standen, B. C. S. (1996). Without a template: The biracial Korean/White experience. In M. P. P. Root (Ed.), *The multiracial experience: Racial borders as the new frontier* (pp. 245–262). Thousand Oaks, CA: Sage Publications, Inc.

Stanton-Salazar, R. D. (2004). Social capital among working-class minority students. In M. A. Gibson, P. Gándara, & J. P. Koyama (Eds.), *School connections: U.S. Mexican youth, peers, and school achievement.* New York: Teachers College Press.

Stewart, J. (Writer). (2010, June 23). Samuel L. Jackson scale of black emotion [Television series episode 15082]. In J. Stewart (Executive producer), *The daily show with John Stewart.* New York: Comedy Central. Retrieved from http://www.thedailyshow.com/watch/wed-june-23-2010/samuel-l--jackson-scale-of-black-emotion

Takaki, R. (1998). *Strangers from a different shore: A history of Asian Americans.* Boston: Bay Back Books.

Tatum, B. D. (1997). *"Why are all the black kids sitting together in the cafeteria?" And other conversations about race.* New York: Basic Books.

Telles, E. E., & Sue, C. A. (2009). Race mixture: Boundary crossing in comparative perspective. *Annual Review of Sociology, 35,* 129–146.

Thompson, A. (2003). Tiffany, friend of people of color: White investments in antiracism. *International Journal of Qualitative Studies in Education, 16,* 7–29.

Thompson, B. (2001). *A promise and a way of life: White antiracist activism.* Minneapolis, MN: University of Minnesota Press.

Torres, C. A., & Mitchell, T. R. (1998). Introduction. In C. A. Torres & T. R. Mitchell (Eds.), *Sociology of education: Emerging perspectives* (pp. 1–18). Albany, NY: State University of New York Press.

Trueba, E. H. T. (2004). *The new Americans: Immigrants and transnationals at work.* Lanham, MD: Rowman & Littlefield Publishers, Inc.

REFERENCES

Valenzuela, A. (1999). *Subtractive schooling: U.S.-Mexican youth and the politics of caring*. New York: State University of New York Press.

Van Maanen, J. (1988). *The tales of the field: On writing ethnography*. Cambridge, MA: Harvard University Press.

Wade, P. (2004). Images of Latin American mestizaje and the politics of comparison. *Bulletin of Latin American Research, 23*, 355–366.

Walker, R. (2001). *Black, white, and Jewish: Autobiography of a shifting self*. New York: Riverhead Books.

Weber, M. (1978). Economy and society (Vols. 1 & 2, G. Roth & C. Wittich, Eds.). Berkeley, CA: University of California Press.

Weis, L., McCarthy, C. & Dimitriadis, G. (Eds.). (2006). *Ideology, curriculum and the new sociology of education*. New York: Routledge.

Wijeyesinghe, C. L., Griffin, P., & Love, B. (1997). Racism curriculum design. In M. Adams, L. A. Bell, & P. Griffin (Eds.), *Teaching for diversity and social justice* (pp. 88–104). New York & London: Routledge.

Williams, K. M. (2008). *Mark one or more: Civil rights in multiracial America*. Ann Arbor, MI: University of Michigan Press.

Williams, T. K. (1997). Race-ing and being raced. *Amerasia Journal, 23*(1), 61–65.

Willinsky, J. (1998). *Learning to divide the world: Education at empire's end*. Minneapolis, MN: University of Minnesota Press.

Wise, T. (2005). *White like me: Reflections on race from a privileged son*. Brooklyn, NY: Soft Skull Press.

Wolk, S. (2007). Why go to school? *Phi Delta Kappan, 88*(9), 648–658.

Yamada, M. (1983). Invisibility is an unnatural disaster: Reflections of an Asian American woman. In C. Moraga & G. Anzaldúa (Eds.), *This bridge called my back: Writings by radical women of color* (2nd ed., pp. 35–40). New York: Kitchen Table Women of Color Press.

Young, R. J. C. (1995). *Colonial desire: Hybridity in theory, culture and race*. London: Routledge.

Zack, N. (1993). *Race and mixed race*. Philadelphia: Temple University Press.

Zinn, H. (1980). *A people's history of the United States*. New York: Harper & Row.

INDEX

CPSIA information can be obtained at www.ICGtesting.com
Printed in the USA
BVOW040008101011

273214BV00003B/2/P